'An extraordinary read – intriguing,
enlightening and funny.'
Jan Ravens

'Sara Gibbs absolutely nails the disorienting experience
of growing up with undiagnosed autism.'
Joanne Limberg, author of _Letters to My Weird Sisters_

'Will resonate with anyone who has ever felt
misunderstood.'
Rosie Holt

'A fast and hilarious memoir about love and
acceptance. Razor sharp and so very touching.'
Lizzy Dent, author of _The Summer Job_

'For a Drama Queen, Gibbs is sparklingly hilarious.'
Desiree Burch

'Full of warmth, insight, heartache, and seemingly
effortless humour. It grabs you by the lapels
and doesn't let go.'
Nick Pettigrew, author of _Anti Social_

'Incredibly intelligent . . . I cried laughing.'
Shappi Khorsandi

'Funny and uplifting.'
Isy Suttie

Sara Gibbs is a UK-based comedy writer, graduate of the National Film and Television School's Writing & Producing Comedy course and prolific tweeter. Her credits include *Dead Ringers*, *The News Quiz*, *The Daily Mash*, *CollegeHumor*, *The Now Show*, *The Mash Report* and *Have I Got News for You*. She is co-founder of satirical online women's magazine, *Succubus*, and the founder of The First Laugh Comedy Writing Competition for new writers.

SARA GIBBS

DRAMA QUEEN

HEADLINE

First published in the UK in 2021 by
HEADLINE PUBLISHING GROUP

First published in paperback in 2022 by
HEADLINE PUBLISHING GROUP

5

Cataloguing in Publication Data is available from the British Library

ISBN 978 1 4722 7436 6

Designed and typeset by EM&EN
Printed and bound in Great Britain by Clays Ltd, Elcograf S.p.A.

Headline's policy is to use papers that are natural, renewable and
recyclable products and made from wood grown in sustainable forests.
The logging and manufacturing processes are expected to conform
to the environmental regulations of the country of origin.

HEADLINE PUBLISHING GROUP
An Hachette UK Company
Carmelite House
50 Victoria Embankment
London
EC4Y 0DZ

www.headline.co.uk
www.hachette.co.uk

This book is dedicated to the memory of my dad, Zvi, who would be so proud and so annoyed.

CONTENTS

INTRODUCTION

Hi. Hello. *Salut.* Yo?

OK, you've got me. I've never figured out how to introduce myself. Maybe just imagine you're chatting to a friend and there's a pale ginger woman loitering nearby, staring creepily at you, before choosing an inexplicable moment to jump in, bellowing, 'I COULDN'T HELP BUT OVERHEAR; I'M SARA BY THE WAY.' Great, now that we're introduced, I'll break the ice with a joke. Given that I write jokes for radio and TV for a living, this should be a piece of cake. What do you call an undiagnosed autistic girl? Oh God, first rule of comedy – never start a joke when you don't have a punchline. But I've already announced, out loud, that I'm going to tell a joke, set your expectations really high by telling you I do this for money and now you're all looking at me expectantly. Or with pity in your eyes. I honestly can't tell.

In actual fact, in the absence of a diagnosis, many autistic people who grew up being socialised as girls are made to feel like walking punchlines, and that's no joke. We are among the least understood people on the planet. We're up there with people who choose the middle seat on the plane and . . . Wait, don't walk off! I'm just a little nervous. Honestly, I'm not that bad. You'll see! You just have to spend the next ten years getting to know me.

I kid, but actually 'I'm not that bad' is one of the kindest things I've ever said about myself and it took years of therapy to get here. Until I was thirty years old I thought I was the most uniquely terrible person in the world. Nobody in existence was as selfish, lazy, incapable, weak, dramatic, inappropriate, ridiculous or out of sync with the world as I was.

My whole life I strongly suspected there was a top-secret handbook for how to person and I was the only one without a copy. Just as well. I've never been able to keep a secret. While other kids were playing games, making friends and doing whatever else people do but don't tell me about, I was always trailing behind, looking in the wrong direction or saying things that made the room descend into an awkward silence. Why is it that when Fleabag overshares about her sex life, it's a witty anecdote, but when I do it everyone goes ashen-faced and asks me to stop talking because I'm upsetting Grandma? One of life's many mysteries.

Ironically, as autistic people are so often told we lack empathy, I am going to ask a lot of you in the coming pages when it comes to attempting to put yourself in my shoes (they're very comfy and I've bought several pairs in case they wear out). I'm going to ask you to imagine that all the things that you take for granted you are able to do in life are significantly harder for you than for everyone else – but because there's nothing *visibly* different about you, nobody believes you.

Worse, imagine that while you're struggling with extreme sensory sensitivities, muscle weakness, exhaustion, food aversions and a whole other laundry list of physical difficulties, you're being told that you're putting it all on for attention and are often scolded about how you really *should* be able to do these basic things. While you're struggling with severe executive dysfunction, you're told off for being lazy and useless. When you try to explain yourself, your body language and facial expressions don't match your words, adding to the perception that you're not to be trusted. When you finally meltdown because you are overwhelmed by your environment or frustrated at not being heard, you're berated for being dramatic. Everything you do to try to fit in or, at the very least, articulate why you can't, makes people less and less likely to believe you.

Now take those struggles, and many more, and set them against the backdrop of a weird and wacky world of New Age woo. Imagine your chances of diagnosis growing up in a tight-knit hippie community where you're more likely to be taken to a Reiki healer than a psychologist. Imagine surviving your formative years, being too weird to be accepted by people who believe in fairies, gnomes and, most preposterously, homeopathy.

Imagine then that years later, after spending your whole life working overtime to pretend to be just like everyone else, you finally get an answer – a diagnosis! But you've done such a good job of convincing yourself and everybody else that you're just a useless, dramatic human being that nobody believes you – you barely even believe you – and every person who challenges your diagnosis only reinforces your own doubt and confusion. Welcome to my world.

When I first looked into getting diagnosed, people asked me why I needed a 'label'. The answer was that living with just one label would be a blessed relief. By the time autistic women reach adulthood, diagnosed or not, many of us have accrued a lifetime of labels that form the basis of the way other people see us and, by extension, the way we see ourselves. Peeling those labels off can be as tricky as peeling off literal labels. It's fiddly, sticky, time-consuming and, no matter how hard you try, there will always be some leftover residue.

So, this is my story. Before I get started, I want to be clear that it comes with a giant disclaimer – if you've met one autistic person, you've met one autistic person. And, yes, I choose to say autistic person, rather than person with autism. Other people are welcome to identify differently but given that I can't leave my autism at home while I pop to the shop to get a few bits done, this is the way round I prefer it. Before you start complaining that I'm nothing like your autistic brother, child you once saw at the supermarket or goat, that's OK. I don't have to be! This is *my* story with all the gory, mortifying and, hopefully, entertaining details.

Another thing it is important to make clear is that this is the story of a lucky autistic person. I survived my upbringing relatively unscathed. There are autistic people out there who have been subjected to unimaginable cruelty – the torture of controversial 'behavioural therapies', their most vulnerable moments filmed and put online without their consent to demonstrate how 'difficult' they are, dangerous attempts at 'cures', like bleach enemas and incarceration in institutions, with some autistic people placed in isolation, unable to see their families. Some autistic children never become adults. In rare and extreme cases, some are killed in their homes by the people who are supposed to love and care for them. A tiny percentage are killed in their schools by teachers attempting to restrain them. Autistic people are at significantly higher risk of dying by suicide than their neurotypical peers. There are many autistic people who, for a multitude of complicated reasons, are not able to tell their own stories and so have false narratives and limitations imposed upon them.

I am also uncomfortable with the idea of this book being held up as an example of what autistic people can achieve without explaining first that the worth of autistic people should not be judged by their ability to work and 'contribute', whatever that means, and secondly that all I have achieved in my career would not have been possible without an incredible amount of support.

My circumstances have been unique and blessed. Again, I am lucky. Even with the extraordinary care and financial safety net I have been privileged enough to enjoy, working at a high level has often come at a huge emotional price. Autistic people can and do thrive professionally, but it would be irresponsible of me to ignore that this success is often facilitated by the right support, understanding and accommodations.

That, and I am clearly a comedy legend. Why have you all stopped laughing?

There will be moments in this book where I draw upon my extensive study and immersion in the autistic community to describe anecdotally common traits or experiences. I in no way wish to claim that these are universal, nor that I speak for all autistic people. At points in this book, particularly when reporting my early diagnosis, I refer to terminology that is now outdated or defunct in order to accurately describe my experience as it unfolded at the time. Asperger syndrome in particular has been widely retired as a diagnostic label, although many people still use it, as it was their original diagnosis.

I can't teach you about autism. All I can offer is a tour inside this one autistic brain. Please come in. I'm so sorry about the mess, but there's plenty of comfy seating. No, not that seat. That's my special seat. Ahhh, that's better. This is the story of one autistic woman in a world that does everything it can not to recognise us.

1

CRYBABY

It's January 1998. My dad is begrudgingly driving me and a girl from my class to see *Titanic* at the cinema for what is clearly a friendship audition. My dad, a diligent rule follower, has taken a lot of persuading to be complicit in what he calls 'committing fraud'. *Titanic* is graded twelve and I am, as he has repeatedly reminded me, eleven and a quarter. I've pulled out all the stops to convince him to aid and abet my pre-teen rebellion. I've begged, I've pleaded, I've reasoned. And by reasoned I mean I've burst into tears and shouted 'Why are you ruining my life?' Against the odds, I've worn him down and he has reluctantly agreed to buy our tickets and then leave us to it.

'But if they ask how old you are,' he warns us, 'I won't lie.'

My dad goes ahead to the booth to buy the tickets while I hide conspicuously behind him with my potential new friend, like a cartoon character behind a lamp post.

The ticket guy eyes my visible limbs suspiciously. 'Is that your daughter?'

'Yes.'

'How old is she?'

There is an uncomfortably long pause. A dead giveaway of a pause. Nobody in the history of time has ever paused for that long and then gone on to tell the truth. It goes on so long I can't actually be sure I haven't turned twelve in the interim.

Finally, my dad speaks up entirely unconvincingly. 'I don't know.'

A few months later, *Titanic* was released on VHS. My dad came home one afternoon to the sound of hysterical sobbing and wailing. He ran into the living room, braced for whatever life-changing disaster he might find when he got there. A dead pet? The charred remains of the house? One of his mistresses up the duff?

'Are you OK?'

I paused Rose and Jack's devastating parting words, looked at my dad through my swollen eyes, blew my snotty nose and bawled, 'I am. BUT THEY'RE NOT.'

My dad may have cost me one friend, but ultimately I was grateful that he saved something much more valuable: my dignity. Already nicknamed 'crybaby' by my classmates, the last thing I needed was the mortification of having an audience to my reaction to *Titanic*.

I have never been able to understand people who can stop themselves crying. If I'm upset, my face instantly resembles something that's just been pulled out of the ground by its leaves. My tears are constantly simmering close to the surface, waiting for the slightest nudge to come spilling out of my face. 'At the ready, men, she's just watched a video of a puppy making friends with a duck!' My emotions are too big. Or I'm too small. I'm just an oversized bag of emotions wearing a human skinsuit.

To the uninitiated, my weepies can be a very uncomfortable thing to witness. But anyone who spends any meaningful time around me has to just get used to it. I cry. A lot. About everything. To my loved ones it's like the weather. 'It's a bit windy outside.' 'Oh, Sara's leaking again. What is it now, Sara?' 'I suddenly remembered the Cadbury's drumming gorilla. So passionate. So noble.'

I tend to be at my soggiest when other people are upset. Empathy is a physical experience for me. I viscerally feel other people's emotions. They possess me like little hormonal demons and it can often be hard to discern what's mine and what's theirs. It's incredibly draining and, worse, it's wasted emotional energy, but I couldn't turn it off if I tried. I often imagine the good I could do in the world if I wasn't busy feeling devastated that my third cousin has to have a root canal.

This overactive empathy chip can be so overwhelming that I can rarely find the appropriate reaction. If I engage with someone else's emotions, tears are inevitable. I can't say so much as a kind word without opening the floodgates. This is incredibly inconvenient when I'm in a writers' room and all I want to do is say 'Nice sketch, mate', but it comes out as 'You're just such an extraordinary shining light of a writer; this sketch is exemplary of your talent and this industry would be poorer without you,' while tears stream down my face.

The only way to avoid being absolutely terrifying when it comes to any kind of emotional exchange is to shut down completely. Then it looks like I don't care at all. This is inconvenient when, say, my husband comes running in to tell me about his promotion at work, but I don't have the energy for a sobbing session so all I can manage is an eye-contactless 'well done'. Maybe a perfunctory handshake. I have two modes: sobbing wreck or heartless robot.

Anyway, they say to become an expert in anything you have to put in your 10,000 hours of practice. If that's true, then by now I have surely earned my PhD in weeping. I'd go so far as to say that I'm a leading global expert. I should be called upon as the definitive authority on the ol' waterworks whenever they need one on the news. 'We now go live to our Crying Correspondent, Sara Gibbs . . . Sara . . . can you calm down a bit? We can't understand anything you're saying. Do you think you can take a breath and compose yourself? Uh . . . we seem to have lost Sara there, sorry. Here's the weather.'

The first thing I did when I arrived on this planet? You can probably guess.

Now, normally nothing strikes fear into my heart like the words 'tell me about yourself'. Without specific instructions on precisely how much information I'm expected to share, I'll start from the beginning, the very beginning, and continue without pause until someone manages to get a word in. 'That's all fascinating, Mrs Gibbs, and I'm really glad you got through the trauma of your first period, but I'm more interested in your experience of writing press releases . . .' On this occasion, however, by reading this book, you *have* asked for my life story. That's the deal. Holy shit, a captive audience.

I will go so far as to spare you the details of my conception, of which sadly I am also aware. I am not, it would transpire, the only oversharer in my family. Cheers, Dad.

'Come on, Sara. It's a beautiful story. What's wrong with two people making l—'

'LA, LA, LA, NOT LISTENING.'

'You don't want to hear how we made you?'

'Did the stork bring me?'

'No, we made l—'

'LALALALALALALA, CAN'T HEAR YOU. GOING TO THERAPY NOW.'

I was born in Israel to an English mother and a very Israeli father. Israelis are well known for two things – a lack of social graces and extreme paranoia. My dad was so Israeli he always reverse-parked in case he needed to make a quick getaway (I still have no idea from whom). He was so Israeli he'd show his appreciation for a good meal by licking his plate in the middle of the restaurant. He was so Israeli he taught us Morse code as kids in case we were kidnapped and needed to tap for help.

My parents met after my mum had left university to move to Israel in the name of love, only to find the man who had encouraged her to move there had already moved on with another woman by the time she arrived. My dad, according to many, many people, who have told me in a number of inappropriate ways, was an exceptionally handsome man. He was a photography student who had been a helicopter captain in the Israeli Defense Forces and came complete with a harrowing near-death experience after a helicopter crash had broken nearly every bone in his body. My mum was also a beauty, but she didn't quite know her currency in the same way my dad very obviously did. My freshly heartbroken mother met my probably-a-bad-idea-but-appealing father because my mum's sister was marrying my dad's brother. It's not incest. As a result, though, I share all four grandparents with my first cousins. It bears repeating – IT'S NOT INCEST.

I was born in 1987, shortly after my parents moved with my older brother from a transcendental meditation community at the top of a mountain, where they lived with my aunt, uncle and three cousins (still not incest), to an anthroposophical kibbutz in the Galilee region. Transcendental meditation, for those who haven't had the pleasure, is a spiritual practice, some proponents of which believe that at a certain stage of enlightenment literally enables you to fly. Anthroposophy is, according to Google, an educational, therapeutic and creative system created by Rudolf Steiner. It postulates the existence of an objective, intellectually comprehensible spiritual world that is accessible by direct experience through inner development. If you didn't understand a word of that, don't feel bad. I went to a Steiner school, which is also called Waldorf education, until I was seventeen and I have no idea what it's supposed to mean. Friends who grew up with TVs have suggested it might have something to do with the Muppets. I don't know about that, but the system does tend to attract a few. If this all sounds very weird, that's because it is. Much of my childhood involved prancing about in silk robes. There is a huge organic movement within the Steiner community and it tends to attract people who believe in every type of quackery on offer. We're talking the full vaccine-sceptic, homeopathy-loving, technology-eschewing monty. According to Steiner philosophy, we choose our parents, so in all likelihood I only have myself to blame for all of this.

When my mum was six months pregnant with me, she discovered that my dad was having an affair. Not only that but he'd had numerous other affairs over the years – even when they were trying to bring me into the world. Thanks to overexposure to damaging New Age philosophies, my poor mum spent much of my childhood attributing what everyone saw as my 'hysteria' to emotional damage inflicted by her, in the womb, because she had a totally normal emotional reaction to her husband, and father of her toddler and unborn child, screwing around behind her back.

I was born at home, the product of two bohemian kibbutzniks whose greatest desire was to grow organic vegetables and organic children. My parents have told me many times that I came to them both in respective dreams asking to be called Sara. On this claim I call bullshit. Not even because of the implied mysticism, but because I refuse to believe that my disembodied spirit would actively request a self-inflicted lifetime of people mispronouncing my name.

'It's S-A-R-A, no H. Say it like you're really frustrated, like S-ARGH, uh!'

'Oh, Zara?'

'No . . .'

'Nice to meet you, Sarah.'

My four-letter name is apparently such a challenge that it's misspelled several times in my baby books – by my own mother. I have friends of over a decade who still call me Sarah because I was too polite to correct them and it's definitely too late now. I guess this is the least embarrassing way to tell them.

Another dubious claim made by my parents is that, when placed on my stomach as a newborn, I raised my own head and looked around me. My dad used to proudly tell everyone that from then on they never had to support my head, which may go some way towards explaining my lifetime of neck problems. But this I can absolutely believe – upon looking around me I apparently decided 'fuck this place', because I spent the next five hours screaming my head off. Perhaps because the first thing I overheard was my parents' plans to plant a tree on my placenta. Years later, I would visit my birthplace for the first time and go in search of a tree bearing fruit with my angry red little face on them, but I never found it. But I digress. You'll notice I do that a lot. It wouldn't be a complete tour of my brain without enjoying the bouncy walls. BOING! Off topic. BOING! Back on topic again – I never lost the original thread; I just took a little detour. You'll get used to it.

When I was eight months old, we moved from Israel to England, where we set up home just outside what's affectionately known as the cult capital of the UK. East Grinstead is home to the mystic order of Rosicrucians, the ultra-Catholic order of Opus Dei, the Christian Scientists, the Ashworth Dowsers, the Pagan Federation, The Church of Jesus Christ of Latter-day Saints and Scientology's UK headquarters. My parents were lured there by the Anthroposophical Society, having been sent away by the Israeli kibbutz to train in Steiner-approved professions in order to be truly worthy of living within the community.

We moved into a little flat in Forest Row, a quaint village that time forgot, where everybody knew everybody and their business. It was the kind of place you'd be punished the moment you even contemplated misbehaving because your parents would somehow already know about it. The village was mostly inhabited by Steiner types, anthroposophical shops and, its crowning glory, the local Steiner school, inconveniently located opposite the local Scientology school so the parts of my childhood not spent explaining that I was not a product of incest were instead spent insisting that I wasn't a Scientologist. After a short spell there, we moved to a larger family home in East Grinstead itself where we would spend the rest of my childhood. My parents stopped speaking Hebrew directly to us and used it instead to argue with each other, so these days my Hebrew hurtles jarringly from toddler-like idiosyncrasy to all the bad words. 'Can I have some ice cream, YOU CHEATING SON OF A BITCH?'

As soon as I was old enough, my parents put me into a Steiner playgroup. It was a gentle, naturally lit space with weird, crooked architecture. Steiner architecture studiously avoids using right angles for reasons that have never quite been made clear to me. Because of this everything looks a bit like the *Simpsons* episode in which Ned Flanders lost his house in a hurricane and his incompetent neighbours did a half-arsed job trying to rebuild it, tipping the usually chipper character into a nervous breakdown. Whenever I see a Steiner-sanctioned building with its unnecessarily complicated geometry, I can't help but think, *They did their best . . . shoddily-iddily-iddily-diddily . . .*

Tales of my early boo-hooing have traditionally been framed as more comic than tragic. Growing up, my parents would tell anyone who would listen about 'Sara's little tantrums'. As my mum describes, I didn't like to hear the word 'no'. According to legend, the tantrums would come with a warning system: an angry little bump appearing between my eyebrows, my mouth drooping into an upside-down 'u' and then a three-second grace period (counted down by my parents in unison for effect) before I started screaming my head off.

As a toddler, the crying began to be a noticeable problem and frankly, given what you know so far, can you blame me? The waterworks made their most frequent appearances when I was away from my parents, when I would do all I could to prevent them from having anything resembling a social life. Babysitters and playgroup teachers alike were in for hours of meltdowns, where I would insist that I was dying and my mum needed to come back and tend to me before my batteries would run out.

Socialising has never been intuitive for me and so it's been a lifelong process of trial and error. In my beta-testing phase, also known as playgroup, I learned that constant crying fits fell into the category of 'error'. Showing weakness doesn't win you friends – but it does inspire the other kids to throw sand in your eye.

I was a sensitive child. I know this because I was frequently told to stop being so sensitive. Is there a product for that? Like an extra-gentle toothpaste for your emotional wellbeing? Sensodyne for the soul? This sensitivity manifested itself in extreme attachment issues. I would very easily become fixated on everything I encountered: people, places, inanimate objects. And I couldn't separate out emotions that were appropriate for humans and meaningful relationships from attachments to random stuff.

I would get so attached to toys in shops that I would pick them up and refuse to put them down. Often I would latch on to stuffed animals with whom I'd formed an instant deep and meaningful connection. By the time my mum said 'no', I'd already fleshed it out with a whole personality and backstory. Most of the time I was wrenched from the object of choice, wailing my little heart out, but occasionally it was easier for my poor mum to just pay for the damn thing and get me home without a fuss. Once I had them in my possession, I nurtured each of these inanimate objects with an obsessive maternal passion. Each one had its own character and unique role in my little organisation.

'Sara, do you really need all these toys? Let's have a clear-out. What about R2-D2? You don't even like *Star Wars*.'

'No. He's the night watchman.'

'Well, you never play with this teddy.'

'So you're just going to separate her from her kids?'

Every evening before bed, I would painstakingly organise my toys into pairs so each one had a designated sleeping buddy. This wasn't arbitrary, mind; there was a deep and complex thought process about compatibility and companionship behind each pairing, based on their personality profiles. Brave toys would be assigned to look after the timid ones. Sick toys would be placed with toys with medical qualifications. Every now and then they'd be switched around to let the caregivers in the pairings have a night off – I didn't want to forget their needs either. The important thing was that none of them would be lonely or frightened during the night.

Leaving places was also a problem, particularly places where I'd formed happy memories. When we went on holiday and it was time to go home, I found the idea that I might never return unbearable. I would walk from room to room saying tearful, melodramatic goodbyes to each fixture. 'Bye, lamp. Thank you for lighting the room for me. Bye, carpet, I really enjoyed walking on you. Bye, picture of a sailing boat, I only just noticed you, but I think I'll miss you most of all.' Then I'd take a souvenir, like a handful of gravel, or a twig from a tree outside – something to make me feel like I'd keep that place with me forever. In my heart. Or, if that proved impractical, in a little jar on my windowsill.

OK, I admit it, I'm kind of a hoarder. Things have to be prised from my devastated hands in order to be thrown away.

'You don't understand – this is the milk carton lid I was holding when I last talked to my mum on the phone.'

'Sara, your mum's fine.'

'Yes, but what if one day she's not and I've thrown away one of my most important memories?'

My house is so full of clutter that if it weren't for my husband quietly disposing of things like the empty conditioner bottle that 'served me so well', I'd probably have to build a fort out of it to live in. I have four giant memory boxes full of things with sentimental value. Birthday cards from people I haven't spoken to in years – some from people I can't actually remember at all but who 'must have meant something at some point if I kept this'.

For the most part, people around me protect me from myself. Useless pieces of crap I'm likely to forget about go missing without fuss or fanfare. But sometimes I get so attached to things that extreme measures have to be taken to prise them from my unwilling hands. One such example was my *bakbuk* (pronounced 'buck-BOOK'), Hebrew for 'bottle', specifically a baby bottle I'd had for years, which I hung on to long past the stage of it being sanitary. It was no longer just a vessel for milk, I would only drink out of my bakbuk, like a paranoid former secret agent who only drinks from a hip flask in case someone tries to poison them. I wonder where I learned that. It would seem the apple doesn't fall far from the placenta tree. The rubber end of my bakbuk was chewed into oblivion.

My parents tried waiting for me to tire of my bakbuk of my own accord, but when I became the almost-school-age child gnawing on a rubber nipple they took decisive action. When regular bakbuk interventions proved ineffective, my dad sat me down and explained, 'There's a family who have just had a baby. They're very poor and they don't have enough money to get their baby a bakbuk. Without a bakbuk they can't feed their baby and the baby will starve and die. I know it's a lot to ask, but if you give up your bakbuk, you'll be saving the baby's life.'

Well, that did the trick. I didn't want a starving baby on my conscience.

'You're doing the right thing,' said my dad sagely, before waiting until I was at a safe distance and throwing it in the bin.

The loss of my bakbuk left a hole in my life that took three years to fill. I was eight when my heart was finally won by Piggy. Piggy is a hot-water bottle cover, given to me for Hanukkah during a family trip to Israel for my cousin's bar mitzvah. Piggy's head, it turned out, was the perfect size on which to rest my chin. For twenty-four years Piggy has been my dirty little secret. When I say 'dirty', I mean that literally; he's very delicate and I don't like to wash him too often. Piggy is my most treasured possession. He is more welcome in my bed than any man. I am so paranoid about leaving Piggy behind or losing him to an overzealous customs agent who assumes he must be full of drugs (because why else would a woman in her thirties be carrying this monstrosity around?). I never take him anywhere. When I go on holiday, I leave him in a fireproof safe. If I ever got burgled, I can only imagine the thieves' disappointment when they smash the thing open and the loot is just a tattered old pig with three decades' worth of inbuilt diseases. I'm not saying Piggy is responsible for the coronavirus outbreak, but I can't say the same for swine flu.

If my attachment to inanimate objects seems unhealthy, it's not a patch on how I feel about people. During my early childhood, I would walk past strangers and suddenly feel a pang of agony that I would never see them again. That was the lowest bar. If someone was kind to me, I clung to them like a little weepy limpet. Clinging would be another great life skill I would hone over the years. I had, and still have to this day, great trouble letting people go – even to the bathroom.

I've been described as intense, which is totally unfair, and I'd really like a list of reasons why people think that and then to discuss each one in detail over a special weekend I've planned for us at a remote cabin in the woods. It's not that I'm scary; I just have a different notion of friendship to most people. Once I consider someone a close friend, they might as well be family. I'm the kind of friend that rushes to hospital bedsides or sends flowers when pets die or shows up to a casual hangout with a platter of cupcakes. OK, I'm a lot, but I'm also the kind of friend who will be there for the hard times, even if I'm crying all over your tragedy.

Being an overly sensitive crybaby with an empathy chip on the fritz comes with countless hazards. I cannot bear to hurt anyone, even when it's well deserved. I cry when an out-and-out monster dies because 'they never got a chance to redeem themselves'. Fortunately for me, I'm not always aware of my impact on others (thank you, low self-esteem and general obliviousness) and so I'm not always conscious of when I've upset somebody, but when I realise it's absolutely crushing.

In playgroup I was friendly with a sweet, quiet little girl, let's call her Sally, who was due to attend my upcoming fourth birthday party. But one day Sally came into playgroup with a huge globule of goo on her inner eye. It was all I could see, looming, sticky and snotty on her face. Looking at it made me feel nauseated. After she had removed the offending gunk, I informed her that while I had enjoyed our friendship, she was no longer invited to my birthday party because I simply couldn't risk another oozing during the festivities. If she reacted, I didn't notice, because having dispatched with the unpleasantness, I continued my day, happily oblivious.

That evening my mother got a phone call. It was Sally's mother, rightly calling to tell my mum what her horrible child had said to her daughter. My mum sat me down and asked me to remember a time when someone had said something to make me feel sad and made me cry. 'Now,' she said, 'remember how that feels, because Sally is sad and crying because of what you said to her and that you excluded her from your party.' The world came crashing down. It hadn't occurred to me that Sally's feelings might be hurt by not being allowed to attend my stupid party. I had *hurt* someone. I didn't even want my stuffed toys to feel left out but here I was leaving out a real person. I burst into big heaving sobs of remorse. My mum told me I had to say sorry to Sally and reinvite her. There was no argument from me. I was relieved that she had told me what to do to make it right. At my party the following weekend she was the guest of honour. To be honest, I probably overdid it. I just about stopped short of singing 'Happy Birthday' to *her*.

From then on I decided to do my best to be kind and put other people's feelings first. This desire stemmed from an unhealthy mix of altruistically caring too much about how other people felt and selfishly caring too much about what other people thought of me, and I started to overcompensate. Oversharing took on a whole new meaning. I couldn't bear for anyone to miss out on something I had, so I would give out my food, toys, items of clothing other people liked (mercifully this rarely happened), whatever I had going. What was mine was anyone's.

Maybe that sounds like a nice quality on paper, but when you'll give anything away to anyone, it makes people uncomfortable. To me, stuff is just that – stuff. What I didn't realise was that other people have all sorts of ideas of power, status and control attached to *stuff*. By giving it all away upfront and trying to please people, I've scared off more friends over a lifetime than I can count. This is also, sadly, a trait that attracts an unpleasant cohort of manipulators and users. People who take advantage of a good nature and unwillingness to offend anyone. These days, though, I pre-empt the problem by warning everyone I meet how easy I am to take advantage of, so they know not to take advantage of me. What could possibly go wrong?

Before you feel too sorry for me, there are benefits to being overly sensitive. I'm the first one people phone with things like job or baby news, because they know they'll get a satisfying reaction. I never have something in my eye for long before it's washed away with the tide. Oh, and it's very handy for getting out of parking tickets and rail fines. When it came to getting through my childhood, however, being the school crybaby turned out to be the tip of the iceberg.

2

CHATTERBOX

I'm twenty-seven years old and I'm late for an evening improv class. Despite having no time or energy to travel into London once a week, I've decided to 'challenge' myself by staring uncomfortably into a stranger's eyes for ~~1,000 years~~ a few minutes every Tuesday night. My blood sugar is dangerously low and bitter experience has taught me that as my energy dwindles so do my social skills, so I dart into Sainsbury's to grab a banana.

The shop assistant offers me a bag. The sentiment I want to express is: 'No thank you, I'm going to eat it now.' What I actually say, in a tone that is meant to sound friendly and winning but comes out sex-pest creepy, is: 'No thanks, I have big plans for this banana.'

I have spent many years in a love-hate relationship with words. By the age of one I had learned a hundred of them. In my thirties I still haven't figured out how to use them without pissing someone off.

If my early vocabulary was a clue to anything being different about me, my parents didn't spot it. People don't take their kid to a psychologist because they're clever; they competitively humblebrag to their other insufferable parent friends – kind of like I'm doing now, obviously as an example of what humblebragging looks like and not because I want you to know that I'm a genius. I wasn't really aware of just how amazing I was (I'm not sure I'm doing this right) until I was twenty-nine, speculating with my mum about when my baby nephew might start talking.

'I don't know.' she said. 'You had a hundred words by the age of one. It's all in your baby book.'

'Ah yes, the sacred, infallible baby book in which you misspelled my name?'

'It was a transliteration. I knew your name.'

At seventeen months, according to this baby bible, little Sarah started talking in full sentences. Excited for a play-date my mum had arranged, I answered the door to my friend with 'Hello, Jerica, would you like to come in?' I take this claim with a pinch of salt. Not the talking in full sentences bit – that I believe – but that I had a friend.

Recently my mum unearthed a pile of long-lost childhood videos, including a short snippet of our early days in England. I am around thirteen or fourteen months old, playing with my brother on the floor of our small flat above the Circle K. I have a toy remote-control rabbit, and I'm talking into the controller as if it's a phone in a mixture of Hebrew and English while my brother answers into the toy rabbit as if it's the other line.

''LO?' I yell. ''LO? *Yodea* [Hebrew for 'I know'], fine.'
I pass the receiver to my mum and announce to her
that I'm a 'good girl'. (I AM SO GOOD AT HUMBLE-
BRAGGING.)

My parents and brother start quizzing me. My brother
is a . . .

'Boy,' I answer.

'Sara is a . . .'

'Boy,' I say.

Everyone laughs. They try again. This time I say 'girl'.

'*Abba* is a . . .' they prompt.

'Boy,' I respond.

'*Ima* is a . . .'

'Girl,' I say, and so on.

The gender-normative brainwashing aside (hey, it was
1988), I was stunned to see that at what couldn't have
been more than fourteen months I could understand the
concept of binary gender and impose it on everyone in
the room. My parents were delighted.

It's always struck me as confusing how babies spend
the first few months of their lives being relentlessly
encouraged to talk, then the rest of their childhood being
told to shut up. I was no exception – the only problem
was the shutting-up bit. I was as good at that as I am at
humblebragging (I think that might be a humble-neg –
oh God, it's all so confusing). Equipped with my new
extensive vocabulary, I set about irritating everyone who
crossed my path by becoming, as a boss would one day
describe me as I sat red-faced with the vain effort of

repressing tears in my appraisal, a 'constant generator of noise'. I liked saying things. I liked finding a thousand different ways to say things. I wanted to do everything in my power to make myself understood.

Being understood was a rare phenomenon for me. It didn't matter how much effort went into explaining myself, somehow everyone around me seemed to get the wrong end of the stick. Trying to make my facial expressions, body language and tone of voice line up with the words that were coming out of my mouth felt like patting my head, rubbing my tummy and juggling fiery knives. I was completely uncoordinated when it came to emoting. If I tried to smile, people told me to stop smirking. If I was being sincere, people told me to stop being sarcastic. If I was being sarcastic, people took me literally. Whatever I tried to communicate through the unspoken language that everyone else was using, my face and body stubbornly refused to play ball. They intuitively knew that people like me are supposed to run away from the ball. It was enormously frustrating and frightening, like being in a nightmare where you're trying to speak but nothing comes out of your mouth, except instead of nothing coming out of your mouth, everything comes out of your mouth – and it comes out all wrong.

In the absence of the 'correct' body language that seemed to come so easily to everyone else, I clung to my words as my most valuable tool. They were like floatation devices in a vast ocean of misunderstandings – something to hang on to while I kicked furiously and tried not to fall into the confusing chasm of everything that can be mistranslated between two people. Words, to borrow a few from the Bee Gees, or, if we're being heretical, Boyzone, were all I had.

If the definition of madness is trying the same thing over and over and expecting different results, I was certifiable. Words didn't make me friends, or make people believe me when I was telling the truth or make people understand my experience when I was stating it as clearly as I possibly could. I felt like a tiny defence lawyer, always on the back foot and sounding like I was protesting too much. When my words weren't received the way I'd intended, I reached into my arsenal for more, making them bigger and bigger until they just sounded like . . . well, drama.

Another reason I was helpless to stop words pouring indiscriminately from my face was that they took up all the space in my head. My brain has never, for a single moment, been quiet. It is constantly chattering to itself, analysing everything into oblivion, second-guessing itself, second-guessing the second-guessing, reliving an argument, reminding me of that dumb thing I did, which reminds me of all those other 'dumb things' I did, finally thinking of the perfect comeback in that argument I was reliving ten minutes ago, and SUDDENLY REMEMBERING I'M GOING TO DIE ONE DAY. It's constantly bouncing from topic to topic and back again, taking detours, changing the subject and switching back without warning in a way that only I can follow. If it's frustrating for the people around me, I CAN NEVER SWITCH IT OFF. Trust me, nobody is more exhausted by me than I am.

My brain is like a malfunctioning automated word factory, constantly overproducing words and it's my job to find places for the overflow. The only way to quiet them down for a moment is to put them in a proper place, but the second I've finished arranging one set of surplus words, I return to the warehouse to find fresh chaos has stacked up in my absence.

Early on, I learned to deal with the cacophony of noise in my brain in two ways. First, I made them a part of my rich inner world. I used them in stories and poems and essays and articles and manifestos and diaries and anywhere else I could find to stuff them. I memorised them from books and repeated them like mantras. I used them in long, elaborate fantasies and make-believe worlds, which I would inhabit in such great detail that it sometimes became difficult to distinguish them from reality.

The second way I dealt with the chatter was to just say whatever was in my head at all times, whether or not it was appropriate. It is rarely, I've learned, appropriate. My words would barge in like tiny unwanted tech billionaires in their mini submarines announcing that they were there to save the day, while getting in the way. They were always there. The nervous fillers of comfortable silences. The blunt deliverers of uncomfortable truths. The valiant diggers of unnecessary holes. My words wouldn't quit – even when people were screaming at me to stop talking. Which people did. A lot. One of those people was my dad.

My dad loved peace and quiet. He did not love coming home to a high-pitched little motormouth who couldn't make her words slow down. Knowing intellectually that I ought to speak more slowly and quietly, or not at all, did nothing to hold back the verbal diarrhoea. It was compulsive and beyond my control. Even when I could feel the pressure building in the room, even when I could see him start to turn red, I was helpless to make it stop. If anything, it prompted yet more word spillage – nervous chatter with no aim or purpose. Until he erupted.

My father's outbursts would often happen over dinner, after he'd had a long day at work. He would come in exhausted, at the very upper limit of his tolerance for sensory input. We would sit down to dinner and I would start squeaking away about everything and nothing while my mum nervously tried to calm me. And then the explosion would happen. When he shouted, it felt like he was shaking the room, charging the air and shattering the windows.

I could physically feel his anger like an earthquake. Sometimes this was metaphorical, sometimes it was literal – a smashed plate and spaghetti sliding down the wall. I was very aware that I was the trigger for these outbursts and it seemed very much as if my dad didn't like me. I crystallised this as the truth and held it inside my heart for so long it became part of my identity. I was frequently punished by being sent away from the family dinner table. I vividly remember sitting at the top of the stairs, watching through the gaps in the banisters as my dad chewed with his mouth open. I would observe his mouth opening and closing, blistering with rage. Why did he get to blatantly break the household rule of 'eat politely' when I had just been sent away from the table for the far lesser crime of talking? To this day people chewing with their mouths open sends me into a visceral rage.

I know now that my dad loved me. But at that formative age not being good enough for one of my parents became the shaky foundation on which I would build whatever I would one day assemble of my self-esteem. My dad was never once physically abusive. But I still spent a large chunk of my childhood feeling absolutely terrified of him.

Nevertheless, I adored my dad. It would have been a lot easier if he was simply the villain of this piece and I could transfer all this self-loathing on to him and blame him for everything, but in many ways he was a fantastic parent. He was responsible and diligent, working a job he detested to give me and my brother what he felt was the best possible life. He was charming, clever, creative, kind and fun and always encouraging of us, our interests and our dreams. An immensely likeable man, his attention felt like what I imagine basking in the sun must feel like to people who aren't pale, photosensitive vampires whose worst nemesis is that fucking cosmic fireball. When he felt like it, he was an incredible parent. The problem was, he didn't always feel like it. Or perhaps, invoking that fickle beast hindsight once again, he didn't always feel up to it. During my childhood, he rationed out his love and approval in glorious little snippets, there one second and maddeningly, devastatingly gone the next. Loving my dad gave me emotional whiplash. As a result, I tried desperately to earn his approval. I was constantly terrified about being dumped or replaced. When my dad introduced my brother as his son, I wailed, 'but I'm your MOON!' When my dad announced he was getting a work laptop, I burst into tears and yelled 'I'M your laptop!' I had imagined that his laptop, whatever it was, would take my rightful place being read stories on my dad's lap.

To say my dad had lots of interests would be the understatement of the century. Much of his life was defined by a series of consuming obsessions. Some were long-term loves that stayed with him his whole life, others were passing fads. Lots of them, to the obvious detriment of our little family unit, were women. Between guitars and cycling and celestial navigation and slide rules and sailing and watercolour painting and creative writing and meditation (and did I mention the women?) it was hard to get a look in.

I so desperately wanted to be the focus of his universe with the ease and unconditional knowing that I felt from my mum. My mum was my constant. We argued, like mothers and daughters do, but I never worried my mum would disappear or stop loving me. She wasn't a ticking time bomb, kind one moment but liable to blow up in my face if I connected the wrong fuse. I craved that stability from my dad, but unfortunately the only way I knew how to communicate this to him was with more of my unwelcome words. Love, I decided, was only worth anything if it was hard to earn. Unconditional love, love easily won and kept, was garbage.

Because my nervous chattering was working out so well for me at home, I decided to deploy it in a whole new setting – school. I started at the local Steiner school having graduated from playgroup to kindergarten to Class One. The 'big school' building, much like playgroup, eschewed evil right angles. It smelled delicious, like beeswax and lacquered wood. Abstract watercolour paintings covered every inch of the warm yellow walls. Each classroom contained multiple hand-crafted nests of felt gnomes. Gnomes, by the way, would feature big time in my early education. Science and mathematics not so much.

The welcoming womb of the Lower School building was set at the top of the vast, idyllic school grounds. At the time the school owned acres of land, boasting picturesque woodland, waterfalls, gardens, lakes, a perpetually freezing outdoor swimming pool, an actual listed manor house known to us as 'The Mansion', which teachers and students alike agreed was 'seriously haunted'.

Class sizes were small, with around twenty kids per class. On paper it sounds like the perfect environment for a sensitive, easily overwhelmed child and, in literal terms, it was. But with so few kids to interact with and the length of time we would be travelling together, usually around twelve years, it meant no second chances. If you blew your goodwill with the group, you blew it forever.

I found this out the hard way when I tried to sit with the other girls at breaktime on the first day of school. Within seconds it was obvious who was boss – a pretty snub-nosed little girl, let's call her Talia (not her real name, but, God help me, I'm thirty-three I'm still kind of terrified of her). Talia had an aura of menacing authority and, like the guy who punches the biggest dude in prison to establish a reputation, she wasn't messing around. She didn't need to physically punch me to establish dominance. Talia had the gift of punching with her words. 'You can't sit here,' she informed me. 'This table is for cool people.' I wasn't old enough or socialised enough to know what a cool person was, but I could extrapolate from context that I wasn't one of them. From that moment on there was no bigger prize in the known universe than becoming one. 'Cool' became an elusive, coveted status on which I wasted the most precious years of my childhood and teens, chasing the impossible and trying to impress people who were objectively unpleasant and not worth impressing.

My interminable chattering did not go unnoticed and I was immediately branded 'annoying', a label I internalised but still could do nothing about. The more I tried to explain that I wasn't annoying, the more annoying I came across. Is there anything more annoying than someone trying to explain why they're not annoying?

From the ages of eight to fourteen my teachers sent home frequent complaints about my talkative nature via my school reports. 'Sara needs to concentrate on her work and talk less' and 'She has been curbing her periods of chatting and her impulses to start or respond to provocative remarks. If she can manage discretion and the wisdom of withdrawal from a foolish fray, she will gain in social ease and the respect of her classmates'. One school report opened bluntly with the sentence: 'Phew – what a talker! And only when it suits her.'

I tried shutting up, I really did, but I was a compulsive wordaholic. I'd often find myself staring enviously at the shy, quiet kids who, with hindsight, probably had their own shit to deal with, but to me came across as paragons of self-control. While they abstained from chattering, they had the luxury of time. You can always come out of your shell – it's a lot harder to stuff yourself back in.

The bullying, because of course there was bullying, was a mixture of active bullying – mostly taunts, name-calling, taking my things, playing unkind pranks on me and, most deliciously, trying to make me cry (I have to say they really lost my respect here – they could have at least given themselves a challenge) and rejection. I was a social leper. To interact with me was to be contaminated with my inherent loserness.

Talia established her territory around a furry red tree known as 'the Monkey Tree'. She declared herself, quite progressively for the mid–late nineties, 'Quing She-He of the Monkey Forest'. The Monkey Forest was *the* place to be and the hive of all social activity in our class and Talia was its undisputed, all-powerful ruler. Quing She-He would sit on their throne in the boughs of the Monkey Tree, surrounded by assorted henchkids, deciding who was and wasn't worthy of entering the small enclave of trees. If you were out, you were *out*. Nothing – not bribery, not begging, not even crying, would grant me entry to this gender-neutral Eden. Attempts to sneak in were met with firm resistance by her bouncers and, being a scrawny little weakling with poor muscle tone and a terror of, well, everything, I stood no chance in a physical confrontation.

The thing to do when you're being bullied is to tell an adult. So, I told my parents, prompting my dad into the overreaction of the century and a masterclass in Making Things Worse. Once, when a girl kicked me in the shin, my dad stormed into the classroom the following day, dragging me with him and, in front of the whole class, pulled up my trouser leg and shouted: 'LOOK WHAT YOU'VE DONE TO MY DAUGHTER'. From then on I decided to confide in my mother.

My mum and I turned to the teacher for support. When I say the teacher, I mean *the* teacher, because in Steiner education you have one teacher for most subjects until you're fourteen. The class teacher, let's call her Miss

Clarke, was a young, softly spoken woman who mostly wore flowy earthy-toned dresses and pashminas. She had a gentle sing-songy voice and a kind, round face. On paper, this very nice lady was absolutely the right person to tell. The problem with very nice people, however, is that they are not always the most effective at kicking ass and taking names. I remember many parent-teacher chats about the problem but very little meaningful progress being made.

Before long, it wasn't just an issue of compulsively overtalking, I was being told off for talking *back*. This confused me because I could see no discernible difference between talking and the *verboten* 'talking back' for which I was always in trouble. In my head talking back was just answering the teacher. They had spoken, I was replying. Why was what the teacher had to say more important than what I had to say? Particularly if they were wrong, which, in my mind, they frequently were. The concept of an unspoken social hierarchy was, at times, painfully clear to me, especially when it came to the ranking of popularity. But when it came to authority, it was utterly lost on me.

There was also my pesky sense of moral responsibility. I did not like it one bit if something was unfair. I hated it if someone was mean for no reason, whether it affected me or not. That meant I butted in. A lot. I despised it if one person, child or adult, got away with something that would have had consequences for someone else. That made me a tattletale or a troublemaker. If there was an injustice unfolding in front of me, I would stop everything to confront it.

And finally there was my troublesome belief in facts over feelings. I said things as I saw them – no sugarcoating. If someone was wrong, I corrected them. If a tense situation was unfolding in front of me, I was the one to bluntly name what was happening. If someone asked me a question, they got an honest answer. It took me many years to work out that other people need the truth gift wrapped for them.

My school reports were packed with complaints about my argumentative streak: 'Sara does not tolerate fools gladly and the resulting arguments prevent her getting down to work as quickly as she might' and 'She is not shy to speak her mind if something is not "fair" and this can sometimes interrupt lessons' and 'She has proved a prickly neighbour in the ring and is often involved in little disputes.'

The consensus was clear. I was an abrasive and disruptive influence and, yes, I had problems interacting with the other kids but . . . well, could you blame them? According to Steiner philosophy, kids have their own karma to work out and when it comes to bullying adults are not to intervene. Also, I really was very annoying, had I thought about maybe not trying so hard, talking so much and being less annoying?

Admittedly, I'm not great at getting the message, but this one was crystal clear. I was too annoying to sit with my family at the dinner table. Too annoying to sit with the other kids at school. Too annoying to even be thought of as a legitimate victim of bullying. At seven years old I began to hate myself.

3

SCAREDY-CAT

I'm seventeen years old and my mum is away on holiday. My friend and honorary godsister, Rhiannon, has come over to keep me company and we've decided to prove how tough we are by watching *The Blair Witch Project*. After we finish the movie, we somehow goad each other into going for a long walk in the woods. We get lost. Rhiannon finds the whole thing hilarious and I'm trying to match her nonchalant energy, but I am the opposite of nonchalant. I am positively chalant. The forest starts spinning with every passing second. Every rustling leaf, every moan of the wind, every animal scampering past is enough to freeze me with fear. A twig snaps somewhere in the distance and I burst into tears and start hyperventilating. It is then, as I sink to the ground with my head between my legs, that Rhiannon sheepishly, full of remorse, admits she's known how to get home the whole time.

After Rhiannon leaves, I sit in the living room, rooted to the spot in pure terror. It is still daylight and I am in for a whole night of this at home alone. The central heating gurgles and creaks into action and I let out a blood-curdling scream. I run full pelt from the house, looking wildly around and behind me for an assailant on my tail. It is one of the only times in my entire life that I have ever run at full speed. I keep running, despite developing an excruciating stitch in my side, and I don't stop until I reach my dad's house (spoiler alert – can you believe those two crazy kids couldn't work it out?). He opens the door to find me doubled over, panting, tears running down my face.

'The witch,' I gasp, as if that's an explanation. I stay at his place, sleeping on sofa cushions in the living room, until my mum comes home.

I've often been asked why I'm so terrified all the time. To that I say why isn't everybody else terrified all the time? We are all in constant danger every second of every day. You might think you're safe, snuggled on your sofa watching *Love Island* but at any second a plane could just crash right into your house. Reckon you're secure there at the kitchen table, flicking through the *Guardian*? At any moment you could get a paper cut that turns septic, develop septicaemia and die. 'Fine,' I hear you say, 'I'll just sit here and do absolutely nothing.' Up to you. Enjoy your deep vein thrombosis.

Congratulations, you now have my debilitating anxiety disorder. You're welcome. I told you I was good at sharing.

I was six months old when I first discovered that the world isn't a safe place. We were still living at the anthroposophical kibbutz and eating our meals, I assume, out of a communal trough. I haven't fact-checked this and frankly I don't want to. I managed to slip an olive from the dining table and swallowed it, before starting to turn purple. My dad held me upside down and slapped my back until it came loose, saving my life. To this day I'm so afraid of choking I can't even chew gum without a lifeguard present.

A few months later, shortly after our move to England, when I was just learning to walk, my mum fell down the stairs with me in her arms. Physically, I was unharmed, but I decided there would be no more of that hazardous walking nonsense for a while. I didn't walk again until I was eighteen months old.

That was fine, though, because I didn't need to walk. I had my dad to carry me on his sturdy, safe shoulders. How free I felt, six feet tall, my curly strawberry-blonde head in the clouds, taking in the beauty of the . . . SMACK! That was me going headfirst into a sign my dad had failed to notice. I peeled backwards and landed with a thud, again miraculously not seriously injured. I swear I survived my unsupervised, unvaccinated childhood by sheer luck.

Most children bounce back from early traumatic experiences, get up and try again. Not I. I would file these incidents away in a permanent folder of things that are decisively not for me. I didn't go through mere phases of hang-ups and phobias that passed in their own time – I accumulated them. The contents of my brain very much resemble my external environment: cluttered with things I haven't needed or used in decades. A hoarder inside and out. Other kids collected Pogs and Beanie Babies; I collected neuroses. Each new nightmare scenario would be neatly filed away in the Disaster Directory. And every night my brain would flip through the pages, ordering an ordeal to ruminate over until morning.

I will die on this hill – a full night's sleep is a lie invented to make people feel bad for never having been able to attain it. When someone says they sleep like a baby, I have no point of reference for this. As a baby I woke up every hour on the hour, like a broken alarm clock sent from hell to torture my parents. My sleep did not improve as my childhood progressed. I still woke up on the hour every hour, but now with enough self-awareness to torture myself as well as my parents. It was, and still is, impossible to sleep through the constant whirring and chattering of my brain. When it wasn't busy berating me for all the mistakes I'd made during the day, it was hard at work convincing me that every terrifying paranormal phenomenon I'd ever heard of was real and coming to get me.

Great efforts were made to limit my access to things that might terrify me. Steiner communities generally discourage screen time and so we didn't have a television. Instead we had a monitor with its aerial removed, a eunuch of a television, which would be turned on for occasional treats after carefully supervised trips to the video shop. The monitor was covered in a silk cloth and topped with crystals, either to ward off evil spirits or, more charitably, so my parents could tell if it had been tampered with in their absence.

In any case the Steiner goal of letting a child develop their own imagination was an unmitigated success, one that backfired spectacularly. My parents believed in homeopathy, so perhaps they should have predicted that tiny doses of TV would actually be the most potent. I couldn't cope with the mildest of gore, having to look away for any scene that involved blood, guts or pain. I was terrified of everything. After we rented *Mars Attacks!*, I became obsessed with the big-brained aliens from outer space, convinced every passing car was a spaceship coming to beam me out of my bed. *Dracula: Dead and Loving It* was another notable mistake, and not just for Leslie Nielsen's career. To this day, even in the most oppressive of heatwaves, I sleep with my blanket tightly over my neck, lest a fanged comedian sneak in through my window to bite me. Let's face it, in my line of work these days that's not unreasonable.

The bedroom I shared with my brother was a weird mishmash of his stuff and mine. A symptom of too little space for two very different kids on to which neither of us, an awkward three and a half years apart, could comfortably assert our fledgling identities. Perhaps we had just been aggressively gendered by society, but my fairy princess aesthetic was totally killing his industrial vehicle-focused vibe. My Little Ponies shared a shelf with *Star Wars* figurines. Pictures of fairies hung behind dangling model aeroplanes. We slept in bunk beds, my brother on the top bunk and me in the bunk below.

My parents tried everything they could to make the environment as safe and comforting for me as possible. On my bunk hung a pink silk sheet, which was supposed to protect me from the outside world but, in reality, made me feel like a sitting duck, vulnerable to any psychopath who could easily disguise themselves as a parent or caregiver because of the gauzy haze separating us. Could be Mum, could be *a chainsaw-wielding maniac*! Perhaps the biggest menace of all was my own imagination.

Fear, my parents thought, was simply the absence of information. If I was scared of the dark, it was because I couldn't see what was in it. A night light ought to do the trick. It certainly did *a* trick – a visual trick of elongating the shadowy silhouettes behind the silk gauze so they flickered like horror-movie special effects. Perhaps, with hindsight, it wasn't the best idea to replace imagined danger, like night ghosts, with actual danger, like a naked flame next to a dangling piece of fabric. We found this out the hard way when the whole thing went up in flames – literally. My brother and I peered anxiously out from our bunks as my dad worked to tackle the blaze before it burned the house down with us in it. That was the end of the night-light experiment.

Desperate, my parents put a pouch under my pillow, which they filled with crystals, basically a hippie replacement for Xanax, and Guatemalan worry dolls, tiny little dolls made out of thread, which they insisted would protect me overnight. The way they're supposed to work is that the child tells the worry doll their specific worry, which is then transferred to the doll, leaving the child's mind clear for sleep, but nobody told me this. This is probably for the best as my list of worries was so long I would have been up all night talking to my worry doll. 'And another thing, Worry Doll, I'm worried I've been talking too long, and I've bored you and you're not going to want to be my friend any more. It's just that you haven't said anything in a really long time and I realise I'm kind of dumping all my problems on you. Is there anything you want to say to me? Are you mad at me? Worry Doll?'

When the crystals, worry dolls and narrowly averted house fire mysteriously failed to work, my dad wrote a bespoke poem for me to say every night to try to ease me into a state of relaxation and create the right frame of mind for me to get to sleep. He wrote it up on a beautiful background he painted himself and hung it by my bed. Every night, we would recite it together:

> Fairies, angels, wind and waves
> Flowers, yellow, red and white
> Gently close my sleepy eyes
> Cover me with love and light.

Fear, I've none, I'm strong and brave.
Sun and moon, stars shining bright
Take me to a paradise
Of golden days and silver nights.

Then, having calmed me down, he'd wind me right up again with a nightly epic performance of 'Golden Slumbers/Carry That Weight/The End' by The Beatles, complete with a manic a cappella instrumental. For sensitive Steiner kids with no access to TV, this was our Glastonbury. We'd get to the last notes of 'The End', flushed from jumping up and down in our beds, hyperactive balls of adrenaline, and that would be the energy on which we were expected to drift into a peaceful sleep.

The moment my parents left the room, my brain took charge.

'What was that sound?'

'Nothing. Just the heating. Go to sleep.'

'Are you sure it's the heating?'

'Yes, it sounds the same every night.'

'But if someone wanted to put snakes in your room, wouldn't they use the fact that they sound like the heating to their advantage?'

'I . . . I hadn't thought of that.'

'*IMA! IMA,* THERE ARE SNAKES IN MY ROOM!'

'No, darling, it's just the heating. Go to sleep.'

'Not until you've checked every corner of the room for snakes.'

'I've checked. No snakes.'

'What about the cupboards? Did you check the cupboards?'

'No snakes in the cupboards either.'

'How do you know unless you turn on the light? OW! THE LIGHT'S TOO BRIGHT.'

'OK, but there are no snakes. Go to sleep.'

'OK.' (Pause.) 'What's that dripping sound?'

'Probably just the tap. It sounds the same every night.'

'But what if tonight it's BLOOD?'

My parents' final act of desperation was to bribe me. Sugar was a hard-to-come-by commodity in a New Age environment, unless you faked an ailment, so your parents would give you useless, delicious homeopathy. Morning Chocolate, a luxury previously reserved for birthdays, became a reward for not disturbing my parents during the night. The problem was, you can't actually bribe a child out of legitimate terror. I very quickly stopped bothering my parents, but nothing had changed for me. I still lay awake night after night, locked in a chamber of horror created by my own mind, but now I was too ashamed to ask for help or comfort. Project Morning Chocolate, on the surface, was a great success and, in my parents' minds, evidence that I had been putting it on for attention. It fixed the behaviour – my parents no longer had to deal with my night terrors interrupting their much-needed sleep. But for the little sleep-deprived scaredy-cat in the room next door, all it meant was that I understood that I was inconveniencing others and that now I was in it alone.

As I got older, my phobias ballooned out of all control. The world around me felt like the Upside Down from *Stranger Things* – a shadowy, uncanny replica of the real world where everything safe and familiar to me was rotting and full of hidden horrors. I couldn't look in the mirror because I imagined I would see a rotting, maggot-infested corpse looking back at me, or a ghost instead of my own reflection or I would accidentally think the name of a horror movie villain three times and they would appear behind me and gut me. I couldn't turn on the tap when I was alone in case blood came out instead of water. I began to develop little rituals to cope with the fear. If I flushed the toilet and there were no adults around to guard me, I had to be fully in bed before the end of the flush or the toilet monster would crawl out and get me. And, once in bed, I couldn't have so much as a toe exposed in case I was grabbed by a zombie hand and dragged down to hell. I know that's not what zombies do, but I was working with some pretty limited cultural references.

I could not be left in a room alone. To be left alone was to be doused in an icy bucket of terror. Being left alone felt like being in mortal peril. I would stand stock-still, too afraid to move a muscle in case I woke the undead or angered a malevolent spirit. When I was at home, I would follow my mother everywhere, from room to room, like an anxious little shadow. I followed her to the bathroom. I clung to her clothing. I begged her not to let me out of her sight. She started to lose her mind with the lack of privacy and alone time. And the more she tried to take space for herself, the harder I clung.

That was until I found out about paranormal possession. The idea that someone could look like your loved one and use that safety and familiarity against you gripped me like my own personal demonic possession. It stole the idea of my parents as safe people. Every time I felt tempted to call for them, I'd imagine them turning slowly with sinister grins on their faces, their eyes glowing red and telling me 'There's nowhere to hide now'.

When I was about five years old, there was a rare occasion when my mum had put her foot down about me following her into the bathroom. I waited outside, shivering with terror until I heard her flush the toilet. Once I was confident the toilet monster hadn't surfaced, and she emerged, I went to use the bathroom myself. That's when I saw it – a tiny bit of blood on a tissue. It's easy now, as an adult, to see that my mum was so harassed by the whimpering little girl waiting outside for her that she simply hadn't fully flushed. But all I saw was validation that my mum had been possessed, killed someone in the bathroom and flushed away the body.

'MURDERER!' I screamed at her. 'You're a MURDERER!'

I'd like to say I hurtled down the stairs away from her but descending a flight of household stairs was one of my many fears, so I wobbled away as fast as I could manage, hiding behind my dad as soon as I'd reached the landing.

And that's how it fell upon my poor dad to teach his bawling, horrified daughter about periods.

For the most part, I felt safer at school. It was a bright, warm environment and despite my social issues I was glad to have so many other people around. Safety in numbers was a genuine comfort, even if those numbers were full of jerks who didn't like me. But then there was the Mansion – the building that had become its own urban legend. There were many conflicting stories about the ghost (or ghosts) in the Mansion, but here is the version that I've remembered: there was a noblewoman who once lived there who had died in a tragic boating accident. The details are fuzzy. Both teachers and students who lodged in the Mansion claimed to have seen her. I became convinced that if I ever saw her, I would instantly die.

It was in that frame of mind that I began weekly piano lessons in the Mansion. I know now that I probably could have just asked the kindly piano teacher to come and meet me in the hallway and walk me through. But I was too scared to articulate my fears in case the ghost got wind of them and killed me for being a snitch. So once a week I would stand in the Mansion's hallway with its black and white chequered flooring, drenched in dread, trying to summon the courage to run the twenty or so metres from there to the Long Room, where my piano lessons took place. I would arrive week after week, blinking back tears of panic, out of breath from the sprint.

I began to develop Mansion-related safety rituals. To get across the chequered hallway I had to step on only the black tiles. If I stepped on a white tile, the ghost would get me. I created an imaginary friend – a *good* ghost, named Tiddlypong, whose job it was to protect me from the evil Mansion ghost. For a kid who kept her myriad fears so closely guarded, I was extremely loose lipped about Tiddlypong and made the mistake of telling the whole class about her and our antics. I was immediately branded a liar (fair, I guess) and, in my humiliation, sent Tiddlypong away, never to be seen or heard from again.

When I was ten, I read *The Witches* by Roald Dahl. I believed every last word of it. I decided that I was not going to suffer the same fate as the little eejits who got themselves turned into mice or trapped in paintings. I was going to be hyper-vigilant for the rest of my natural life. I started looking out for witches everywhere. I was a one-girl witch hunt. And if I ever saw one, I wasn't going to try to take them down. There would be no foolhardiness, no heroics, no grand showdown with the head witch. If I ever saw a witch, I would run as fast as my scrawny little legs would carry me (not very fast at all). I dutifully memorised all the warning signs that I might be in the presence of a witch.

Witches, according to Roald Dahl, always wear gloves to hide the fact that they have claws. They are bald, but wear wigs to hide it, so might be scratching their heads. They have large nostrils and children smell terrible to them. Their eyes flash purple. They have no toes, so would likely be wearing closed-toed shoes, perhaps glamorous ones to throw people off the scent. And, most damning of all, witches have blue spit.

One day, after my piano lesson, my mum was a few minutes late to pick me up. Rather than braving it back across the building alone to wait outside, I took refuge in the small administrative office. As I sat on a chair several sizes too big for me, kicking my legs back and forward, I heard a sweet, cooing voice. 'Are you OK, dear?' I looked up. I had never seen the woman before, which was unusual in a community of just a few hundred people. She looked at me kindly. A quote from *The Witches* echoed in my ears. 'She might even be your lovely school-teacher.' I said nothing but started to scan her for telltale signs. She lifted a gloved hand and scratched her head in bemusement. My blood ran cold.

'You know, I think I teach your brother,' she continued. That's exactly what a witch would say. I refused to look at her, staring instead at her glamorous pointy-toed boots, blood pounding in my ears, the room spinning. 'What's wrong?' she persisted.

I glanced up at her quickly and in that moment I could have sworn her pupils flashed purple. My teeth began to chatter. After what seemed like an age, my mum showed up, made polite conversation with my brother's teacher (poor, gullible Mum) and then left. I clung to her, pale and trembling, refusing to let go until we were safely in our car, looking behind us the whole journey home, half expecting to see the witch in hot pursuit. For the rest of my school life each time I saw that nice woman who was, in fact, just my brother's teacher, I ran and hid.

On top of my internalised fears of all things mystical and mythical, I had a whole other minefield of peril to navigate – the real world. The real world, as I've already mentioned, is brimming with countless mortal threats and I am a human risk assessment.

I never run too fast in case I fall over – unless I'm running from witches. I've never climbed a tree. I've never done a wheelie on a bike. I've never jumped out of anything attached to a cord or a parachute. I've never stuck pieces of wood to my legs and slid down a snowy surface. I was never that kid sitting at the top of the waterslide, too scared to let go, because there was no way in a million years I would have been persuaded to go anywhere near the top of that waterslide in the first place.

As I got older, every accident that happened in proximity to me, every death I heard about in my circles or on the news and, eventually, the near or total loss of actual loved ones, validated my fears. Life is so fragile. Anything can happen, no matter how careful you're being, so why increase those odds by chucking yourself out of a plane with just a flimsy piece of fabric standing between you and the reaper? I have no idea how everyone else walks around like the next day, or even the next second, is guaranteed.

We know two things for certain in life. First, that death will one day come for us all, no exceptions, and, second, that we have no idea when. To me, death is like a house guest who says they'll pop by 'at some point' but fails to specify a time. I can never relax knowing that the doorbell might ring at any second and catch me make-up-less in my pasta-stained pyjamas. The sound of every passing car has me jumping to my feet, turning off the telly and shoving the last of the clutter under the sofa. I see death in everything. Perhaps that is why I'm so sensitive to seeing dead animals. A two-second encounter with roadkill can send me into fits of tears and ruin my entire day. I recently had to abort an entire day out because I saw a dead pigeon by the side of the road.

I see death waiting for me in a speeding car as I cross the road. I see death ready to nudge those loose rocks to crush my car. I see death in every stranger who glances in my direction – who knows what they're capable of? I see death's grinning face reflected in every slippery surface, every unattended flame, every glance in the rear-view mirror. I say goodbye to my family before every hospital appointment, every routine flight, every time I do anything out of the ordinary that might make me vulnerable in a new way. Yes, I am a walking risk assessment or, as people around me put it, the Fun Police.

Death is there for every happy moment – every cuddle with my husband, every game with my nephew, every phone call with my mum. I'm not sure I've had one moment of pure joy in my adult life that hasn't been laced with the hyperawareness of my own mortality.

I continued to develop little rituals to cheat death. Some were sensible rules, like never doing dangerous things unsupervised, being extra careful when doing anything that might break so much as a nail, waiting for the lights to change before crossing the road (my life could be summed up in a montage of impatient companions waiting on the other side of the road having crossed ages ago, while I diligently wait for the little green man). Others were superstitious.

If I step on the cracks in the pavement with one foot, I have to balance it out by stepping with the other. That'll show you, reaper! Drains have their own system. Walking over one drain is neutral, walking over two is good luck, walking over three is a catastrophe. If I see an empty plug socket, I have to turn it off in case some unwitting passer-by sticks their fingers in it or it somehow starts a fire. I know the science isn't on my side here, but the impulse is powerful. Radio and TV volumes must always be on an even number. Five, for the purposes of this quirk, is an honorary even number. If I think a positive thought about the future, I must immediately pay for my hubris by tapping my head three times to show that I understand I'm not guaranteed a future. I have a ritual with my husband where every time he leaves the house I have to say 'Be careful' and he has to say 'I will'. If he says anything to me after that, we have to start the ritual all over again until we get it right. And, usually, I am the one annoyed with him for holding me up. I am at the mercy of countless compulsions, each developed over a lifetime to keep me and my loved ones here and breathing for another day. I could go on for hours. Yeah, fuck you, death. I'm winning.

4

SPOILED BRAT

It's a very special day. My grandma is receiving an award for ten years of volunteering at the Royal Free Hospital and she's asked me to go along as her date. She's in her eighties and spends every Friday there, using her experience as a now retired teacher to entertain kids receiving treatment. For an event hosted in a hospital cafeteria it's a surprisingly glittering affair, complete with a band, balloons and a lavish posh spread for the volunteers and their guests.

For most people this would be a treat. I, however, approach the buffet with growing, silent panic. There is literally nothing here I can eat. I stand with my empty plate, anxiety bubbling inside me, my brain working in overdrive to figure out what I could safely try, or what could be deceptively pushed around my plate. Usually, I would surreptitiously swap plates with my husband and let him have my leftovers. It's a symbiotic relationship and a system that has always worked exceptionally well for us. I'd go so far as to say it forms the foundation of our marriage. But he's not here to be my human dustbin and to cover up my mortifying food issues.

My grandma looks radiant in her sequined top, glowing with pride and enjoying the evening with all her volunteer pals. I desperately don't want to embarrass her or ruin her special day. She clocks the worry on my face, takes me aside and whispers, 'Don't fret, dear. I brought pizza for you in my handbag.' It's worth mentioning that I am thirty years old.

I have always been described by exasperated adults as a 'picky eater'. Perhaps, my parents wondered, it was because they had raised me vegetarian, narrowing my options? Or maybe, I countered, it was because when I was a toddler my mum used to chew up nuts and regurgitate them into my mouth like I was a baby bird, forever putting me off the very idea of food?

The truth was, almost all food was completely unpalatable to me. There was something wrong with everything. Either the taste was too strong, or the combination of flavours all wrong, or the texture made me gag. If someone were to write a fairy tale about me it would be 'Goldilocks and the Three Hundred Bears'.

Like most kids, junk foods like pizza and chips were always safe bets. But, unlike most kids, for me the healthy options weren't just inconvenient gateways to more delicious pastures; I physically could not force most food down. The resulting tearful stalemates with my parents went on for years. Could I not just *try* to eat what was put in front of me? Could I not just manage *one* more bite? Why did I have to be so *fussy*? I didn't have an answer. All I knew was that nobody else seemed to have a problem eating their greens. Other people disliked certain foods, but they could *make* themselves eat them if they needed to. But no matter how much I told myself that I just needed to try harder, I couldn't find a way to push through the nausea and discomfort.

Dinnertime was a nightly ordeal. Not only did I have my dad's mood swings to contend with, but nightly arguments were erupting over my diet. I tried self-advocacy, pulling out the only food I could eat, pre-packaged junk food, going through the ingredients list and explaining that my parents had underestimated its nutritional value. Pizza-flavoured cheesestrings, I argued, were actually healthy because they had herbs in them and herbs were green. I rest my case.

My parents tried every trick in the book. They bribed me. They punished me. They tried hiding vegetables in my food by blending them into something I *would* eat. As if my ultra-sensitive taste buds wouldn't immediately pick up on their treachery. I am so aware of what I'm eating that in another time period it would have been my job to test food for royalty to make sure it wasn't poisoned. Of course, I would have been promptly fired for refusing to eat anything but royal pizza.

Eventually, my parents gave up trying to make me eat healthily and settled for me eating, full stop. It wasn't an ideal solution, but it was better than me starving to death.

They supplemented my diet with teddy bear vitamins, which tasted even more like sweets than homeopathy did, and hoped I wouldn't face any horrific long-term health repercussions.

I had worn my parents down, but I still had to deal with the nightmare scenario of being invited to eat at someone else's house. Even today, dining outside the safety of my home is a frenzy of anxiety. I can't count the number of times someone has pointed out my safe choice in front of everybody, or insisted I try something outside of my comfort zone while everyone stares at me judgmentally.

I grew up in a community full of health-food enthusiasts, so the fact that pretty much everything I ate was pizza, or a variant thereof, was a source of great shame for my parents. I couldn't count on there being a Sara-friendly option at restaurants or friends' houses and I definitely couldn't count on the understanding of my hosts. When I was about ten, a family friend invited me for dinner. My parents weren't there as a buffer and I was in my usual spiral of panic about how I was going to get around my food issues when I was presented with a big slice of vegetable loaf. There was no getting around it. There was no other food, no family member to surreptitiously pass it to, nobody to speak up for me. I took a big bite and instantly threw up on my plate.

Everyone assumed, of course, that I had made myself sick to get out of eating my vegetables. But being sick was one of the many, many, *many* things I was terrified of. There is no universe in which I would intentionally vomit. It would have to be a gun-to-my-head, threat-to-my-family's-lives scenario and even then, I'm not proud of this, I'd hesitate.

The list of things everyone else could do which Princess Sara apparently deemed beneath her grew the more I interacted with the world. In PE we started to do handstands and forward rolls. I was terrified of the sensation of turning upside down. I couldn't bear the feeling of being turned on my head, the room spinning as I came back down, the utter loss of control. Every week, a class full of fed-up kids would line up impatiently behind me as I refused to take my turn. Eventually, I would be removed from the production line entirely and put to the side to sit stubbornly on a gym mat like a broken-down car on the hard shoulder, tearfully shaking my head while everyone else progressed to cartwheels and backflips.

Sports, in general, were where people seemed most exasperated with me. I was so allergic to anything resembling physical activity that it seemed too extreme to be true. I *had* to be putting it on, because nobody in reality is quite that puny. In gym warm-ups, when we were made to run laps, it was not uncommon to see me chugging along at snail's pace while the class sat in a group, waiting for me to finish my first lap of the field when they had all done their third and just wanted to move on to the next activity.

Unfortunately for me, the next activity was usually some sort of team sport in which I was an active liability.

Much of the lesson would be wasted as two almost full teams stood in their groups, with the two team captains yelling, 'You take her!'

'No way, she was on my team last time.'

'Well, I'm not having her.'

The ideal solution for everybody would have been for the teacher to agree I shouldn't be picked at all and to let me hide out in the library where I belonged until it was all over, but participation was mandatory.

The fastest running I did was away from the ball, which suited my teammates just fine. The only game where anyone would let a ball anywhere near me was dodgeball, where the pack would round on me as the easiest target while I curled up on the floor, trying to camouflage myself as a ball, while everyone threw theirs at me. You'd think my years of experience in running away from the ball would have at least given me a head start in dodgeball but sadly that was not the case. In games of rounders, when it was my turn to bat, the entire field would take about twenty paces forward in an act of collective mockery.

When I was sixteen, the gods took pity on me and I developed a tiny benign tumour in my hip. The second the doctor explained to me what 'benign' meant, I was over the moon. This innocuous little growth was my get-out-of-gym-free card. I was even more thrilled when they explained it would need a small outpatient keyhole operation. No gym teacher worth their salt could argue with the word 'operation'. I didn't even mind that the other kids laughed at my limp. Enjoy your push-ups. I'll be laughing all the way to the library.

In addition to being a picky-eating weakling, I started to have unusually strong reactions to physical sensations. In summer, as all the other kids excitedly dived into the school's outdoor pool, I got as far as tentatively dipping a toe into the Arctic water. On the one occasion I summoned the courage to submerge myself, I stood rigid, my teeth chattering, acting like I was waiting to be rescued from the debris of the sunken *Titanic*. The local leisure centre was no better. The pool was thankfully heated so that it could be tolerated by people who weren't actual penguins, but I was still too frightened to venture beyond the shallow end, shielding my eyes from the other children as they splashed and dived around me. 'STOP HAVING FUN!' I shrieked at the little bastards. This only seemed to spur them on more.

As the other kids learned all sorts of fancy strokes and techniques, I couldn't even put my head underwater. In my entire life my head has been fully submerged twice and one of these was when my cousin held my head underwater during one of the dreaded leisure centre excursions in a fun game of 'drown the cousin'. Swimming teacher after swimming teacher swaggered in, full of bravado. 'I'll have her swimming underwater in no time,' they'd promise, insisting there was no child they couldn't conquer, before declaring me to be 'unteachable'.

Unfortunately for me, getting your head wet is kind of an unavoidable part of life. Like most kids, I had hair.

Quite a lot of it, in fact, and it needed washing. My parents would limit hair washing to once a week because none of us wanted to go through the trauma more often than necessary. I was so terrified of the feeling of water in my ears and eyes that there was very little I wouldn't do to avoid it. I would cry, wail, throw myself on the floor, pretend to faint. If all else failed, I would howl at the top of my lungs, 'MURDER! I'M BEING MURDERED!'

'Sara, please,' my mum begged. 'Do you want the neighbours to call the police? They'll take you away from us.'

'Good,' I answered back. 'Then you won't be able to wash my hair.'

Another reason I hated leisure centre visits was the noise. The pool was a cacophony of echoey splashing, shrieking and whooshing scrambling my brain, as background noise always does. 'Just tune it out,' people often advise, cheerfully, as if they've just suggested something that has never occurred to me, an idiot. Noise affects me in a number of ways and the cumulative effect of this can be debilitating.

Think of a noise you can't stand. The kind of noise that sends shudders through your soul or sets your teeth on edge. Maybe it's nails down a blackboard or squeaky brakes. Everybody has one of those noises. I have thousands. Feet scraping on gravel. Sweeping. Machinery. Electricity in the walls. Cutlery scraping on plates (particularly unfortunate for me as this tends to happen when things get awkward). The list is endless. Everyday humdrum noises, which most people wouldn't notice, cause me physical pain. Then there are the noises that illicit a rage response. They call it misophonia, when everyday noises, like the sound of someone else chewing, or snoring, or even breathing, can make you irrationally livid. For some reason it's not considered socially acceptable to tell others to stop breathing.

Noise, in general, is louder to me than it is to other people, so when a waiter clatters plates or somebody raises their voice near me it feels like being smacked in the ear. It means I notice things that pass other people by. Sometimes it's a blessing. I am always the first to know when visitors have arrived because I can hear their cars pulling up outside before anyone else, including my four cats. Other times, it's a curse. I could identify the sound of my husband sneezing from space.

Add to that the confusing crossfire of multiple competing noises and you have yourself an unbearable environment. Trying to have a conversation in a noisy room is like listening to a detuned radio. It is almost impossible for me to process what is being said. Almost all my energy is going into hearing what someone else is saying to me and by the time I've heard it my brain has forgotten to extrapolate any meaning from it. Add to that the fact that there will be multiple other sensory factors, like bright lighting or strong smells, to contend with – and the added social pressures of the situation, the expectation of eye contact and conversing in that context feels like lifting a car over my head and then holding it there for the entire interaction while trying to blend in and look normal.

It's easier for me to listen when I'm looking away, or fiddling with something, but then it looks like I'm rude or not interested. I've often been told that I'm not listening, so I've learned how to enthusiastically perform listening, with a lot of smiling and nodding, which is fine until my brain manages to catch up two minutes later and I've been smiling inanely while someone tells me the tragic story of how they lost both parents in a freak speedboat accident.

Given how uncomfortable everyday life was for me, it's probably no surprise that people around me started to notice that I either seemed to be complaining or unable to do things altogether. I was averse to such an epic list of textures, noises, smells and experiences that the list of things that didn't bother me was significantly shorter than my list of grievances.

The Steiner educational system relies heavily on activities that require physical strength and coordination. The syllabus is packed with messy or intricate arts and crafts and time in the great outdoors. Teachers reported back that I refused to participate in gardening lessons, not just because I saw the fact that we were tending to vegetables that would later be sold in the school shop as child labour, but because the work was, according to my school reports, either 'too arduous or too messy' for me. Handwork lessons were a weekly battle. Sewing and cross-stitch are not great activities for the woefully uncoordinated. I'm someone who struggles to open a packet of crisps; I just paw at it helplessly until someone else takes it off me in frustration, so it's no great mystery as to why I found it hard to muster enthusiasm for a class where I'd spend the vast majority of it trying to thread a needle. As my handwork teacher, clearly a paragon of patience and with that unique ability to transmit her love of the subject to her less able students, so sweetly put it: 'Sara needs frequent reminders to get on with her work. Progress is slow on her cross-stitch. Her design is simple and reflects that she is not interested in it.'

As we moved up through the years, woodwork was introduced. This was an activity forged in the fires of hell and sent straight to me as a gift from Satan himself. The elbow grease required was one thing, but the entire sensory experience was intolerable. I found the texture of the wood on my hands excruciating and the sensation and noise of sanding it down dentist-drill levels of unbearable.

I avoided 'getting on with my work' by nervously chattering at everyone around me. It was the verbal equivalent of moving food around my plate without actually eating any. Sand my piece of wood for two seconds, chat for twenty minutes. It took me a record-breaking three years to make a small wooden egg. While everyone else moved on to spoons, bowls and other fancy contraptions, my reports came back year after year from my kind but bemused woodwork teacher, reporting generously that I was making 'good progress' on my egg. When I finally finished it, nobody celebrated harder than he did. I felt like I'd won the Grand National of wooden egg-making in the 'good effort' category.

Given how many things I detested, it seemed logical to my parents and teachers that my frequent periods of sickness were put on, but the honest truth is that I have never really felt well. I have always battled with exhaustion, unexplained sickness and pain. I seemed to experience things more intensely than everyone else. While my whole family would be infected with the same cold, I would be the only one who found it impossible to focus on anything but how that cold was making me feel.

I was wrestling a mixture of hypersensitivity and extreme anxiety, which meant that every small ailment was felt to the extreme, and I believed I was at death's door on a daily basis. I quickly got a reputation as a faker. People assumed I always *needed* something to be up because God forbid the spotlight should be off me for a minute and I should have to do anything I didn't want to. I heard 'What's wrong *now?*' so often that if I were a cat, I'd be forgiven for thinking that 'now' was my name – in much the same way my now departed cat Lily, who used to habitually pee on the curtains, thought her name was 'Bad Cat, No!' Nobody, myself included, asked the obvious question, which is *why the hell would any child choose to be excluded, stigmatised, ridiculed and humiliated if they could simply make it stop?*

My reputation as an overindulged brat was compounded by the fact that I didn't help out much around the house. There were two reasons housework was such a drain. The first was that I was tired. Not just your usual 'I've had a long day, give me a cuppa and five minutes' tired. I was shattered. At the end of a long school day I couldn't understand how any of the other kids had any steam left in them for things like homework and chores. I was running on an empty tank. The second reason was that, hand on heart, I had no idea how to help. It is assumed that just by observation or osmosis, children know how to clean and tidy things, and maybe most do, but I didn't. When adults think something is intuitive, they neglect to teach it to you. Aside from the times my poor godsister, Rhiannon, would come over and, having been told we couldn't play until I tidied my room, did it for me while I cheered her on from my bed, my room was a permanent bomb site.

I am now in my thirties and I can still see no obvious and quick way to get rid of mess. Either I will simply shove the aforementioned mess somewhere out of sight to deal with later, à la Monica's closet in *Friends* or I aimlessly move piles of junk around the room, achieving absolutely nothing.

Part of this is down to my indecision. As a child, in the rare event we had to take two cars to travel somewhere and I was told to choose which parent to ride with, I would run back and forward between the two cars, getting more and more distressed as I weighed up the options. A sincere effort to put things away triggers that overthinking, as well as my compulsive need to categorise everything and bizarre attachment to inanimate objects. All in all, a perfect storm of overwhelm.

Early in our relationship, my then-boyfriend-now-husband and I did a big spring clean. He took the upstairs and I took the living room. I started with a small pile of mess and began organising it by category. An hour later, he came downstairs, having finished his jobs. I was still sitting over my little pile of mess in floods of tears trying to decide if a tinted moisturiser belonged with make-up or skincare. When he asked if the pile of empty bottles I'd accumulated were for the recycling, I said they were in theory, but I'd spent so much time with them while tidying them up that we'd bonded, and I couldn't bear to throw them away. I had achieved precisely nothing and yet the room was swimming with the effort of it. I had to lie down and recover.

On the odd occasion I tried to help as a child things would go wrong. I would stack the plates poorly and they'd come crashing down, or things would be Sara clean, not *clean* clean (I couldn't see a difference). I desperately didn't want anything to go wrong because that would trigger one of my unexplained episodes. They would happen when I was very distressed, tired, emotional or overwhelmed. Sometimes there would be a catalyst, like an argument with my parents or a bad day at school, but often they would just erupt for no real reason. Something tiny would open the floodgates – an offhand comment or an unexpected change in plans. Long gone were the days of the comical downward mouth turn and the angry eyebrows. Either I would shut down entirely, lying on the floor 'playing dead', not moving or responding to anyone, or I would explode in a fit of hysterics. At home these events were noisy, angry and seasoned with hours of uncontrollable tears. They were almost exclusively met with eye-rolling or ridicule from my family. On one notable occasion I remember falling to the floor, feeling if I had to absorb one more thing from my surroundings, I might die. 'Help me,' I sobbed from the floor. 'I'm dying.' My family stood around me, laughing in bemusement and telling me to stop being dramatic and just get up.

If I was alone, I would hit myself, smacking the side of my head or slapping myself hard across the face. I would be taken over by a terrible rage. I would break things I loved, rip up stories I'd written or throw my toys at the wall. Worst of all, if anyone crossed my path while I was in that state, I would say terrible, unforgivable things and barely remember them afterwards. Whenever I had broken something irreplaceable, whether a beloved toy or a fragile relationship, the remorse and shame that filled me afterwards was indescribable.

In public I managed to contain the meltdowns to convulsive sobbing. This would happen a lot at school, or at family events, anywhere busy and overwhelming. Something would set me off and I would cry my heart out. I would cry until I was sick, until my head pounded and my eyes protruded from my skull like red, watery golf balls. The kind of crying that looked, from the outside, like an insane overreaction. I was completely helpless to stop it.

I'm talking in the past tense, of course, because it's easier to talk about it with wise detachment, as if it's all over, it never happens any more, and I've evolved beyond it all. Because honestly, who wants to admit that they're the grown woman who still has these fits? But these episodes never went away. They have been a consistent part of my life, like early spring storms, raging through me, unstoppable, hurricane-force winds, beyond all control and shelter and leaving terrible destruction in their wake.

Sometimes I am unaware of what's happening, or, like I've been administered a heavy sedative, have trouble remembering them afterwards. But more often than not, I am present somewhere far away, watching the disaster unfold, my voice echoing from the bottom of a very deep pit: 'Stop – you're ruining everything.' But I am not in the driver's seat. I've been metaphorically carjacked and taken along for the joyride, like the demonic possessions I spent my early childhood fearing would happen to those around me. There is nothing to do but sit in the back seat while this maniac without a licence careers into my life. I listen helplessly to the terrible things this monster is saying to the people most important to me, watch it slap and berate me, witness it breaking everything I cherish and then flee, leaving me to explain it away and clean up the aftermath.

I have always done my best to hide my meltdowns. Until recently, they were so shameful I never even allowed myself to voice them. I comforted myself with soothing lies. Everyone probably does this behind closed doors. They just don't talk about it. It never occurred to me to seek an answer, because that would mean admitting something was wrong and telling somebody about it.

Over the years, my meltdowns brought abrupt ends to important relationships, especially as I entered my teens. Boyfriends would be besotted with me until the first meltdown, after which they would be repulsed by me. Friends would enjoy my company until we went out somewhere and the night ended in tears. Workplaces would think I was extremely professional and competent, until I cried in the office for the first time. Sometimes people would stop calling, or dump me, or fire me. But most commonly I would pre-empt them by disappearing or burning bridges out of shame. I would run the moment I had been 'found out'.

Under normal circumstances, with understanding and robust support networks in place, it would have been tough to come to terms with myself, but I came from a New Age mindset where I was expected to magically heal myself. Your thoughts, I was taught growing up, manifest your reality. Imagine telling a kid who's already a walking ball of anxiety that their anxieties will *cause* the things they're anxious about to happen, so they're not only anxious but anxious about being anxious about being anxious, like an infinite self-destructive ripple.

This underlying ideology, never quite explicit, but always floating obnoxiously around the circles we mixed in, like a fart smell everyone in the room seems to be enjoying but me, made it incredibly difficult to admit weakness. If I'm manifesting my own reality, then all my problems are my own fault. It's a powerful message. To this day I berate myself for simply not being able to *think* myself better. I lie in bed with devastating chronic pain or too overwhelmed by the stimuli I've encountered during the day to even open my eyes and castigate myself. 'What have I done wrong?' I ask my husband, on a near-daily basis, even though I *know* it doesn't work that way.

One thing I *am* good at is spotting patterns, weighing up evidence and coming to logical conclusions. So, you can understand how growing up there was a tsunami of evidence that all pointed to one conclusion, which I internalised without question. If we were in a court of law, it would prove beyond reasonable doubt that I, vomiter on plates, abstainer from gym classes, shirker of messy responsibilities, thrower of epic tantrums, was a spoiled brat.

5

WEIRDO

It's 31 May 1998 and my little world has just been torn apart. No, my parents haven't decided to put us all out of our misery and just get a divorce (yet). This is a much bigger catastrophe. Geri has left the Spice Girls.

At ten years old 'obsessive' doesn't begin to cover my feelings about the Spice Girls. I can tell you anything you could ever hope to know about them. And by 'hope to know', I mean politely listen to while thinking about the weekly food shop. And by 'can', I mean will, at great length, without any prompting.

My mum has just broken the devastating news to me and, after an hour spent screaming 'LIAR' at her and another hunched by the radio listening to Geri's statement on repeat, like a war widow desperate for news about my lover in the trenches, the terrible truth is starting to sink in.

I flee the house, howling with grief. 'Oh, Geri,' I sob. 'Is it something *I've* done?' I wander the neighbourhood in my neon-green leggings and age-inappropriate orange Spice Girls crop top like a tiny, scrawny town crier, wailing at unsuspecting dog walkers and old ladies putting out the bins, 'SHE'S GONE!'

That evening I try, to no avail, to convince my parents that I can't possibly be expected to go to school the next day, given the circumstances. But 'lady leaves pop group' is apparently not considered a legitimate bereavement and so I do go to school the following day, wearing a makeshift black armband. I spend break and lunch hours circling the playground in a slow hunch-shouldered shuffle, à la Charlie Brown. If I had been allowed to bring a boombox along with my own tragic soundtrack, I would have.

A couple of months later, the Spice Girls release 'Viva Forever', the last song featuring Geri, and my months of healing are undone in an instant. 'Goodbye' is released a few months later sans Geri – a tribute to their departed friend. To this day I still can't listen to either of those songs without being triggered into fits of convulsive sobs. Perhaps now is the time to mention that Geri is my least favourite Spice Girl.

I have always been weird, a quality I spent my formative years blaming on my upbringing, but that didn't account for the fact that I didn't exactly fit in there either. To understand exactly how weird that is, it's important to understand the setting against which I was judged too weird for the other weirdos. By now the more perceptive among you may have picked up on some hints that my school wasn't exactly . . . regular. All the things I took for granted as fundamental truths as a child were, to put it mildly, completely bananas. It's also important that you know the details of my education so that you understand why there was absolutely no chance of someone like me being diagnosed with anything other than, say, misaligned chakras or bad karma.

First of all, to be fair to the Steiner system, there are some notable positives. For a kid who struggled with sensory input, the sweet smell of beeswax, the soft lighting and the reduced class sizes were ideal. We learned from old-fashioned blackboards, instead of whiteboards and markers. We wrote with pencils and then fountain pens. Biros were banned – as was football. TVs in the home were discouraged. Basically, anything that connected us to the modern world was a no-no. If an alien landed on Earth wanting to get a sense of the time period and the first thing they encountered was a Steiner school, they'd have more questions than answers.

We were taught French and German from the moment we arrived. I loved learning languages. Perhaps because of some subconscious inherent understanding that, in a way, I was speaking my own language and the fact that other languages and cultures could be translated and understood gave me a strange sort of hope. Languages also gave me an 'in' with the foreign exchange kids, who had to default to me as a friend because I was the only one who could communicate with them. With hindsight I provided a lot of foreign students with an added incentive to learn English.

The school was set in acres of beautifully landscaped grounds, where we would take regular class walks among the fields, woodlands, lakes and waterfalls. We had wonderful facilities. There was a fully equipped theatre that, when it wasn't in use for school plays and assemblies, was regularly hired out to local amateur dramatics productions. Outside the 'seriously haunted' Mansion was an outdoor Grecian-style amphitheatre, where the older kids staged productions of Shakespeare plays.

A typical day in Lower School (ages six to thirteen) would start with us crossing our arms over our chests and reciting a morning verse. I got through this by pretending someone had pressed pause in the middle of the 'Macarena'. We'd then do a round of singing or recorder playing. As six-year-olds we started off on a pentatonic recorder, which is a uniquely Waldorf thing, a recorder on the pentatonic scale, which basically means it doesn't have enough notes to play any actual songs apart from most of 'Walk Like an Egyptian'. This was just a gateway recorder. Once we proved we could handle that, we were entrusted with a recorder with the full octave. Some of the more hardcore kids even got to play alto and bass recorders. As most of us weren't allowed near any kind of technology, this was the closest we had to upgrade-itis.

After recorder time, we would settle in for Main Lesson, a two-hour class on the same subject every day for three weeks, usually taught by our class teacher. Learning about one subject for three weeks meant, quite literally, dancing around it. For example, a maths Main Lesson would have us singing multiplication tables or throwing beanbags to each other. The crowning glory of every Main Lesson cycle was the Main Lesson book – an in-depth hand-drawn and written book on whatever topic we had learned about. A Main Lesson book was not considered complete unless it was adequately decorated. We probably spent more time drawing Celtic border patterns around our work and rubbing colourful pencil shavings into the background than we did actually learning anything. I could never see the point of it. If all the information was there, why did I need to waste my time on bells and whistles? It is still a great source of pride that in my entire Steiner career, I never finished a Main Lesson book.

In the early years our Main Lessons were focused on fairy tales, fables and mythology. We were strongly encouraged to believe in gnomes and fairies. Gnomes came to define a lot of my early education. We put on plays where half the characters were gnomes. We went on walks to look for gnomes. We were so busy learning about gnomes, they almost forgot to teach us science, which they introduced tentatively around the age of nine, by which point I had to unlearn my overriding belief that the gnomes did it all by magic.

According to the Steiner system, children shouldn't begin to learn to read until the age of seven, when they become spiritually ready. Unfortunately, I had already taught myself to read and write fluently at around three or four. While the other kids were learning the alphabet, I had multiple contraband novels stashed in my bag. I wasn't allowed to read them while the children all marvelled over the letter 'A'. Instead I had to sit through a three-week Main Lesson about the alphabet in which I was told to be quiet and not to ruin it for the others. I'm still not sure what they thought I was going to do with what wasn't exactly the spoiler of the century. 'Hey, guys, you won't believe what happens when you get to Z.'

The weirdest thing about my upbringing, weirder by far than the gnomes, the forbidden literacy and the school ghost, was eurythmy. Eurythmy is a trippy form of movement and performance art that Steiner types claim has therapeutic purposes and helps with things like balance and spatial awareness. Eurythmy is so weird that even as the weirdest weirdo that ever weirded, I knew it was weird. A typical Eurythmy lesson as a small child would have us walking around a large studio – lacquered wooden floors, Ned Flanders architecture, stained-glass windows – in white rubber-soled slippers. We would walk in a circle while a teacher, dressed like she'd got lost on her way to a palm-reading convention, chanted 'short, short loooooong. Short, short, looooooooooong' as we took the corresponding steps (two short steps followed by a slightly longer one, in case that wasn't intuitive).

Then we'd be put into pairs with another child and given a copper rod, which we would chuck to, or, more commonly, at the other kid. As if having a copper rod you don't have a hope in hell of catching flying towards your face isn't traumatic enough, sometimes the teacher would introduce a second rod, so you had to both throw and catch at the same time. For me Eurythmy classes were just forty-five minutes of flinching and falling over.

Eurythmy has its own visual alphabet of exaggerated arm movements. It's the sign language equivalent of your elderly relative who texts in all caps. The performance part of Eurythmy had us prancing around (in silk robes, if we were on stage) to piano music or a Steiner poem, waving our arms around. The entire art form was highly gendered, with dainty movements for girls and wooden scimitars for boys. To be fair, they were just preparing us for the real world in which men haven't got a hope in hell of landing a job without scimitar skills.

Christmas festivities came with a Steiner-sanctioned series of events and plays. Some of them, like the annual advent fair, which boasted a fairy garden, gingerbread house decorating, candle-making, a lovely market selling handmade gifts, mulled wine, a fairy grotto, an actual donkey, chestnuts and the best damn waffles you've ever tasted, were genuinely magical. But then there were the more troubling Yuletide traditions, like one parent of an Aryan-looking Dutch family who would visit our overwhelmingly white class once a year dressed as a character from Dutch folklore, Zwarte Piet (Black Pete), in full-on blackface. When the parents weren't blacking up, the teachers took up the mantle in a play they put on about the three kings. It speaks volumes about the levels of diversity in our community that none of us had any idea this was anything but our teachers playing innocent dress-up.

Perhaps our teachers were just that clueless. But then there's the uncomfortable fact that Steiner believed in racial hierarchies and that all our teachers had been through extensive Waldorf training. Steiner saw black people as distinguished by 'instinctual life' as opposed to Caucasians, who represent 'intellectual life'. Oof. He believed that races should stay in 'their' geographical locations and thought of black people in Europe as 'a nuisance'. Eek. But don't worry, folks, if you were born as a member of an 'inferior' race, you might be reincarnated up a level next life as a white person. I wish I was joking.

Proponents of Steiner education insist that while anthroposophy does propagate ideas of racial hierarchies, none of these ideas are present in Steiner's educational philosophies. However, there have since been reports in the media of these ideas filtering down through the faculty in other Steiner schools. One training day, according to a 2014 BBC News article, saw four white teachers tick every ethnicity on the diversity form as they believed they had ascended through the races. It's worth noting here that most casual Steiner parents are, or certainly were at the time, blissfully unaware of those aspects of anthroposophy. My parents definitely were, as my mum's horrified reaction when I put all of this to her confirmed.

I was one of a handful of kids from a minority background and it was at school that I got my first real taste of antisemitism. Talia (of course it was Talia) hissed at me that I had killed Christ, so I lunged furiously at her and earned myself a detention. I'm still not sure why I attacked her. I didn't really understand the loaded connotations of what she had said to me. Perhaps it activated some deep-seated subconscious Jewdar in me ingrained over millennia of persecution. The early experience, however, taught me that if you make a fuss about prejudice, you will be the one who gets in trouble.

One of our jolliest school traditions was Pancake Day. It was an exciting day of pageantry and dress-up where the whole school was in costume and lessons were replaced with a fun assembly, an afternoon of pancake races and, most importantly, pancake eating. An opportunity to express ourselves in costume, however, was more revealing than intended. One year, a teacher came in dressed as AN HONEST-TO-GOD NAZI. When parents complained, he insisted it was a historical re-enactment for educational purposes, but I have to wonder: WHO HAS A HIGH-QUALITY, AUTHENTIC NAZI UNIFORM JUST LYING AROUND? There was also the absolutely lovely teacher who dressed in drag, which caused a vicious whisper campaign among both parents and children about him being 'gay', delivered in a tone that made it clear to us that this was definitely not OK. Looking back on it and his bravery, persisting in being himself even in the face of horrific discrimination, I feel nothing but admiration.

Our midsummer festival was another magical celebration with a daytime fete, boasting a coconut shy, fairy grottos, musical entertainment, cake and strawberries and cream. The younger kids would then be sent home while the older years and parents settled in for the outdoor evening performance of that year's Class Ten Shakespeare play. The festivities would end with everyone assembling in the dark, two fields down from the Seriously Haunted Mansion, as that year's outgoing Class Twelve, officially the final year in Steiner education, made their way from the Mansion to the gathered crowds in a procession dressed in, erm . . . white and carrying, uh . . . God this is awkward . . . blazing torches, which were eventually plunged into a bonfire. I'm pretty sure it was an innocent ritual and that they were ignorant of the KKKonnotations, but given the system's dicey record on race, the aesthetic is more than a little squirmy.

As there were no uniforms, it was left to us to work out exactly what the dress code was and how to attain the ever-elusive status of 'cool'. I had no problem with that at all. I am great at reading unspoken social cues and came to school every day looking chic and put together. I am, of course, kidding. I was the kid with massive dry, frizzy hair. Of course, it could have just been lovely curly hair if I, or either one of my parents, had the first clue of how to manage it. But we didn't. My hair was brushed out after it dried, taking all the definition out of my curls, amplifying the volume by about five hundred thousand. 'Five hundred thousand what?' you ask. I have no idea. For some reason I don't know any science. Five hundred thousand gnomes? Whatever the metrics, I had the permanent look of someone who'd just received an enormous electric shock, which explains the fear of open plug sockets. That and the fact that I don't know any science.

A little girl who's already acquired the nickname 'frizzhead' would probably be wise to try to find other ways to blend in. So naturally I came to school dressed in neon colours, conspicuous eighties throwbacks my mum had found in charity shops and my brother's hand-me-downs. In an environment where half the faculty looked like they were dressed for Ascension Day, I still managed to stick out as an oddball.

Never judge a book by its cover, right? Except we already know that once you got past the fact that I perpetually looked like I had got dressed in the dark from a selection of clothing chosen by someone who hated me, you would be assaulted by a flurry of verbal diarrhoea. If you managed to withstand the unstoppable barrage of word bullets, you would find a didactic, pedantic kid who was a walking 'well, actually'. OK, so maybe I wasn't great chat, but perhaps I was a good person to hang out, play sports, eat some fine cuisine, go on adventures and try new things with. Ha! Just checking you've been paying attention.

My time at school as I remember it was defined by bullying, but these days I wonder if it was as black and white as it always felt to me. I'd love to recall with crystal clarity a satisfying narrative in which I'm the poor put-upon kid who just wanted to be left alone, but the picture I have in my mind is murkier than that. For one thing I didn't want to be left alone. I wanted to be everyone's best mate.

I am no expert in child development, but as someone who survived the self-esteem battering of social alienation, these questions keep me up at night. Is exclusion actually a form of bullying? We constantly and correctly tell adults that they are allowed their boundaries. So why should it be different for children? And if exclusion doesn't count as bullying, was I really bullied at all? Were exasperated kids simply asserting their right to befriend or reject whomever they damn well liked?

Talking to my friend Barbara, another Steiner survivor and now a teacher, who was always kind to me at school, we mulled over this question.

'Barbs, was I really bullied or was it just fair enough that the other kids didn't want to hang out with me?'

Barbara, always thoughtful, took a long pause before she answered. 'That may have come into it, sure,' she said. 'But . . . and I don't want to hurt your feelings or anything . . . you were definitely also bullied.'

'Are you sure?' I asked.

'Oh God, yeah,' she said certainly. 'Sorry.'

It wasn't that I didn't have any friends at all. I had my godsisters, Carys and Rhiannon, two impossibly beautiful, tall and popular sisters in the year above and below me respectively. We had known each other since we were infants, our parents were all godparents to each other's kids and their home was my second home. Years later, they would be maids of honour at my wedding. But within the school ecosystem, they had their own friends and lives and there wasn't a lot of mixing between year groups.

I survived by forming a loose coalition with other kids who were having trouble fitting in. The nerds, oddballs and freaks gravitated together like pack animals finding safety in numbers. It was an uneasy alliance. We weren't natural friends – the only thing any of us really had in common was our status as social rejects. We spent half our time squabbling, falling out and shooting bitchy little jibes at each other. Weirdly, the majority of our little network of survivors is still in touch today and we're now great pals. Maybe at the time it was the acute knowledge that we hadn't chosen each other that caused all the friction.

I tried everything I could to make the bullying stop. When my aggressive attempts to befriend my tormentors proved fruitless, I tried to appeal to their empathy. Instead of trying to hide my hurt feelings, I wore them as conspicuously as my neon outfits. Weeping openly, I'd say things like 'Please stop, you're hurting my feelings.' It genuinely hadn't sunk in that this was their aim. When that didn't work, I sought advice from my parents. 'Just ignore them,' my mum explained. 'Don't let them get a rise out of you.' The problem with the 'ignoring them' strategy is it requires time and patience. It's a subtle art. You can't ignore someone loudly. When one morning of quietly ignoring the bullies didn't produce immediate miraculous results, I resorted to shouting at them 'I'M IGNORING YOU AND YOU'RE NOT GOING TO GET A RISE OUT OF ME.'

Talia continued to terrorise me, the gatekeeper of the social utopia to which I so desperately wanted access. Things came to a head on my ninth birthday. At my school it was customary for the birthday kid to bring in a cake. Most of the kids were on strictly organic, sugar-free, joy-free diets, so birthdays were hotly anticipated events and my mum just so happened to make the world's best chocolate cake – undisputed.

Birthdays represented something more for me personally. Birthdays were the one day everyone *had* to be nice to me. My birthday was *my* day, and everyone had to treat me like The Birthday Girl, whether they liked it or not. It was the law. And even if it wasn't, I was the one with the cake – so there. This might, I've just realised, be why I compulsively feel the need to bring along a home-baked version of people's favourite cake wherever I go, a flimsy alternative to just saying 'please like me'.

On this particular birthday, my cake was displayed on the teacher's desk for the morning with the promise of a slice at lunchtime. That morning, however, Miss

Clarke was called away from the classroom for a couple of minutes. The moment she had left the room, Talia ran to her desk.

'Don't!' I shouted. 'It's not lunchtime yet!'

Talia smiled wickedly, delighted to be getting a rise out of me, even though I'd specifically told her that she was not getting a rise out of me.

I ran to the front of the class to try to stop her, but it was too late. Her finger was already making its way through the thick layer of icing. She licked it in satisfaction. 'Mmmm,' she said victoriously.

Miss Clarke returned to find a cake with a conspicuous finger track and me and Talia facing off at the front of the class. 'Who did this?' she asked, furiously.

'Sara did it,' Talia responded coolly. 'I tried to stop her.'

Immediately, tears sprang to my eyes and I became inarticulate. The nerve of her! In front of an entire classroom full of witnesses! But that didn't seem to bother Talia one bit – the witness intimidation was implicit.

'It wasn't me!' I protested.

Miss Clarke looked from Talia, cool as a cucumber, to me, red, flustered, almost hyperventilating with the injustice of it all. While Miss Clarke's attention was on me, Talia surreptitiously licked a little stray icing from the side of her mouth. 'For the love of God,' I wanted to shout, 'breathalyse her! You can still smell the chocolate!'

I sobbed silently as Miss Clarke laid down my punishment. My cake was locked away and nobody would be allowed any until after school hours. I was to stay inside at lunch and sweep the classroom. When lunchtime came around, Talia skipped off outside while I spent my one glorious 'everyone has to be nice to the birthday girl' break torturing myself with the sound of the broom scraping along the floor.

*

I had always had a vivid imagination but faced with an unpleasant external reality, I retreated inwards. I had an enormous, intricate inner world that often bled into my reality and left me struggling to distinguish between the two. I developed my fantasy worlds in part to escape being bullied by day at school and rejected by night at home, and partly as a form of harnessing and controlling the huge imagination that haunted and tortured me. I grew up on a diet of romance and magic. Fairy tales, Enid Blyton books and later an obsessive love of Harry Potter. My fantasies were vivid, elaborate and involved a mixture of people I knew and celebrities I loved, set in a world where magic was very real. More often than not, my fantasies collided with my obsessions – bands or films and frequently boys I happened to be infatuated with at the time. Most importantly, in these fantasies I was beautiful, witty, popular and skilled at everything I tried. I'd like to say I was the best version of myself, but the truth was fantasy Sara didn't bear so much as a passing resemblance to real-life Sara.

My inner universe was vast and complex, with rules, regular characters, sets, props and storylines. It was forever being developed – sometimes the pleasure was more in the world-building than the story itself. I'd spend so much time setting the scene that on many occasions nothing else would happen at all. It was a delightful world to live in and a spectacular gift – the ability to create a sanctuary inside my mind that I could escape to whenever I needed to. Not that I truly escaped my anxieties – my fantasy worlds always had a full team of medical staff on hand just in case.

An imagination that powerful was, however, a double-edged sword. The stories my mind concocted almost felt more real to me at times than the real world. The temptation was to abandon reality entirely and stay in my happy place. And I did. A lot. But even worse were my attempts to marry my two realities. I genuinely, with all my heart, believed, because I was constantly told that we manifest our own reality, that if I dreamed something hard enough, it would come true. That's a very sweet and very dangerous belief – one that can lead a little girl (and, unfortunately, a big girl) with a tenuous grip on reality to put herself out there in humiliating and life-wrecking ways, and one that transforms what should have been minor let-downs into full-on bereavements.

Sometimes the results would be relatively trivial – like being mocked at school for spending lunchtimes with my 'flying horse', Destrier (an archaic word for a warhorse). While I was charging at a thrilling speed

I'd never dare to go in reality, through the clouds on Destrier's back (clouds that tasted like candyfloss), the other kids saw a bizarre little bundle of neon colours and frizzy hair sitting sideways on a swing, alone, shouting 'Faster, Destrier!' Other times, the results would be more devastating, especially as I got older and deluded myself into believing boys who had been nice to me once were an active and willing part of our entirely fictional love affair.

This heady, addictive and perilous mix of fantasy and obsession was the world I lived in for my entire childhood and most of my young adulthood. My obsessions were your garden-variety little-girl interests, but the intensity with which I focused on them and clung to them was on another level. There were lots of them. Some short-lived fads, others lifelong loves. My first and truest love was animals. Specifically, cats. As I type these words, my beloved cat, Tilly, one of the four little lions with which I am currently sharing my home, life and bed, is draped contentedly over my arm, fast asleep, having given up on her goal of trying to move me to the sofa for a cuddle. My arm is slowly going numb but moving her is out of the question. In my world it's felines first. Cats in the Gibbs household are treated with the reverence, respect and adoration they would have enjoyed in ancient Egypt.

What's weird about that? I hear you ask. Lots of kids love animals. True. But not all kids start to believe that they *are* their favourite animal. When I was playing with my cats, I *was* a cat. I boasted to everyone at school that

I could talk to cats. This did not increase my human friend count. I recently found a note written to my cats when I was six years old. It reads, with rather sinister undertones: *To kittys, be at my bed at five aclorc in the morning tommorrow from Sara*. The 'or else' was implicit. The note pretty much sums up the contradictions in my personality – smart enough to *write* the note, not grounded enough in reality to understand that cats can't read.

As I got older, it became increasingly impractical to keep me away from popular culture. While we didn't have a proper TV until I was around eleven, I had figured out how to game the system by spending afternoons at my god-family's house, where we tuned in to BBC1 every evening to watch the Australian soap, *Neighbours*. It was my first experience of serial television with an ongoing plot and I became completely transfixed. To this day I am one of the last avid *Neighbours* viewers and am a clandestine member of two ironic *Neighbours* 'art' groups, a regular listener of two *Neighbours* podcasts, a lurker on several *Neighbours* forums and can recite from heart pretty much every storyline going back to around 1997.

When I was eleven, Disney released the remake of its classic *The Parent Trap*, starring Lindsay Lohan. The film completely enthralled me. Everything about it, from the popping blue and yellow colour scheme on the box to the cheery, bright locations and music and the luxurious lifestyles of the characters. I decided that somewhere out there I might have an identical twin – someone who *had* to like me no matter what because they basically *were* me.

I watched the VHS every spare moment I was allowed, every time my parents went out and left me unattended with the video player, carefully getting the exact position of the silk sheet and crystals right so I wouldn't get caught. When I wasn't allowed to watch *The Parent Trap* all day every day, I hijacked my dad's work computer and braved the screech of the dial-up to find the script, before printing out all 132 pages. My parents were livid, and I was paying for printer ink out of my pocket money into the next millennium, but I stapled the thing together and treated it like my Bible, carrying it everywhere with me and reading it at every spare opportunity. It wasn't long before I had the entire film memorised.

I idolised Lindsay Lohan, just over a year my senior, with her vivid red hair and expressive face. I wanted to be exactly like her – more precisely, the cool Californian twin, Hallie, who played poker, drank wine with dinner and ate chocolate chip pancakes for breakfast. I raided the shelves of Superdrug, buying the same electric blue shade of nail polish worn by Hallie in the movie and 99p sachets of red hair tint, which I hoped to enhance the vague 'maybe-if-you-squint' ginger notes in my once strawberry blonde, now tragically mousy hair. I cut myself a little side fringe, like the one Hallie cuts for Annie in the movie so that it sprang out in a frizzy triangle that could only be subdued with about five thousand hair clips. The red hair tint failed to take on my hair but did leave a gruesome red ring in the bathtub, which, even though I *knew* I had caused it, still made my heart skip with panic that a murder really had taken place in my bathroom. I had no idea how to apply nail polish, so I walked around with globs of congealed blue gunk on my nails. I was less Californian cool and more 'quarantine her before we all catch it'.

My childhood would have been an extremely lonely experience if I hadn't met Rob. When I was eight years old, it was time for my brother to start bar mitzvah lessons. A bar mitzvah is a Jewish rite of passage into adulthood. Boys have their bar mitzvahs aged thirteen and, in more progressive strands of Judaism, girls have their bat mitzvahs at twelve. The nearest Reform synagogue was half an hour away in Brighton and so we would attend once a week as a family. I was enrolled in the Jewish equivalent of Sunday school, *cheder*, pronounced like you're coughing up a hairball, not like the West Country cheese. That's where I met my best friend.

Rob and I met in the synagogue's makeshift playground. Rob, six months older than me, was a shy, gangly kid who struggled to connect to the cheder crowd and, while I don't remember the specifics of our initial meeting, I imagine I had just gone from kid to kid like a street seller who puts a bracelet on your wrist before you can argue, then charges you for it, bellowing 'I'M SARA BY THE WAY' until somebody responded. That somebody happened to be Rob.

Rob was unlike anyone I'd ever met before in that he actually liked me. Until then, I thought a friend was just someone who let you stand next to them for more than five minutes without telling you to 'fuck off', or someone whose parents forced you to play with them. Rob and I had something more than just proximity and parental guilt – we both loved pop music. The idea of bonding over a shared interest was, to me, revolutionary. Rob and I had actual conversations – for hours on end. And when the day ended and cheder was over, we still had enough to say to each other that we would wait until after six in the evening, when non-local phone calls would become free, and continue our discussions. Chats about the charts paved the way for talks about our lives, our feelings and our dreams.

Having a friend who actually liked and wanted to be around me felt like winning the lottery. Everything that other people mocked about me only seemed to endear me to him more. He loved my gobbiness. He was amused by my bluntness. He was flattered by my neediness. He thought my cloud of fluffy hair was hilarious and delightful and loved brushing and playing with it. He helped me turn my army of imaginary friends into little plays and songs that we would perform together.

Rob lived in a big house in Brighton with a spectacular view over the landscape and parents who sincerely liked each other. It was a place where civilised conversation was made and nobody stormed away from the dinner table in a rage or threw plates at the wall. Rob's family always had pizza ready for my visits and would watch me in gentle bemusement as I got more of it on the table than I did in my mouth. While many of my toys at home were hand-me-downs, Rob, being an only child, had all the latest gadgets, which he was pleased to share with me. I assume. I didn't give him much of a choice. Many an afternoon was spent happily jumping around the living room to Britney Spears or fighting over the mic on his karaoke machine.

We got our clumsily uncoordinated crushes on each other out of the way early in the friendship. I took the early shift, crushing hard from the ages of about nine to ten, before moving on to the next victim and leaving poor Rob to nurse his newly burgeoning unrequited crush, which was quickly snuffed out after he suggested we become boyfriend and girlfriend and I awkwardly responded, 'You're more like a brother to me.'

Rob and I had humble ambitions. We wanted to be superstars. We wanted to be as big as Marvin and Tamara. 'Who?' you say. I guess in a roundabout way we managed it! Once I was allowed a TV, Rob and I scheduled a once-weekly phone call, just after *Top of the Pops* aired on a Friday evening, to dissect everything we'd just watched with a view to emulating it. We took a forward-thinking, multimedia approach à la S Club 7 and Cleopatra. As well as writing chart-topping hits (there's still time), we wrote a corresponding TV show, playing ourselves as aspiring pop stars, which we recorded with Rob's camcorder. We didn't actually have the patience to write a whole script before filming, so we wrote a few lines and made a taster tape. To the best of our recollection the script went like this (I've added formatting and stage directions for your benefit):

INT. ROB'S LIVING ROOM, DAY
Rob and Sara are sitting on the sofa in silence,
    staring directly ahead, because that is normal
    human behaviour. The phone doesn't ring.
    Rob picks it up anyway.
ROB: Hello? You're joking. OK, thanks. Bye.
SARA: What is it?
ROB: We've won a recording contract and a
    million pounds!
SARA: Wow! Awesome!

Tragically for the world, our TV show did not get an after-school slot on ITV. Probably because we never sent it to anyone, otherwise by now we would be washed-up has-beens who have both been featured on *First Dates* because we aren't famous enough for *Celebrity Big Brother*. But it did give me a taste for the glitz and glamour of showbiz and I was instantly hungry for more.

6

SHOW-OFF

It is the day of my bat mitzvah, my twelfth birthday. I have spent months preparing, learning my Torah portion, planning my party and, most importantly, choosing the perfect outfit. I have gone with an inappropriately short skirt for synagogue, one that really shows off my knobbly knees and pale chicken legs. I am wearing a dark grey cardigan with sparkly threads that make my arms itch. My loose hair is so big, I look like I am so electrically charged I should be cordoned off. *Danger of death*, the sign would read. *Approach the bat mitzvah girl at your own peril.*

After the ceremony, a lunch is held in my honour at a local Italian restaurant. It is a long, overwhelming day full of noise, bustle and I'm the centre of attention. I'm confused, because I have always been told I love attention, but I don't love this at all. To survive the day I play a character – a confident, outgoing young woman who *really* loves all her presents. All this is caught by

Rob's camcorder. I have decided that the way to exude confidence is to overuse words like 'professional'. 'This is the professional way to do it,' I bleat obnoxiously at the camera, showing Rob how I've styled my fuzzy mane with my new butterfly clips.

The moment I think eyes are off me, I visibly slump. I stroke my hair approximately twenty thousand times a minute. I fold my arms protectively round my skinny body. When I speak, I sound like someone reading from a script without really understanding what the words mean. 'I love it,' I say mechanically of every present. 'You know me so well.' My parents taught me growing up that it's polite to open a card before you open your present and more than once, when opening a present, I say to myself, 'Card first.' At one point I forget and go for the present, before berating myself. 'Always card first!' I scold, even though nobody has said anything.

No party is complete in my family without a variety show of performances from the various actors and singers in our ranks. It is expected that I, too, will stand up and sing. 'Sara just LOVES the stage,' announces my cousin at the end of her set, before everyone starts cheering for me to get up and perform. I stay in my seat for a while, nervously stroking my hair and ripping the edges of a small lyric sheet in my hands. Finally, I wobble to the microphone and, in a shaky voice, my scrawny knees knocking together, sing 'Kiss Me' by Sixpence None the Richer while my brother accompanies me on the guitar. I barely look up from the lyric sheet even though I know the song by heart. The second it's over, my posture hunches and I run back to my seat like I've been caught in a sudden downpour. The camera zooms in on my mortified little face as I try to ignore the clapping and intense focus on me, leaving me wondering: *Did Sara actually love the stage?*

It was completely understandable that everyone, myself included, assumed that I enjoyed the limelight. There were several reasons for this. First, my apparently insatiable need for attention. After all, why else was I constantly complaining and making a fuss? I was typecast into the role of an attention-seeker and so I played up to it. I covered up my shyness with gregariousness. If I was in the room, I made sure everybody knew I was there. If I couldn't control my behaviour and make myself quieter, I could make being noisy and visible my thing.

There was also my natural love of singing – and the equally natural desire to get recognition for something I was good at meant that I sought out opportunities to perform, even if I didn't particularly enjoy the resulting attention. And finally, my desperate need to be liked. Everybody liked and admired celebrities. Nobody liked and admired me. When I was eight years old, I hatched a plan. I was going to become famous and then everyone would have to be nice to me.

According to my baby book, little Sarah was a natural entertainer. I sang as much as I talked and discovered early on the thrill of capturing an audience. I also enjoyed getting a laugh. As a toddler, I would strip butt naked, put on a woolly hat and dance around the living room. As I got older and my hair got bigger, I discovered I could thrash it around to great comedic effect singing 'Wild Thing'.

It was reinforced early and often that singing was something I was Very Good At. Teachers, adults and even the other kids started to comment on my voice and, realising it was a way to get positive attention, I turned all my efforts to music. My mum, a keen singer, started to coach me at home and enrolled me in the local youth choir, which I treated like a competitive sport, doing my level best to out-sing the other kids, win every solo and generally piss everyone off.

At the end of Class Three a small miracle happened. Miss Clarke announced that she was pregnant. That is not the miracle to which I'm referring. The miracle was that she would therefore would not be able to see our class through the full eight years of Lower School. That's when we were gifted Mrs Low.

Mrs Low, who has sadly since passed away, was a stern woman of seventy who slept four hours a night like Margaret Thatcher and still put us all to shame with her energy and physical fitness. A veteran teacher of many years, Mrs Low was old school in many ways. Her methods might not have passed an Ofsted inspection by today's standards, but I've never since met anybody so competent. She could silence a rowdy class with one death stare, delivered with a flourish of chewing on the end of her glasses. Nobody messed with Mrs Low.

Mrs Low provided something that the other teachers had never quite managed: firm and clear boundaries. She had no interest in fawning over the popular kids. Even if I despised her at times, I could never accuse Mrs Low of being unfair and I quickly learned I didn't have to argue the toss with her. I knew exactly where I stood in her classroom at all times and it revolutionised my experience at school. Even in moments I didn't like her, I always respected her, and, in turn, she treated me with a respect I'd never before experienced from an adult.

Among her many, many, talents, which included doing the splits, a skill revealed to us during a Pancake Day assembly as she donned a showgirl outfit and slid seductively to the floor, all our jaws following her there, was singing. Mrs Low was a former opera singer and she brought music into every aspect of our education. She quickly picked up on my passion for singing and made it her business to praise and encourage me. In school plays she made sure to include a song, even if it wasn't in the original text, to give me a chance to perform. Desperate to impress her, I worked constantly on my singing and started clumsily accompanying myself on the piano and tentatively writing proper songs. That's what I was going to do with my life. I wouldn't rest until I became the sixth Spice Girl.

I made my singer-songwriter debut at the age of nine at my cousin Adam's bar mitzvah with a song I'd written in his honour. I liked Adam very much, but we lived in different countries, so I didn't actually know very much about him. The song consisted of a very literal account of his birth, which included inspired, highly personal lyrics such as 'once he had long hair, then he cut it short' and continued to the present day with 'now it's his bar mitzvah . . . isn't that cool?'. My dad enlisted the entire band to back me as he proudly played guitar and sung backing vocals behind me. The song was received with polite applause and a big, gracious thank-you hug from my cousin. Presumably for all the lovely things I said about him in the song. That was encouragement enough for me.

Ever the shrewd businesswoman, I started to seek opportunities for publicity wherever they presented themselves. Having read in one of my pre-teen pop magazines that Shola Ama was discovered because she was singing on a train station platform, I made a habit of loudly singing wherever I went, raising the volume exponentially if someone looked remotely record company executive-y – so, basically, belting out numbers at anyone nearby who happened to be wearing a suit.

The moment my parents gave up on their TV prohibition and hooked our TV up to an aerial, I began making frequent appearances on it in the role of 'nuisance caller'. Saturday-morning breakfast shows had freephone numbers and the at-home audience was invited to call in with inane questions for that day's guests. I had a knack for memorising phone numbers and 0181 811 8181 was dialled so often I can still recite it in my sleep. If you were a regular viewer of *Live & Kicking*, for example, you might remember me from such butt-clenchingly awkward moments as asking H from Steps 'do you ever get fed up of your hyperactive image?'. I'm not entirely sure what I hoped to achieve from these encounters. In my wildest fantasies, which, as we know, quickly became firm expectations, the celebrity on the other end of the line would recognise my innate star quality and offer me a recording contract on the spot.

Despite my foolproof strategy to become famous by proximity failing to bear fruit and, worse, Geri crushing my big dream of becoming the sixth Spice Girl by leaving a vacancy for the fifth (why, Geri?), I stuck with music and acting and joined a local amateur dramatics society.

In my sleepy hometown activities were few and far between. You did one of three things: sporting, culting or June Easther. June Easther was a small theatre school run by its namesake. It offered dance, singing and drama classes and I signed up for absolutely everything. I have never been any good with directions. When I did my Duke of Edinburgh award and was charged with navigating, I accidentally led my team through a massive shortcut because I thought the way to use a compass was to follow the needle. After a few frustrating dance classes, the teachers stopped trying to help me with the actual steps, which the other kids were doing in perfect synchronisation, and just let me happily flail about doing my own thing somewhere towards the back.

Then, at the grand old age of eleven after a lifetime of preparation, I got my big break. June Easther announced it was putting on a production of *Oliver!* at the Hawth theatre in Crawley, an 855-seater auditorium that I would later loftily tell people was 'basically the West End'. I set my heart on playing the Artful Dodger and ran home, dizzy with excitement, to tell my parents I was going to audition.

My dad's reaction was muted. 'There are forty kids auditioning,' he explained. 'That's a lot of competition. I don't want you to be too disappointed if you don't get it.'

'But,' I responded, 'didn't you have dreams when you were younger, and everyone told you they were impossible?'

He laughed. 'Right you are, baby,' he said. 'Go out there and get the part.'

For the first time in my life my propensity for confusing fantasy with reality worked in my favour. When I walked into that audition, I was brimming with unearned confidence, which June and her panel evidently mistook for stage presence, because they actually gave me the part. My dad was over the moon with pride and a new lesson was learned – performing is the way to get my daddy to love me. As we know from every Hollywood biopic ever made, this is an emotionally healthy, foolproof life strategy.

The next few months were a blur of learning my lines and rehearsing the same damn song over and over until my entire family were humming it in their sleep. But there was just one problem – dancing. I was still bad at it. Really, really bad. I am nothing if not consistent, and the lack of coordination between my emotions and my presentation was replicated a thousand-fold in my attempts to move to music. I hit stumbling blocks at every stage. I couldn't copy the teacher's movements. It took hours to teach me something that would have taken a more adept kid five minutes. I could master the arms, or the legs, but never both at once. On the rare occasions I did, I would show up the next day having completely forgotten it all.

When, by some miracle, I managed to learn the basics, recalling them in fast sequence was a nightmare. If only everyone would pause for a moment to let my brain catch up, I would have been hunky-dory – but apparently that's not how dancing works. Then there was the small matter of executing the steps convincingly. My body moved with all the grace and fluidity of the Honey Monster. Instead of standing up straight and beaming in a classic showbiz 'tits and teeth', I'd be hunched over, my eyes glued angrily to the floor, so I could see where I was going.

I'm not quite sure why I thought the dancing part would be a doddle. Maybe my expectations had been mismanaged because a few months earlier I had entered a dancing competition and won. The fact that I had been the only child to enter in that category for my age group? Details. I was an 'award-winning dancer'. Having won a lead role, there was to be no hiding at the back and only slightly ruining the performance. I had a devastatingly short amount of time before I would have to be front and centre with all eyes on me, simultaneously hopping from side to side with confidence and singing. Not only that, but the entire company would be doing the same dance routine behind me, so if I messed up, everyone would know.

I was rescued by my Artful Dodger alternate – a girl a few years older than me named Sarah who was a fantastic dancer and an incredibly kind soul with infinite patience. Sarah had a knack for teaching the unteachable. Calmly and compassionately, she spent days on end with me showing me the same steps over and over. Hop step, hop step, hop ball, hop step. Hop step, hop step, hop ball, hop step. It didn't matter how spectacularly I was making a pig's ear of it, Sarah was nothing but encouraging. Slowly but surely, under her magnificent tuition, I started to get it. I practised that routine everywhere I went. I hop-stepped and hop-balled around the playground, I step-ball changed to the car every morning, I pirouetted clumsily around my living room. I nailed it.

Finally, opening night arrived. I felt like a shaken-up Champagne bottle – positively ready to burst with nerves and excitement the moment I was uncorked on to the stage. A gaggle of volunteer mums helped me into my raggedy suit and top hat, steered me to my mark (I never would have found the correct side of the stage unaided) and I swaggered out in front of the wide world to make my big debut. I launched into a rip-roaring rendition (if I do say so myself) of 'Consider Yourself' – the number that included the big, troublesome dance section. I braced myself to cock it up but amazingly I remembered every single step and executed them all with expert precision. When I came off the stage, I was flying. I'd done it! I'd really done it! Nobody had the heart to tell me until many years later that, as I proudly led the entire cast in the dance routine, I was cheerfully and confidently dancing in the wrong direction.

Still, my slight misstep wasn't held against me for very long and a little over a year later, now an angsty thirteen-year-old, I was cast as Blousey Brown in the June Easther production of *Bugsy Malone*. The part barely required any dancing and, aside from an American accent, which, despite months of practice, sounded stubbornly Welsh, I had a much easier time learning my role. Opening night came round like a bullet and the show went off without a hitch. As I stood on the stage singing 'Ordinary Fool', lit by a single spotlight, I managed to catch a glimpse of the front row. There was my dad – sobbing his eyes out.

One of the things about having a lot of early success is that it can be a very long way to fall. Yes, I'd heard mutterings about the cruel, competitive world of showbiz, but so far I'd achieved everything I'd attempted. Maybe showbiz was cruel to OTHER people, but not me. I'd never heard of big fish in small ponds, I just assumed I would either grow to fit my new enclosure or eat all the other fish. It all came crashing down when I decided to dip my toe in a brand-new pond. I know fish don't have toes; I guess I just ran out of steam with that analogy.

The small performing arts community was abuzz with the news that a different theatre company was coming to town with a production of *Annie*. I was ecstatic. *Annie* was my favourite musical. I'd watched the movie version so often I'd worn out the VHS. At thirteen I was already a little too 'buxom' for the role, as my mum so delicately put it, so this was my last chance to play the iconic part. I wish I could say I worked hard and prepared, but the truth is I was resting on my laurels. I assumed, given my past successes, that some innate quality would land me the role and that, without very much rehearsal at all, some rush of adrenaline would see me through the audition.

The audition song, 'Tomorrow', however, was a different beast to songs I'd tackled in the past. It required a big, belty West End voice, not a 'basically the West End if you're listening through a door' squeak. It was a note or two out of my comfortable range and the climactic end notes were in that pesky range where my chest voice broke into a feeble head voice.

My dad drove me to the day-long audition process at the local theatre. I looked around at the literally *hundreds* of children auditioning and suddenly I felt a lot less sure of myself. The judging panel was nothing like the smiling, familiar faces of the June Easther company. They were cold, unforgiving and gave absolutely nothing away. I wasn't walking into a room where everyone already knew me. I was handed a number, by which I would be referred to for the rest of the process.

It took approximately thirty seconds into the first singing audition, 'It's the Hard Knock Life', for me to realise just how screwed I was. These other kids were rehearsed, polished and note-perfect. The panel made their first cuts at lunchtime, dividing the room *X Factor* style and sending half the children home. It was brutal. Children were sobbing in the hallways. *There but for the grace of God go I*, I thought, as I scraped through to the afternoon auditions.

The afternoon session was even tougher. We were given a relatively simple dance routine to learn. I did my best to copy the choreographer's movements but given that we had around an hour to learn the routine, instead of the required four months of private tuition, I stood no chance. At that point I went into some sort of self-protective denial mode. *It's* OK, I told myself. *They won't expect you to be able to learn it on the first go.* As all the other auditionees *had* been able to learn it on the first go without any problems, I'm not sure how I managed to kid myself, but such was my need to preserve my self-image as somehow inherently exceptional.

The final part of the audition was the big number – 'Tomorrow'. By the time my turn came around I was exhausted. I was drained from the loud, confusing and unfamiliar atmosphere, the relentlessly long day and the emotional demands of presenting myself to a panel of strangers with hard faces. I made a valiant effort, but when it came to those final top notes I hit that dodgy point where my belting range ran out. My voice cracked.

My dreams cracked. It was so nightmarish that if I'd looked down and realised I was auditioning naked I would have thought, *That's about right*. Then the next hopeful stepped on to the stage. To this day I haven't forgotten her name, but I won't use it here because it's not her fault she became the obsessive focal point of my jealousy and self-loathing. Let's call her Susie Perfection. Susie delivered a stunning, moving rendition. When it was time to hit that top note, it rang out like a beautiful bell. I even saw one of the robotic panellists crack a smile. Someone wiped away a tear.

Even I wasn't so deluded that I thought I would get the titular role after such a shambolic audition, but nothing could have prepared me for the end of the day when once more we were separated into two groups and my group was briskly thanked and excused. *There must be some mistake*, I thought. *Don't they know who I am? Don't they know who I'm going to be?* And then the sickening truth sunk in. Not only was I not going to play Annie, I hadn't even made the chorus. I had been *that bad*. I wasn't even good enough to stand around in the background only slightly ruining the performance. The ground gave way beneath me. I wasn't special. I wasn't destined for greatness. I'd just got lucky a couple of times. The thing that made me special didn't make me special after all.

I walked out of the audition, terrified to face my dad, who was waiting with the other parents, his face alight with expectation. I shook my head and my face crumpled. I had so desperately wanted to avoid crying in front of my dad and all the other children, but there was about as much chance of that happening as me doing the Riverdance. My dad's face fell with disappointment, but it wasn't his own disappointment. It was worse – he felt sorry for me.

A more resilient teenager might have got up and tried again, understanding that the key to success is hard work, or that good performers have bad auditions. But I took that one rejection as an absolute final judgement. I was shit. There was no point in trying any more. That was the end of my adventures in musical theatre. I never did another production. Instead I would wait until everyone was out of the house, sit at the piano and work on my own compositions, which I performed to an empty living room, vowing never to sing in front of anyone again.

The experience launched me headfirst into my moody teenage years. It was time to put away childish things, like my beloved Spice Girls. My VHS tapes of popular musicals started gathering dust. Instead I started sneaking CDs from my brother's collection. Three and a half years my senior, he had a more sophisticated musical palate than I did, and I desperately wanted to cultivate the air of subtle superiority he had just by listening to cooler music than me. Through careful theft, and learning to burn CDs, I received a thorough education in grunge, punk and pretty much everything decent from the last decade. I inhaled my way through Nirvana, Pixies, Garbage, Skunk Anansie, Weezer, Green Day, Rage Against the Machine and countless other iconic bands of the era. I made myself compilation CDs, which I took great care to blare out as publicly as possible, so everybody knew how cool I was with my cool, cool music. Everybody except my brother, of course. A guilty little part of me felt like I was stealing his identity, as well as his albums.

My disillusionment with performing arts meant I needed to find another way to shine. Fortunately, I had a backup plan. Remember all those pesky words I kept accumulating but had no idea what to do with? Turns out that when assembled in a pleasing order, they weren't so destructive after all. Written words, even those scribbled in a hurry as they tumbled in an avalanche from my brain to my pen, were not permanent statements. They were not etched in stone or, worse, heard by human ears before they were fully considered. Unlike spoken language, written words could be scribbled out, taken back, ripped up, rearranged and presented to the wider world only when they perfectly expressed exactly what I was trying to say.

I had always enjoyed reading and writing, but my early education was rife with confusing messages about when and how I should be doing it. First, I was scolded for reading and writing 'too early' for the Steiner system's liking. Then I was sharply mocked by my classmates and even a little by my teachers, for engaging enthusiastically with my English lessons, earning me a new nickname, 'know-it-all'.

OK, so maybe I spent most of my time in class with my hand as high in the air as it would go, a second hand joining it if I felt the teacher hadn't noticed me, like I was doing aerobics, but wasn't the point of learning to know stuff? 'Sara is always very keen to show how much she knows,' said one of my school reports, scathingly. *Well, why*, I thought, *ask the bloody question if you don't want an answer?*

As I entered my teens, however, I was given something more than just my own satisfaction to cling to – external validation and encouragement. Mrs Low was the first teacher to notice my interest in writing and, despite thinking my chosen subject matter was a bit frivolous (oh, if only she could see what I do for a living now), she urged me to keep going. It was Mrs Morris-Brown, the first English teacher with whom I really connected, who suggested creative writing might play a big part in my future. Mrs Morris-Brown was nothing like the teachers who had preceded her. She was young, genuinely passionate about her job and, the class agreed in hushed murmurs, pretty cool. Mrs Morris-Brown didn't strike me as at all Steiner-ish. She seemed much more real-world savvy. She knew and cared about the great works of literature and had that rare knack of lighting a fire of enthusiasm under whichever class was lucky enough to have her. It was Mrs Morris-Brown who told me I had a 'flair for language'. A turn of phrase I never forgot. It was one thing to be a good speller or a fast reader – but a 'flair', that was a gift. Something special that, while it could be honed, was much harder to teach.

I started writing whenever I could find the time. Mostly short stories and poems, and better lyrics for my angsty teenage songs. I wasn't sure exactly where I was going with the writing thing, but I knew that whatever I ended up doing, it would involve wrangling words, hopefully for money.

Around this time, tragedy struck and Mrs Low retired. Our class was merged with another class of children our age and we were lumped with a teacher who found my enthusiasm and know-it-all-itis beyond irritating. His lessons were littered with factual inaccuracies and, when I raised my hand to correct him, as I was prone to doing, I would find myself unceremoniously booted out of the class.

I decided to take my education upon myself, with my new best friend, TV, as my tutor. This is how I would learn how to be normal, I decided. I invested hours and hours recording episodes of *Friends* and *The Simpsons*, memorising all the jokes and repeating them to get laughs out of my brother and his friends. These shows didn't teach me an awful lot about how to be normal, but they taught me something far more valuable – how to be funny. I had no idea at the time that what I was doing was legitimate research.

Around a year into licking my *Annie* wounds, it was announced that there would be a school talent contest. In a most un-Steinerised turn of events, it would be a variety show where students could enter dance routines, comedy sketches and music from *this* century. The contest was the brainchild of a newer, more contemporary music teacher – someone who had us singing The Beatles instead of Steiner-approved hymns. The contest would be judged by a panel of parents with some vague or imagined showbiz connections.

My brother, an exceptional guitarist, formed a band and sheepishly I asked him if I could join and perform with him. When the answer, to my great amazement was no, my eighteen-year-old brother did not want his fourteen-year-old little sister cramping his style, a sense of furious sibling rivalry overrode any confidence I had lost since the *Annie* debacle. It wasn't about shining, or doing it for the love of music, it was about wiping the stupid smirk off my stupid brother's face.

Filled with a new sense of purpose, I began assembling the best musicians in my year, suggesting we perform a cover of Skunk Anansie's 'Weak'. If I could have a word with my younger self, I'd probably ask me what the hell I was thinking putting myself in direct comparison with Skin, one of the greatest vocalists of all time. Fortunately, barely anyone in the Steiner community had heard of Skunk Anansie, and so despite being guaranteed to come up short, we settled on 'Weak' as our piece for the talent contest. We rehearsed day and night, piecing together each instrument's role by ear. At first it was shambolic, but gradually we gained in confidence and by the time the talent contest came around, we were actually, for a bunch of fourteen-year-olds who had grown up on anthroposophical hymns, pretty polished. The only thing missing was a band name. 'I've got it,' I cried, during one late-night rehearsal. 'Just Add Vodka!' Not letting the minor detail that not a single one of us had ever tried vodka deter us, we all agreed that the name was brilliant, even inspired. At least, that's how I remember it. If you were a member of Just Add Vodka and you disagree – I didn't want to hear it then and I don't want to hear it now.

The period between the contest being announced and the gig itself was a tense one in our household. For me at least. My brother hadn't noticed in the slightest that rejecting me from his stupid dumb, poo-head band had earned him a sworn enemy, but from my end mealtimes consisted mostly of resentful glares and pointed requests to my bemused parents to ask *my brother* to pass the ketchup.

The gig came round in a hurry, as nerve-wracking things often do. I had never felt so cool standing on the stage of the Ned Flanders auditorium, the dimmed lights snapping on to reveal me at the front of the band in a sleeveless black tank top emblazoned with rhinestones spelling out the word 'rock'. The band played the opening notes of 'Weak'. And then something terrible happened. As if they had run out of batteries, the whole band faltered at once and the music petered out before I had sung a note. This had never happened before. The auditorium fell into a loud silence and the lights, which moments before had made me feel like The Shit, shone disconcertingly into my eyes. I turned round to the band, inexplicably calm, and said, 'It's OK, start again.' Start again we did – and this time, perhaps because the worst had already happened, we killed it. My memory of the performance itself is a blur, but the stadium (yes, stadium, OK? Let me have this) erupting into rapturous applause at the end is crystal clear.

I had been so preoccupied with my own entry for the contest that I hadn't noticed Talia was bothering me a lot less than usual. She too was frequently absent during breaks and lunches and, as it turned out, she had assembled a mini dance troupe to perform a routine'. The troupe comprised several of the pretty, popular kids, who did a relatively tame dance routine which was . . . OK. I am in no position to criticise anyone's dancing. Or anyone who can brush their teeth without accidentally punching themselves in the face. But the routine was safe, and, between moves, they all apparently forgot they were still on stage, let their arms flop and stood around looking pretty and bored until it was their individual turn to dance again.

Then my brother's band took to the stage. My brother had cleverly assembled the very best musicians in the whole school to perform Metallica's 'Nothing Else Matters'. His band was fronted by another of his close friends, one of the best-looking humans any of us had ever seen in real life, who, if that wasn't unfair enough, had been concealing a secret talent for singing. As much as I hated to admit it, I was impressed. Their set was, by anyone's standards, excellent. The disappointing sinking feeling that there was no way my band could have matched it was heavily outweighed by pride and happiness for my brother, however begrudging.

As the results were announced, all the acts huddled together on the stage. I found my brother and whispered my congratulations, which he returned, and then, in an event so unprecedented I still wonder if I imagined it, we squeezed each other's hands as they announced the final three. Third and second place were announced. Neither of us were in it. I felt a wave of disappointment crush me as I realised that I hadn't even placed, but never mind. I needed to put on a brave face for my brother. He had clearly earned the top spot. And then first place was announced. It was a tie for first place. We had both won.

A shining sensation erupted inside me, like every organ in my body was tingling with pure joy. It was one of the best moments of my life. We all hugged on the stage, jumping about, humbly commiserating with those who hadn't won a prize, trying to remember to look the right amount of pleased, without appearing *too* pleased. Our parents, in the audience, were beyond jubilant. As we all dispersed in the auditorium, I felt like my wildest dreams had come true. This, I thought, *this* was surely my big break. Not into stardom, I wasn't quite *that* naive, but into the upper echelons of society. Winning something as cool and modern as a *talent contest*, the coveted first prize, in front of the whole school, had to be my ticket in. All my problems, I decided, were now over forever. And for five glorious minutes, it seemed that was true. People who had never before said more than two words to me, and those words had been creative variations of 'fuck off' were now clapping me on the back and congratulating me.

And then I bumped into Talia. She looked pretty much how I had looked after my *Annie* audition, right before I had spent several days bawling my eyes out. 'It's really unfair that you won,' she said, spitefully. 'We spent weeks practising day and night and you just showed up on the day and won first prize without even trying.' I was taken aback. I wasn't sure what was more disconcerting, the accusation that I hadn't tried, when not just I but the whole band had put in such a monumental effort, or her uncharacteristic display of overt jealousy and weakness.

This was not, sadly, the start of some Hallmark heart-to-heart where we reconciled our differences and reached an uneasy truce. Nor was it, as I had imagined, the beginning of my ascent into popularity. The next day, the nicknames and taunts resumed, and it was business as usual. People continued to conflate my love of performing and my 'need for something to always be wrong' and label me a chronic attention seeker who needed to be taken down a few pegs. Talia continued to give me a hard time but somehow, after that conversation, she never quite seemed as intimidating again.

7

KISSY GIRL

I am four years old and my parents have given up on waiting until I'm spiritually ready for the alphabet and bought me a copy of *The Jolly Postman* by Janet and Allan Ahlberg, the tale of a postman with a sunny disposition who delivers letters to a who's who of fairy-tale characters. My favourite bit of all is Cinderella's mail, which contains a proof of a soon-to-be-published book written by Peter Piper about the royal love story. I am so enchanted by this mini story within a story that I have memorised every word, even the ones I can't pronounce yet, let alone understand, like 'the pwinth wath incontholable'.

I love everything about Cinderella's story – the fairy godmother, the beautiful ballgown, the glass slipper – but most of all I am enthralled by the idea that one day the perfect man will come along and fix everything.

Thus began my dangerous addiction to fairy tales. Fairy tales are all about destiny – they teach you that two people are made for each other. Nobody cheats. Nobody shouts. Nobody throws plates of pasta at the wall. The story ends with a beginning – a kiss or a wedding and the nebulous promise of a happily ever after. A fairy tale is not concerned with the messy business of making a marriage work, because when you find your perfect prince, everything just falls into place. I internalised this message with such ferocity that I was almost thirty before I managed to undo my own fairy-tale curse – believing that romantic love is a quick fix for all of life's problems.

My fantasy world was fundamentally at odds with my reality, where my parents very clearly were not each other's happily ever after. But the more their marriage unravelled in front of my eyes, the more I clung to the belief that true love conquers all. Given my propensity for fantasy and my unique inability to discern what was and wasn't real within that, this was the most treacherous belief to hold. It meant every flutter of a crush was a matter of life or death, every spark of a romantic attachment became an all-consuming obsession and, given that I truly thought I could wish things true, my acting on a crush was calamitous. And no matter how many times I crashed and burned, I never, ever learned the next time my crush monster came knocking.

As I got older, my obsession with fairy tales evolved into a more sophisticated palate for romantic comedies. Everything I learned about romantic relationships, I learned from the genre. One thing I had always excelled at was extrapolating data and spotting patterns. Here are the rules of love as I understood them:

— If a man is horrible to you, he secretly really likes you.
— If you're wondering why you'd want such a man to like you, deep down he's actually a sweet, sensitive soul who writes poetry, volunteers with sick kids and saves war-hero puppies from burning buildings.
— Said man is just a bit damaged because he's been hurt before. It is your job to fix him.
— Never take no for an answer. This includes following your crush around, pestering them at their workplace, insinuating yourself into their life at every opportunity and forcing a kiss on them to show them how they really feel about you.
— There are two types of women who men fall in love with: uptight career bitches who just need a man to teach them how to let their hair down and kooky manic pixie dream girls whose personalities are assembled at random by a writer shutting their eyes and pointing at a list of adjectives.
— True love has to be tested with a colossal argument in the early stages of the relationship. The issues that argument exposes don't need to be addressed, as long as one of you is willing to make a grand gesture, which instantly solves everything.
— True love has to be tortuously earned. Love freely given is worthless.
— Once you admit your true feelings for each other, you must immediately get engaged or married.
— If there are other long-term partners involved, they will immediately realise their feelings aren't as

important as your true love and will graciously step
aside and give you their blessing.
— The end of your love story is a first kiss, engagement
or wedding. Possibly a baby. What comes after that?
Try not to think about that too much.

When I was five, my family nearly fell apart. I have a
vivid memory of being in the back of the car and asking
my dad if he was having an affair. I have no idea where
I got that idea from, but as far as I was concerned adults
never lie, so if my dad said 'no', that would be good
enough for me.

'Of course not,' he reassured me.

'Swear to God,' I demanded. I wanted insurance. My
dad wouldn't lie to God.

'I swear to God,' he answered.

A few weeks later, my dad moved out. He had become
infatuated with one of my mum's close friends and had
left to be with her. Ten days into our new life as a family
of three, we walked in to find my dad face down on the
couch, sobbing. Whatever he'd had going with his new
woman had fallen through and he was having a nervous
breakdown. Usually when my dad went away for a while,
he'd come back with a Toblerone. This time, our gift was
ten days' worth (or a lifetime's worth, depending on how
you look at it) of dirty laundry. My mum comforted him
through his loss, nursed him back to health and we all
did our best to move on with our lives, with everything
just a bit more fractured and fragile than before.

My first crush, mortifyingly, was on one of my cousins. I was five years old and I was devastated when I was told that this *would* be incest.

My crush monster's attention was misdirected, but now he was wide awake and ravenous. He flailed around wildly from boy to boy, and occasionally girls, wreaking havoc on my emotional stability. Nobody was safe. Not the local boys who'd play football in the street by my house, not random passers-by who showed me a crumb of kindness, and definitely not the boys at school, who were absolutely terrified of me. I believed in the magical power of true love's kiss. If I kissed the right boy, all my sadness would go away. The only problem was I had no idea which boy was the right boy. So, aged six, I found myself running around the playground after the boys trying to kiss each one on the cheek to see if he was my true love. They would flee my advances, shouting, 'AAARGH, RUN AWAY FROM THE KISSY GIRL!' Fortunately for all of us, I was not a very fast runner.

Despite my forward approach, I didn't have a very high early success rate. In my first few weeks of school, aged six, I managed to score a couple of boyfriends, but soon scared them off with immediate proposals of marriage. I was turning seven, after all. I didn't want to end up an old maid. I adjusted my strategy to obsessing over boys who were way out of my league (so, basically all of them), going bright red every time that person's name was mentioned and writing fan fiction about my own life in my diary. This was more convenient because

I could project a whole personality I'd invented on to totally mediocre boys, instead of having to wait around for them to develop ones on their own. After months of pining, creepy staring and intense relationships conducted entirely inside my own head, I'd finally pluck up the courage to approach the boy in question and blurt out 'WILLYOUGOOUTWITHME?'. I was always shocked when the answer was no. I had spent months daydreaming about things going very differently. I had made it so real that despite the answer *always* being no, the gulf between fantasy and reality was so vast, I fell into it every. Damn. Time.

There would then be a period of mourning when I would sit in my bedroom, weeping into my pillow and listening to 'our song' on repeat – songs the oblivious object of my affections had probably never even heard. I can't tell you how many of my favourite songs I've ruined that way. After a few hours, days or weeks, depending on how invested I'd been in that particular infatuation, my crush monster would move on, looking for the next host body to attach itself to. I have a theory that I have only actually ever had one crush. It was just another poltergeist in my world, except I didn't have the self-awareness to fear it indiscriminately possessing whoever it happened to come across. I was in love with love. The first flutters of interest, the long, hazy fantasies where I got to live in a bubble of perfection, the obsessive interpretation of every little sign. *Today his hand brushed mine in gym*, I'd write in my diary, wilfully misinterpreting a slightly clumsy schoolmate walking past me as a declaration of undying love.

My crushes were a bit like buying a lottery ticket. While intellectually, most people don't actually *expect* to win the lottery, people buy tickets for the period of time between purchase and draw when you get to imagine what your life would be like if you won. And because it's such a remote concept, the fantasy is orders of magnitude more magical than the reality could ever be. When you don't win, you feel a little dip of disappointment – and then you buy a ticket for the next draw. But what if, every single week, your fantasies were so convincing that by the time the draw came round, you'd already put down an actual deposit on a Lamborghini and a thirty-bedroom mansion? Despite the huge emotional damage I was causing myself, I never learned.

When I was around eight years old, I became obsessed with the musical *Grease*. I wrote 'Pink Ladies' in chalk on one of my pink jackets and carried a little comb around that I used to slick back my hair, which had the opposite effect of backcombing it to new levels of Sideshow Bob-ness. I was captivated by the epic love story of Danny and Sandy, two teenagers in their mid-to-late-twenties, who had a summer fling before Sandy moved to Danny's high school, where Danny romantically rejected her for being a massive nerd. Swoon! *Grease*, a musical set in the fifties and released in the seventies, seemed to me the ultimate contemporary guide to love. I watched, wide-eyed, absorbing everything I could about how to live my best life. Sandy learning to smoke, dress all sexy and change her entire personality in order to win her man, Rizzo explaining through the medium of song how the very worst thing you can do is flirt with a guy and then not go through with it, whatever *it* was. No self-respecting girl, I extrapolated, would get a guy all worked up and then not do this mysterious 'it'.

When I was nine years old, I fell in love with Zac Hanson. I learned everything about him. Zac was almost exactly two years older than me. He came from a large Mormon family in Tulsa, Oklahoma. His favourite show was *Animaniacs*. I was so fixated on him that I begged my parents to take me to SegaWorld in London, because I'd seen pictures in a magazine of Hanson playing on a motorbike-themed video game and I was convinced beyond all sense that if I touched something Zac had touched, a psychic link would be activated between us, like a medium at a murder scene touching something the victim owned. Having established our magic connection by touching the seat of the very arcade-style motorbike on which Zac had once sat, I managed to gather my whole family for Hanson's 1998 show in London. Before the show, my mum took me shopping and I bought what I thought was a fabulous new dress but which actually turned out to be an extra-large adult-sized T-shirt. I had near-religious faith that Zac would spot me in the crowd, invite me onstage and propose to me then and there, so I needed to be dressed for the occasion.

When we arrived at the massive Wembley Arena and took our seats, I was aghast. We were so far back, Zac and I might as well have been in different counties. We needed binoculars just to make out the fuzzy shapes of the trio, a zillion miles away. But still, I told myself, Zac would see me. It didn't matter how far away I was, he'd spot me in my XXL T-shirt for ladies and fall head over heels in love.

And then something amazing happened. Halfway through track thirteen, 'I Will Come to You', Zac's eyes locked with my binoculars. As if in a trance, he stepped out from behind his drum kit and off the stage, making his way through the crowd like Moses parting the Red Sea. He walked purposefully towards me, everyone cheering as they realised what was happening, and began to climb up the side of the stands, no structure too tall to stand between us. I maintained an innocent façade, putting on my best 'surely he can't mean me' face, even though I knew that of course he did. The jumbo screen, which moments before had been showing close-ups of the band, now flickered between the two of us. Finally, he reached me, producing a single red rose from behind his back and handing it to me with a twinkling smile. 'Mind if I borrow her?' he asked my parents politely, before sweeping me up in his arms and carrying me back to the stage, where he got down on one knee and asked me to be his wife and also to join the band.

Back in the real world, Hanson performed their set, then their two-track encore before we spent several hours trying to get out of the crowded car park. I had set my expectations so high that I had barely registered the gig at all. I had ruined my whole night waiting for an impossible fairy tale at the expense of the already pretty awesome reality.

Years later, in my thirties, I would score second-row tickets to Hanson's *String Theory* gig at the Royal Festival Hall. Zac would be mere metres in front of me. By then Zac and I were both happily married to other people so sadly our moment had passed and I was just free to enjoy the night with my childhood friend, Rob. In the intervening years I had let things slide and lost my crown as the world's biggest Hanson fan. As the screaming, weeping fans surrounding me sang along to every word of the new album I'd only listened to once and began to rush to the front of the stage in the hopes of touching a Hanson, it actually happened. As I was jostled around by the mob of thirsty thirty-somethings and their even thirstier mums, I looked up at the stage to see Zac looking at me. I gave him a look that said 'yikes, can you believe these desperados?' and he returned my expression. 'I know,' his eyes said, and then he added, 'Just so you know – it would have been you.'

Having learned a valuable lesson from the Zac Hanson debacle, I immediately erased it from my memory and went on to ruin all the other formative moments in my life. When I was eleven, I met a boy at a friend's bat mitzvah. That is the entire story of my face-to-face contact with him: I met a boy. I fell head over heels in love with him and embarked on the hard work of devising him an imaginary persona and complex backstory. I didn't catch his name at the time, but when the bat mitzvah girl sent out a thank-you email, there were only a couple of boys copied in. I took my best guess and emailed the boy whose name vaguely rang a bell, let's call him Adam Cohen. I started bombarding that email address with long, mortifying missives about my day-to-day life, my feelings, my hopes and dreams. I cannot stress enough that I'm not even sure this was the same boy I'd fancied, but in the absence of certainty I settled on delusion. I decided that my bat mitzvah was my big chance to have that romcom perfect moment and sent him an invitation. He didn't reply. *That's OK*, I thought. *He's not supposed to reply. He's supposed to show up at the eleventh hour and surprise me.*

I kept up my overconfident, abrasive persona well into the evening party, to which Adam Cohen had been invited. In my bat mitzvah video one of the other children compliments my Groovy Chick bat mitzvah cake (the fondant Groovy Chick figure apparently modelled in my own likeness) and I point proudly at myself while positively bellowing in their face, nearly sending the smaller girl flying across the room, 'I DESIGNED IT.' I strut unconvincingly across the room in my New Look lavender strappy polyester number, complete with veil, balancing on my platform heels like a wobbly baby deer. I say things like 'We have to get the party going'.

A playlist of absolute tunes from the era blast in the background as I flit between the awkward patchwork quilt of everyone I've ever met – kids from drama school, elderly relatives, classmates whose parents forced them to attend. Even Talia had been strong-armed into going and from the footage she doesn't seem pleased about it. This did give rise, however, to a satisfying moment, caught on camera, where Talia tries to nab the piece of Groovy Chick cake with 'my' face on it and I quite firmly tell her she can't have it before asking the kitchen staff to ensure that I am given that slice in a move that really said 'Not this birthday, bitch'.

What the tape doesn't show is that I kept nervously glancing at the door, waiting for the mysterious Adam Cohen to arrive and sweep me off my feet. I had it all planned out, right down to my choice of song for the last dance of the night, 'Save The Best For Last' by Vanessa Williams. Adam was going to stride in at the very last moment, tap me on the shoulder and say, 'May I have this dance?' Cut to a twelve-year-old me standing alone at the side of the dance floor as my parents, aunts and uncles, grandparents and a few of the older kids slow danced to 'our' song, not a knight in shining armour to be seen. I couldn't believe it. How could it have just not happened after I'd lived it so many times in my mind? Set against the might of my own expectations, the reality of my bat mitzvah, which everyone agreed was a roaring success, was an almighty flop.

After the requisite week of wailing and listening to my cassette tape of 'Save The Best For Last' on repeat until it mysteriously went missing, I continued to cycle through crushes like dirty socks. Then, finally, at the age of thirteen, something marvellous started happening to my body: womanhood came to tap me on the shoulder. By the time this happened I was both massively over-prepared and seriously underprepared. I knew about periods from three sources. The first was the 'murder' my mum had committed in the toilet; the second was Anne Frank's diary, where there is a detailed description of what to expect in the run-up to your first period; the third was from an overenthusiastic teacher who sent all the boys out of the classroom one lesson and gave us a harrowing account of her first period, which I can only assume was designed to put us off periods so we'd stay well away from them. Sex education at school was negligible, which is why I learned more about my own body from a young woman who was murdered in the Holocaust than I did from my own teachers.

Finally, the day before New Year's Eve 2000, my period made its first appearance. I was over the moon. Having checked off that milestone, the next item on my list of things to acquire was boobs. Every night before bed I would lie in the dark willing them to grow, but my chest remained stubbornly flat. And then, after what felt like a thousand years of wishing and wait-ing, they arrived. And they didn't stop arriving. I grew out of the training bra my grandma had bought me at

Marks & Spencer in about a month and kept having to trade up as often.

If I thought my new boobs would bring me respect and admiration, I was sadly mistaken. They did, however, invite mockery, staring and lifelong back pain. Be careful what you wish for. But, no matter, I was a proper woman now. I started experimenting with fashion. My tops got a little tighter. I wore low-cut bell-bottom jeans instead of fluorescent leggings. I got an expensive grungey hoodie. I was starting to look the part. And surely that meant the boys were about to start lining up.

That year I received my first and only anonymous Valentine. It arrived in the post in a stiff red envelope and my heart hammered with excitement as my mum put it into my hands over breakfast. I tore it open and stared in disbelief at the pink and red love hearts on the card, the mysterious signature, a single question mark, wondering how Zac from Hanson had managed to get my address.

'Who do you think it is?' I asked my mum in wonder.

'Rob,' she answered.

'But it might be Zac from Hanson,' I offered.

'It might be,' she admitted. 'But it's probably Rob.'

*

When I was around thirteen, a boy from the year above me, let's call him Bob, approached me in the playground. Bob was skinny, pale and spotty. He was odd-looking and, like me, somewhere near the bottom of the popularity pyramid. He would not have been a natural target for my crush monster. But to my delight he told me that he really liked me and wondered if I'd like to go out with him. I was so flabbergasted that a boy was paying me attention and so *desperately* grateful that I said yes without even pausing to consider if I liked him back. We spent the whole day holding hands. It felt like fireworks were going off inside my heart. We arranged to meet at the cinema that evening for our first official date. Despite thinking that Bob was a disgusting teenage boy, my mum helped me to get ready and drove me to the cinema, where I waited for Bob to arrive.

Five minutes passed, but that was OK, I was early. No need to be neurotic about it. Ten minutes. He was cutting it a bit fine if we were going to get good seats for the movie. Fifteen. OK, now he might miss it altogether. And then I saw them – the popular girls from my class walking into the film. They all looked at me and burst into nasty giggles. That's when the penny dropped. I was being stood up and everyone was in on it. I ran to the payphone and burned through all my loose change dialling home. Finally, after about an hour of sitting in the cold cinema lobby, sobbing into my lap, I got through to her. We went through every possible excuse for him standing me up: he'd been struck by lightning. He'd developed amnesia and forgotten who I was. He was being held prisoner by a jealous sea witch. But my worst fears were confirmed the following day when I saw Bob in the playground. 'It was a joke,' he laughed cruelly. 'Like I'd ever go out with you.'

I suddenly recalled that feeling of terror I'd had so frequently when I was younger that someone I cared about might become possessed by an evil spirit and want to harm me. Just one day previously I had truly believed this person liked me and enjoyed my company. It had felt like the first bulbs of spring, making everything fresh, wonderful and vividly colourful. Now it was all withered and dead. I was used to my fantasy relationships but surely I hadn't imagined this one too – or had I? The incident irrevocably damaged my trust in myself and in others and, catastrophically, my belief that anyone could genuinely fancy me.

And then my parents split up.

It wasn't as if I hadn't seen it coming. My parents had never been happy together. I was thirteen years old and sitting downstairs with the radio turned up, doing my best to ignore the screaming and sobbing coming from upstairs. I was so used to those sounds now; they were basically background noise. My mum came downstairs in floods of tears and told me it was really over this time. 'Oh,' I said calmly. 'OK then.' I waited for the inevitable wave of grief and upheaval you're supposed to feel when your parents split up, but I was surprised to find I felt absolutely nothing. With hindsight I should have hugged my mum, asked how *she* felt, comforted her – but it didn't occur to me that my parents existed as independent human beings. I was at that horrible age where I was only really concerned with how their actions affected me. And I didn't feel particularly affected.

I expected my dad would immediately move out and, after a lifetime of treading on eggshells, we would all finally be able to breathe. But it being the sensible, correct course of action made it pretty much illegal in my household. My dad didn't just stay in the house; he stayed in the marital bed. Both of my parents were too paranoid to budge an inch, believing that giving up any territory would be perceived as a sign of weakness in the eventual divorce proceedings. And so that's how we ended up with the nightmarish scenario where my parents would go on to share a bed for two years, in which my dad would come home every Friday, pick up a weekend bag and leave, without uttering a single word to us or even looking at us, to go to stay with his then girlfriend in Scotland. He clearly had a type, because she had been another friend of my mother's.

Around this time, I learned that one surefire way to make people like me, at least temporarily, was to flirt. I continued to hoover up romantic comedies as the ultimate guide to life. I watched *Coyote Ugly*, saucer-eyed, as leading man Kevin romantically followed leading lady Violet home while she romantically ran away from him, threatening him with pepper spray. I watched *Bridget Jones's Diary*, transfixed, as Bridget's boss romantically sexually harassed her and she romantically told him to stop it (she didn't mean it, though). I swooned my way through episode after episode of *Ally McBeal* as our neurotic heroine pined romantically after her married ex-boyfriend while he romantically had an emotional affair with her behind his wife's back and, when it looked like she might have actually met someone, romantically called her a bitch.

My first kiss was with my mum's friend's son. When I was fourteen, my mum and I went on holiday to Atlanta, Georgia. It was our first solo holiday together, and the trip was emblematic of a golden age in our mother–daughter relationship. I was just at the age where I was becoming interested in clothes and make-up and she, newly single, was going through a similar stage in her emotional development. Overcompensating for the turmoil at home, my mum spoiled me rotten. We went to the cinema and watched Britney Spears in *Crossroads*. We scoured the rails of TJ Maxx for the perfect dress for my upcoming Class Eight ball – the closest thing I would ever have to the prom, and found a strapless red sparkly gown that made me feel like Jessica Rabbit. On the last night of the trip our host's thirteen-year-old son and I shared an awkward kiss after our parents had gone to bed and I immediately scuttled off to write about it in my diary, taking great care to romanticise the encounter as much as possible.

I returned to school feeling puffed up and full of myself. Who cared what these children thought of me? I was an experienced woman – I'd done kissing. And I'm sure I would have done that BJ thing my kissing partner had so romantically mentioned, if I'd have known what it was. I started talking a really big game, playing those daft sleepover games with anyone who would indulge me where you choose which boy you would BJ, sixty-nine, have sex with. I had no idea what any of these terms actually meant. The basic mechanics of sex were a mystery to me until I actually did it a good couple of years later. All I'd seen of sex in movies were two people bumping together. All I'd gleaned from school was a vague drawing of anatomy that I couldn't relate to anything in real life and a story about a spirit named Adam who chose his parents. I was a perilous mix of over-compensating with overconfidence and utterly ignorant about what I was saying.

While I was still very much a pariah at school, my social life outside school was starting to pick up a little. I still had Carys and Rhiannon as my anchors, but I also started hanging out with some of the other girls, who saw me as a *Clueless*-style project. One of the wealthier girls gave me her hand-me-down clothes, while others let me tag along on their sleepovers. I never felt quite welcome, or quite 'in', but it was close enough. To my great shame I started treating Rob horribly. Our Friday-night phone call tradition became a nightmare for him as he was passed unkindly around a group of giggling, anonymous teenage girls and I stopped giving him the time of day. Eventually, and quite understandably, Rob became tired of being taken for granted and, as kids that age do, we grew apart.

The summer before I turned fifteen, we went on our Class Eight trip, a Steiner tradition to mark the end of our Lower School years cycling along the Danube, through Austria and ending up in Hungary, where we met kids from a Hungarian Steiner school. I somehow ingratiated myself with the popular clique of our Hungarian counterparts, probably because they couldn't understand a word I was saying, and, because I couldn't walk two metres without falling madly in love, my crush monster latched furiously on to a boy with a giant head. Let's call him Laszlo. Laszlo and I barely exchanged two words, simply sitting in silence together, exchanging shy glances. When it was time to go home, the Hungarian kids came to the airport to see us off. As I was leaving, Laszlo caught my arm. 'I love you,' he said, pulling me into a close embrace and kissing me passionately in front of everybody.

This movie-perfect moment was too much for my romance-obsessed brain. Of course Laszlo didn't love me. He didn't even know me. 'I love you' was possibly the longest phrase we had ever uttered in each other's company. He probably didn't even mean to say 'love'. In Hungarian the world for 'like' and 'love' is the same. But I had just had a proper romantic-comedy moment. An eleventh-hour confession of love with a kiss at the airport. I floated back to London on a cloud. Hungary seemed like a mini utopia to me, an upside-down land where I was popular and desirable. Back at home, I went straight to the building society, took out the small amount of cash I'd been given for my bat mitzvah a couple of years earlier and booked a flight back to Hungary for the following month.

I stayed with one of the pretty, popular girls who had taken a shine to me and on the first night they arranged for me to meet Laszlo at an open-air nightclub, which, apparently, would serve absolutely anybody no matter how blatantly underage they were. I came to discover this was commonplace in Budapest. Laszlo and I spent an awkward, embarrassing evening snogging each other's faces off. The next day, Laszlo dumped me. It's a testament to just how shallow our romance was that he didn't have enough English to explain to me why. I followed him around the unfamiliar streets of Budapest sobbing and begging him to reconsider, but he sadly shook his giant head. My big movie romance was over before it had truly begun. I spent the rest of the holiday a dripping mess. I snotted all over the city, I cried my little heart out on the shores of Lake Balaton and I was so hysterical on the plane journey home, the person next to me asked if they could change seats. My sad-sack behaviour exposed me as a fraud in the eyes of my cool new friends. I clearly was not the sophisticated Londoner for whom they had mistaken me, but an inexperienced loser who had no idea how to deal with being dumped.

The most traumatic element of all was my burgeoning relationship with sex. I was, with hindsight, extremely vulnerable. I was largely unsupervised, in part because around that time there was a serious illness in the family, but also because I came off, in many ways, as more worldly and mature than I actually was. I was also incredibly tactile, overly so, with a very poor understanding of physical boundaries and what was and wasn't appropriate. I didn't always mean to flirt, but I often looked like I did. And I believed that if I'd flirted, I had no right to then say no.

As I had been reliably informed by my new best friend, television, that boys are threatened by intelligent girls, I started playing the ditz. I wore pink pleated skirts and fluffy boots. I dyed my hair bottle blonde. I started saying deliberately silly things. I played the idiot. I played the role so well I even began to fool myself. I stopped trying to achieve in school. My teachers started to call me out on it. 'If you keep up this attitude,' warned one teacher, 'not only will you fail my class, but you'll fail in life.'

'Ah well,' I retorted, 'if I fail in life, I can always come back and teach here.'

By now I had kissed several boys and was getting a bit big for my boots. Carys and I started spending our weekends shopping in Superdrug for cheap make-up and pheromone wipes and excluding poor Rhiannon, who was just a little younger than us, from our little excursions.

'What are pheromones?' Rhiannon asked us one day, as we smeared our necks with little wet wipes that neither of us wanted to admit smelled like cat wee.

Carys and I laughed knowingly as if to say 'What a ludicrous question! It doesn't even deserve an answer'. This had the dual effect of making us feel smug and superior while disguising the fact that we had no idea what pheromones were.

The summer before I turned sixteen, I managed to score a coveted place at a school summer camp. Students in Class Twelve, the final official Steiner school year, were required to do major independent projects as part of the curriculum. The summer camp was organised by one of my brother's friends as an anti-racism project. It was well-meant, but definitely the whitest anti-racist gathering I have ever attended. That's where I met the next big love of my life. Let's call him Luka. I've changed a few details about Luka to protect his identity. Luka was Slovakian, a couple of years older than me with the added bonus of being able to grow a small beard and therefore look even older and mysterious. He was deliciously handsome in an unconventional way, which made him even more memorable. Luka was beyond fluent in English – he was more articulate than I was. He expressed his considerable intelligence in that very toxic, typically teenage way of complimenting me for being able to 'match' him (bleugh) while occasionally dropping in that 'it's easy to forget how young' I was (bleuggggh). We spent several hot summer days glued to one another in the grounds of the school. Luka moved into my tent on day one and that's how I found out what 'it', and all the other naughty terms I'd been throwing around with abandon actually meant. Although this first clumsy attempt at 'it' was not particularly successful, a mishap Luka responded to with surprising gentleman-liness, Luka embedded himself in that special place a girl keeps in her heart for her first. After an emotional goodbye, we stayed in touch via text and phone calls for several weeks.

By now I had my first mobile phone, a Nokia brick that never ran out of battery. I became addicted to the *beep-beep* of an incoming text. My moods became volatile and unstable. I would only be happy if I'd heard from Luka in the last five minutes. If someone who wasn't Luka happened to text me, I would throw my phone down on my bed in disappointment, wanting to reply *How dare you text this number and not be Luka?* Luka played along for a while, until my incessant contact became so irritating he proved himself to be about fifteen years ahead of his time and ghosted me before that was even a thing.

I responded with dignity. If he didn't want to be with me, then I wasn't going to force my unwanted company on him. It was sad, but I deleted his number from my phone and moved on. Ha! Of course I bloody didn't. What I did do was call him constantly, day and night, dialling, letting it ring out and hanging up only when I was sure I'd been sent to voicemail, as if he was just going to answer the phone and be like, 'Oh sorry, I only pick up every five hundredth phone call.' I paused my compulsive phone calls only to text him, begging him to talk to me. The rampage only ended when my dad came over, clutching an astronomical phone bill that ran for pages and pages, demanding to know who I'd been phoning every thirty seconds in Slovakia. I explained the situation and watched my dad's expression change from anger to pity.

'Sara . . .' he said, holding up the mortifying document, 'this is crazy.'

'I know,' I sobbed.

My late teens were a parade of short-term boyfriends, lasting between a few days and a few months, friends with benefits and people I just had no idea how to say no to. In and among this conveyor belt of 'relationships', there were some stand-out wounds. A trail of particularly influential boyfriends for whom I would temporarily adopt an entirely new persona. A lot of boyfriends. A lot of Saras. For each new obsession I would take on a whole new set of interests, mannerisms and wardrobe changes. I dyed my hair so many times, it started to literally fall out. 'You can be whoever you want, bitch,' my hair decided, 'but I'm sick of the abuse – I'm out of here.'

There was my first serious boyfriend, who lived in Dorset, with whom I shared an intense, passionate and obsessive connection. That was until he got bored of having a girlfriend who lived an eight-hour coach trip away with a stopover in Bristol and cheated on me. During the tearful break-up, where I, the cheated-on party, begged *him* not to leave *me*, he explained, 'Imagine you have a watch – and you really love that watch. But the watch only works between twelve and two, so you have to get another watch to fill in for all the other hours.' There was my brother's university friend, on whom I developed a beast of a crush, who had to awkwardly ask my brother if he could gently tell his little sister to stop phoning him every day and talking at him for hours. There was the boy I had a heart-to-heart with on a cross-country coach journey, one of those once-in-a-lifetime connections, before sharing a long kiss goodbye before he left, leaving behind a fake number and taking with him a piece of my heart and the whole of my wallet. There was the boy who described himself as 'punk' and quoted romantic lines from *The* O.C., pretending he'd just come up with them on the spot, who I followed to his sixth form to spend more time with him, only to be dumped the summer before I was due to start.

While I could have stayed on at the Steiner school for my A levels, I felt it was time to move on for a number of reasons. The first was that there simply weren't that many subject options at the Steiner school. I wanted to dabble in exotic-but-ultimately-useless subjects, like Law, which would have been impossible at my small school with a handful of teachers. Nobody has ever needed a Law A level, but I was going through a phase where I wanted to be Ally McBeal when I grew up, and a Law A level seemed like as good a place as any to start. The second reason was that I was just done. I was done with being the school loser, done with the claustrophobia of the now tiny class sizes and ready for a fresh start. My school had, for reasons I'm legally required to say probably have nothing to do with free manual labour, introduced an extra pre-GCSE year where, alongside our regular academic work, we did odd jobs around the school like bricklaying and painting, and so by the time I was due to start my A levels I was almost eighteen years old.

My last year at the Steiner school was rescued by Meredith. Meredith was a pretty, earthy American girl with curly brown hair, enormous eyes and a galactic intellect. If I had ever, for a second, felt smart in my life, compared to Meredith, I felt like a dog who'd been trained to walk on its hindlegs. She, however, saw right through my dumb-blonde act and patiently, quietly, helped me to get back on track with my schoolwork. She was a good influence on me, and I was a bad influence on her. It was a match made in heaven.

For the wonderful year she spent in the UK, we spent all our time together. We lay in the grass on the village green eating Magnums, we talked about books and music, we consoled each other through angsty teenage break-ups. After the infamous 'I need another watch' dumping, Meredith held me in her arms while I bawled my eyes out. 'I can feel the sadness resonating off you,' she said, brimming with empathy. Meredith kept my GCSE year on track, insisting we finished our revision before the fun could start and, thanks to her, the dumb-blonde act evolved into the unexpectedly-high-grades act.

As sixth form approached, another small miracle happened. Rob and I got back in touch. Rob had been thinking about me in the years since I became a horrible little shit and scared him away and decided to give my home number a try and see if I still lived there. Rob remembers being incredibly anxious about getting in touch. What if I didn't remember him? What if we had nothing in common any more? What if I still came with an obnoxious entourage of giggling teenage girls I was desperate to impress at his expense? He even, I recently discovered, made a list of topics in case we had nothing to say.

'Sara,' my mum called. 'Rob's on the phone!'

'Rob? Wait, *Rob* Rob? *The* Rob???'

The truth was, I had often thought about calling Rob, but I was too ashamed of how I had treated him to make the first move. That night we talked for hours and I was delighted when Rob wanted to meet up. By this point I was a highly sexualised teenage girl who thought that the only way to make boys like her was to be as overtly flirtatious as possible. After an excruciating encounter when I hit on Rob in a way that I'm confident he will take to his grave (unless he would like an early one), we settled into a comfortable friendship, both new and exciting, because we were both so much older and completely different people, yet familiar and nostalgic. Rob had grown up to be a sensible, highly intelligent teenager. Top of his class at school, about to go to Oxford, clearly destined for great things. From then on every moment I wasn't with some boy whose name I wouldn't be able to remember in fifteen years, I began to spend with him.

My reconnection with Rob caused divisions with my then boyfriend, the punk boy who could quote *The* O.C.

verbatim. On their first meeting Rob politely offered to buy me a hot chocolate, an act that fatally wounded Punk Boy's fragile masculinity. 'I can get her drink,' he snapped. That evening, over the phone, Punk Boy made his feelings about Rob very clear. He did *not* like our easy closeness, nor how Rob had tried to 'stake his claim' over me by offering me a beverage. As far as he was concerned, Rob had all but peed on me. I tried to explain that it was just Rob, just *my* Rob, that it was a sibling vibe and nothing more, but my increasingly verbose explanations only made him more suspicious. After half an hour of trying to convince him that Rob was no threat, I blurted out a rare lie.

'Rob's gay,' I said.

'Oh,' he said, relieved. 'I didn't know that.'

There are two things you need to know to make sense of my subsequent appalling behaviour. The first is that in my entire life my exposure to gay people had been limited to two things: the teacher at school who had worn drag to Pancake Day, who everyone accused of being gay, as if it were a crime against nature, and shows like *Will & Grace* and *Friends*. Homophobic jokes were still so normalised that 'gay' was still a widespread playground insult. I had no healthy depictions of gay people as a frame of reference. They were completely theoretical to me. I didn't *think* I was homophobic. No . . . I didn't *know* I was homophobic. Because even though I had no consciously bad intentions towards gay people, I definitely saw them as camp stereotypes who existed purely to take me shopping and dancing. The second thing you need to know is that I am an appalling liar. The only reason that I got away with the initial lie was that Punk Boy hadn't been physically there to see the big, shit-eating grin that spread across my face the moment it tumbled out of my mouth.

From that moment onwards I became so paranoid about being caught out that every time Punk Boy was around, I started making a massive deal of Rob's sexuality in the clumsiest, most insensitive way. 'SO, ROB,' I would half bark in a blind panic, 'HAVE YOU HAD ANY DATES WITH BOYS LATELY? HAVE YOU BEEN GAYING ABOUT GAILY? HAVE I MENTIONED YOU'RE GAY IN THE LAST FIVE SECONDS?' I am ashamed to say I asked Rob to 'act more gay' in front of Punk Boy. In the end Punk Boy, significantly more enlightened and socially progressive than me, called me out on it, asking why I was making such a big deal out of it and pointing out how utterly offensive it was to keep bringing up Rob's sexuality. I was mortified. He was absolutely right. The whole episode had exposed a gaping hole in my understanding of what it meant to be gay and how to treat a friend with respect and tact. The fact that I hadn't learned better yet was no excuse. I felt like the big old homophobe I was and vowed from that moment to do better. I felt so awful, I immediately confessed the lie.

'Oh,' said Punk Boy coldly. 'I see.' He dumped me a couple of weeks later. Reader, I was still surprised.

I phoned Rob and apologised for embroiling him in the whole mess. 'You don't have to pretend to be gay any more,' I reassured him.

'Actually,' said Rob, awkwardly, 'I've been meaning to talk to you about that.' And that was the moment Rob chose to come out to me.

I'd like to say I was instantly the perfect best friend and ally, but that would be a lie. It took me a while to get there and I'm ashamed that anybody had to be my learning curve, let alone someone as precious to me as Rob. After I'd accepted that Rob had absolutely no interest in taking me shopping and would still be worse than useless in that situation, my friendship with him settled into a much easier dynamic. Something about eliminating the potential for romantic misunderstandings meant I could open up to Rob in a new, more authentic way.

We hung out non-stop. We attended parties together, then went back to Rob's for drunken sleepovers, where we discussed in depth which boys we had fancied and what we had thought of every single person who had attended. I know this because there are tapes. Long, mortifying videotapes of me curled up at Rob's side on his sofa giving detailed, bitchy analyses of people who I now can't even remember meeting.

Rob and I even went on holiday together, a tour of Italy with a group of his friends. At seventeen Rob and I had very different ideas of how to have an excellent holiday. Rob's idea of a good time was a tour of cultural hotspots followed by an early night. Mine was wild nights out and meeting as many good-looking guys on their gap year as I could pack into a two-week trip. The holiday naturally divided us into two groups – the sophisticates and the partiers. This divide seemed too much for everyone else's fragile teenage friendships, and by the end of the trip Rob and I seemed to be the only ones who hadn't fallen out. Instead Rob and I caught up over dinner every evening, sharing our stories from the day or night before, accepting that different interests didn't mean that we didn't love each other unconditionally.

It took me until I was thirty-two to pluck up the courage to ask Rob if he had sent me that Valentine. He had. I was thrilled. Not as thrilled as if it had been Zac from Hanson, but still.

These days Rob is the party animal and my definition of a party is a visit from the postman, but nothing has changed. Who would have thought that one of the biggest, longest-lasting loves of my life was absolutely right to run away from the kissy girl?

8

SHIT-STIRRER

It's been a long day at work and I am exhausted. I have reached the upper limit of my physical and mental capacity and can't tolerate one more second of sensory input. My sweet, oblivious husband chooses this moment to start telling me a dull story about planes. My husband loves planes. I find them as interesting as a museum dedicated to doorknobs. I love him dearly, but my brain needs a rest and, knowing it's impolite to blurt out 'you're being boring', need to find verbal gift wrapping. Desperate for a way to soften the blow, I scan the room for clues before announcing, 'The cat thinks you're being boring.' Much better.

Ever seen that movie *Liar Liar*, where Jim Carrey suddenly loses the ability to lie, with hilarious consequences? The exact same thing happened to me, except I've been afflicted since birth, and the consequences are more life-ruining than side-splitting. It seems only fair at this point to issue a warning to anyone who might still be considering becoming friends with me after reading this far: do not, under any circumstances, tell me a secret. Especially one that comes with an ethical dilemma. Don't tell me you've cheated on someone we both know. Don't tell me you've committed a crime. Don't tell me you think Rory was destined for Dean on *Gilmore Girls*, you psychopath.

Because I am well-meaning and want to be there for people, I am often mistaken for being a vault. I'm not a vault. I'm a flimsy cardboard box that's been left out in the rain and the second you pick me up the bottom will fall out, along with all your darkest secrets.

Don't get me wrong. I have every intention of taking your ill deeds to the grave. But I won't. Your secret will last as long as it takes for someone to ask me a direct question about it. As I've mentioned, my face will spread into a big, shit-eating grin that says 'I know something you don't'. My voice will raise to a pitch only dogs can hear. A line of questioning will begin. I'll try to lie, but I'll be so absurdly crap at it, I'll be rumbled in about five seconds. All of this is completely involuntary, but try telling that to the many people whose lives I've ruined with my uncooperative fucking face.

'If you really wanted to,' said one furious ex, breaking up with me after one of his secrets was jostled out of me by a nosy friend, 'you would lie. It's as easy or as hard as you make it.'

Not so. Lying physically hurts me. I can't even lie to get myself out of trouble, as I found out in my teens, trying to convince my mum that the empty cigarette packets she'd found in my coat pockets were being kept as a favour to a friend.

While we're on the warnings, here's another one: never, ever ask for my opinion unless you are sincerely prepared to hear an honest one. I could try to lie to you, but, as we've established, that would be an insult to your intelligence. Don't say the words 'What do you think?' if what you're looking for is validation. A friend recently asked me if they should get an undercut. I launched into a long, impassioned rant about what a bad idea it was because it would grow back uneven. It was only later that my husband gently explained that my friend had just wanted me to tell her to go for it.

These two significant stumbling blocks mean that while I can be very good at making friends, keeping them is trickier. I can just about do a one-on-one connection, but group dynamics can get in the bin. One thing I've learned the hard way from a lifetime of non-optional honesty is that the more baldly you speak the truth, the quicker people will be to accuse you of being a liar. And if you are the lone voice of truth, bluntly naming the dynamics of a situation, you become a convenient scapegoat for beef that should have nothing to do with you.

Because of this compulsive honesty in childhood, I got a reputation as an incorrigible gossip, a bald-faced liar and a malicious shit-stirrer. Every time somebody confided in me, I would spend every waking moment, from the second I found out the secret, basically puce with the effort of keeping it to myself. The problem was, if I managed that for any meaningful length of time, I would be so proud of myself I'd have to tell somebody that I'd managed to keep the secret, spilling the secret in the process.

I was also a classic snitch. If someone was horrible to me, I would tell on them. Being the youngest child in a family of one sibling and three double cousins, I was frequently on the receiving end of teasing, hitting and minor attempted drownings. When I would report them back to my mum, the party line was that I was lying for attention. My mum was the only person who always believed me. The narrative that I told tall tales became so deeply embedded in family folklore that even years later, when I was in my twenties, I would have to tolerate the whole family laughing mean-spiritedly at Sara's 'big imagination' while my ever-loyal mum fumed silently by my side.

The autumn I turned eighteen, freshly dumped by Punk Boy, I followed him to his sixth-form college, where he spent a year awkwardly avoiding me. I had convinced myself that leaving the confines of the Steiner school, where my reputation long preceded me, and going out into the wider world, would make all the difference to my social struggles. It took a special talent for self-delusion, but I managed to convince myself that *I* wasn't the problem; it was my environment. Sixth form was going to be my fresh start. And for a while it actually was. I made friends – lots of them. I was almost, although I didn't dare say it, popular.

Academically, I started doing really well. I'd left the Steiner school with a healthy but not outstanding set of GCSE grades, but now that I was focused on just four subjects I really enjoyed – English, French, History and Law – I excelled. Reinvigorated by my interest in the topics and the clarity with which they were taught, I abandoned my dumb-blonde act and replaced it with my old mantle of unbearable know-it-all. I copied down my notes into concise bullet points, illustrated with visual memory aids and bound in large colour-coded binders that I treated with the reverence of holy texts. I reverse-engineered exam papers, figuring out the formula for top-scoring answers. The fact that I was willing to share this colossal cheat sheet with my friends may have gone some way to explaining my sudden popularity.

My English teachers were delighted with me, championing me, signing me up for an Advanced Extension Award and insisting that I was going to be their record-breaking student. My Law teacher was less impressed with my proactive approach, frequently snapping at me and asking if I would like to teach the class. The first time she asked this, I completely missed the sarcasm in her voice and, overjoyed, replied that, yes, I'd love to. I have no idea why but this was not interpreted as enthusiastic participation and love of my subject matter, but as some sort of insinuation that the teacher was underqualified. I tried to fix this by demonstrating an encyclopaedic knowledge of the syllabus, which only seemed to make her angrier. The more I knew, the more she reacted like I was challenging her competence as a teacher.

It was a fresh start all round. My brother headed off to uni, my mum got a new boyfriend, and my dad, having racked up a few more girlfriends since the divorce, met someone special. It was hard to tell at first that she was someone special, because, like me, my dad had his own formless crush monster, which would fall madly in love with whichever woman happened to be in proximity. I had met a few 'the ones' already. It was a running joke in my family that each new woman was his soulmate.

'He must have a lot of souls,' mused my mum over one Shabbat dinner.

'Yeah,' my grandma shot back. 'Arse-souls.'

My dad had a routine for introducing us to new women in his life. We would all go to Pizza Express, where we would sit at my dad's favourite table, he would order a Giardiniera and we would make polite small talk with the latest love of his life. If anyone still has the CCTV footage from the East Grinstead branch of Pizza Express in the mid-noughties, they could put together a montage of us sitting at that table, the only thing changing between each scene being the woman sitting next to my dad. But this one *did* feel different somehow. Maybe because she made an actual effort with us, but Shira, not her real name, was a breath of fresh air. She was warm, kind and open. Shira was Israeli, from a Moroccan

Jewish background, with a large family of her own and a daughter a week apart from me in age. She was a wonderful cook (I have been reliably informed of this, as what she made was not a variant on pizza), a fantastic hugger and, most impressively, she took no crap from my dad. Together they moved into a lovely home in Forest Row and she made a concerted effort to make me feel as welcome and at home there as possible, even though that meant saying things like 'If you have your boyfriend over and want to make love, we can wear earplugs'.

My relationship with my dad, until that point, had been strained to say the least. While he had stayed nearby after the divorce, I wasn't feeling particularly forgiving. It didn't help that any prolonged time spent together usually ended with him screaming at me and me storming home in tears. My dad often thought I was being dramatic or over the top. And I felt like a teenage girl whose dad didn't like her very much. Things came to a head the evening before my nineteenth birthday when, on a shift at my then job, I hit my wrist on the side of the cash register desk. I phoned my mum to come but she was on a date and reluctant to leave to drive me to A & E so, in desperation, I tried my dad, who shouted at me to stop being dramatic. In the end I phoned a friend's mum, who drove me to A & E and waited with me into the night, where I turned nineteen as they treated my fractured wrist.

Shira was appalled and told my dad she couldn't be with someone who treated his daughter like that.

He tried to explain to her what I was like, but Shira wouldn't accept 'you don't know what she's like' as an excuse. I was the child, he was the adult and the onus was on him to make the effort with me. This was a revolutionary notion to my dad, but also to me. I had spent my entire life believing that I deserved to be shouted at. And that was it. That was all it took for my dad to fundamentally change his entire relationship with me.

The next day, Shira and my dad got married. It was a beautiful celebration at which I was a bridesmaid and I couldn't have been happier to be included in the day. Psych! I wasn't there. What actually happened was my dad and Shira showed up at my birthday party and announced that they had got married that day.

'Oh, Sara,' my dad said impatiently as my bottom lip started to wobble, 'it was just a small thing. We only had a couple of witnesses.'

'I could have been a witness,' I pointed out – a suggestion my dad laughed off.

The sixth-form college was a half-hour drive from my house, which meant I had to make use of the college's twice-daily coach service with the other local kids. The week I turned nineteen, I made a new friend. Let's call her Mia. Thanks to the Steiner system screwing with my educational timeline, Mia was a few years younger than me. She was a friendly girl with brown doe eyes and an aura of being much older than her years. I probably initially seemed a little glamorous to her (hey, I could buy the drinks) and my emotional immaturity made us a perfect match.

Outside college, I had begun working at the local Wetherspoons, a job at which I was irredeemably crap, and it wasn't long before I was unceremoniously fired. During that time, I had started hanging out with a group of locals, people in their late twenties and early thirties who had chosen to stay in their home town, mostly lived with their parents and who, by virtue of being older than me, seemed impossibly cool. It was with this group of friends that my college dream began to crumble, when I allowed my two worlds to collide.

It started when I introduced them to Mia who, then aged sixteen or seventeen, began to date a man from my social circles in his early thirties. I didn't know a lot about anything at that age, but my instincts told me that this situation was Not Quite Right. Mia, however, seemed so sure of herself, so confident beyond her years and so delighted with her relationship that I worried I was being overly sensitive. I wasn't sure how to process my discomfort. I could have spoken to Mia but given that I was also friends with her boyfriend, I was just as terrified of his reaction as I was of hers. My tactic so far of simply blurting things out to people's faces had always backfired. So I tried a new approach. I confided in one of the older girls in the group, someone who had known Mia a long time and might be better placed to talk to her. But instead of framing my concerns as discomfort around an older man taking advantage of Mia, I heard the words come out of my mouth in an unexpectedly bitter tone: 'It's all so weird. She's not even old enough to come to the pub with us. I don't like it.'

It wasn't until much later that I realised that I had phrased my anxieties clumsily. My concern was not that Mia would spoil our nice time at the pub, but simply trying to put into perspective how weird I felt seeing what was a perfectly legal but still icky age gap.

The next morning at the bus stop, I waited for Mia. When she showed up, she was with a group of girls I had never spoken to before.

'Bitch!' she spat.

'What?!' I exclaimed. 'Why am I a bitch?'

I had been misread as bad-mouthing Mia. I tried to explain, but a wall had gone up. Mia was furious and unforgiving. As we waited for the bus, she sat with her friends, talking loudly about what an awful person I was and sniggering at my every move. My stomach turned to lead as I shook with anxiety and disbelief. I knew, instantly, that the change was irreversible. Overnight, my sixth-form best bud had turned into my bully. She was an entirely different person.

While I was devastated to lose Mia, I assumed that if I left her alone, she would return the favour. Not so. Mia had a vendetta and, at the end of the first day of her following me around, whispering nasty comments and telling everyone not to speak to me, it became very clear that my fresh start had gone spectacularly south. As much as my friends told me to ignore her, they didn't quite stand up for me either, becoming conveniently very interested in something else happening nearby whenever she picked on me. My social currency had sunk to the value of the pound the morning after the Brexit vote. It was the Steiner school all over again; being seen with me made people pariahs. *This is pathetic*, I told myself. *You're letting yourself be bullied by a child*. But our age difference had no impact on my ability to handle a bully. I was no better at it at nineteen than I had been a decade earlier, shouting 'You'll be sorry when I'm famous' at my tormentors.

After several more days of Mia and her cronies tailing me everywhere I went, flinging insults, like the physical embodiment of my inner monologue, a real-life Greek chorus, I started to feel something I had never felt in earnest before: suicidal.

Like many teenagers, thoughts of suicide had crossed my mind before. Usually during dramatic break-ups. But this felt like a catastrophe from which there was no return. One thing I was even better at than self-delusion was pattern spotting. If I had transferred my social problems from the Steiner school to sixth form, then the problem wasn't them. It was me. And if it was me, I was stuck with me. It wouldn't matter how many fresh starts I got in life, I would always take me with me and I was a liability. It wasn't a feeling of being trapped in a bad situation; it was so much worse than that. It was being trapped with a bad personality.

One morning, filled with self-loathing, exhausted after days of not eating or sleeping, I walked out of my lessons and took the fifteen-minute train journey to Brighton. Numbly, I walked to the beach, where I sat for a while reading Sylvia Plath, the worst possible reading material for a teenage girl already on the edge and writing my own angsty poetry about the burnt-down Old Pier. I decided to wait until it was dark and jump off the pier. I texted both of my parents a dramatic goodbye, telling them what I planned to do. My phone started ringing. My dad. I declined the call. He texted instead. *I'm on my way. Don't do anything.*

I genuinely hadn't expected this. Perhaps from my mum, but my dad? My dad who so often saw my pain as attention-seeking? I assumed he would write it off as drama. But my dad didn't write it off as drama. He did something unprecedented. He told his colleagues, 'My daughter needs me,' and he left work in the middle of the day. About an hour later, my dad pulled up in one of the parking bays by the seafront and obediently I got into the car. I had never been more relieved to see anyone in my whole life. He put his arms round me and I sank my face into his shirt, bawling my eyes out in shame, misery and self-pity.

We drove a short while to the marina, where we ate at a little independent pizza restaurant and I explained what had happened. During that conversation, the situation with Mia started to feel trivial, when just hours before it had felt catastrophic. We wandered around the shops. My dad bought me a handbag I was admiring, which might feel like plastering over the problem to some, or a recipe for a spoiled child, but my dad was an epic tightwad. He never bought me gifts just 'because'. It meant something because it was so out of character.

Mia would not be the last person I would become close to only to wreck it by baldly speaking an unpleasant truth. This trait would go on to dog me my entire life. But in that particular era of my life, as much as I dreaded bumping into her, I managed to rise above her daily taunts and zone her out. I can't say she ever got bored and left me alone, but I survived the onslaught.

Blessed with a bulldozed social life, I focused all my energy into my schoolwork. With my A levels approaching, I applied to do English at Bristol, Durham, Exeter, Sussex and, rather optimistically, Cambridge, and was stunned when I actually got an interview (it was disastrous – I showed up having cried all night because as we know, that's what I do and then I mispronounced 'Proust'). I was thrilled to accept my place at Exeter.

Towards the end of the year, one of the English teachers pulled me aside and informed me that she was relying on me to get a top five national grade.

I laughed. She didn't.

'No pressure,' I joked.

'Ha ha,' she said. 'No pressure. But seriously, I need you to get that grade.' And then she mentioned that she and another teacher had found some of my angsty teenage poetry on the back of my notes and they hoped I didn't mind but they'd typed it up and sent it in to a competition. The competition was to win a place at a prestigious poetry summer school, hosted at Oxford University. And, by the way, they'd received a reply and I had been awarded a place. It wasn't a place at the actual university, but a chance to go there for the summer and pretend I was clever enough to get in, which was good enough for me. I was so excited about the summer school that it didn't even occur to me to be annoyed that my teachers had sent off my private teenage ramblings without my consent.

After my exams were over, I spent a couple of delightful weeks of the summer at poetry summer camp, where for the first time in my life I was surrounded exclusively by other nerds. These kids, I cannot overstate this enough, were already more accomplished than most adults I know (including myself) now that I'm in my thirties. Almost everyone had some sort of genius scholarship, national publication or Nobel Prize. Then there was me with my hyperbolic, angsty poems, my state sixth-form background and my then purple hair. 'Um . . . well, I devised a very effective system of binders for my A-level revision . . . Oh! And I can now correctly pronounce "Proust".' It was my first taste, since I had been beaten to the role of Annie by a much more talented child, of feeling mediocre at something I usually excelled at in my small pond.

When A level results day arrived, I sat by the computer, refreshing the UCAS site until eventually the message appeared on the screen: *Congratulations, your place at the University of Exeter has been confirmed.* A knot in my stomach that had been there all summer immediately loosened. I hadn't even realised how tightly I had been holding on to my anxiety until it wasn't there any more.

My dad arrived to drive me to college to pick up my final results. All I truly cared about was moving on to the next stage of my life. Now I knew that was happening, and that my grades were probably at least AAB, the same as my offer, I felt quite calm about everything. We approached the desk and I gave the woman sitting behind it my name. She leafed through her papers and then looked up, alarmed.

'Has anyone spoken to you yet?' she asked.

Shit. I knew it had been too good to be true. The UCAS website must have made a mistake. I had failed everything. I wouldn't be going to university after all.

'No,' I said, trying to sound calm. 'Why?'

'You came top five for English,' she said, beaming.

'Wow!' said my dad, proudly. 'Top five in the college? That's amazing! It's a big college!'

'No,' she said. 'Top five in the country.'

My dad stood there for a moment, looking dumbstruck. Then, to my great horror and delight, he burst into tears.

9

DEPRESSED

I headed off to university with a new burst of optimism. Ah, my fresh start. No, not the last fresh start, which went horribly wrong, a *real* fresh start. Exeter was far enough from home to convince me I could leave my old self behind, a four-hour drive away. I pitched my fresh start to myself with the confidence of a dodgy salesman trying to convince your nan that a four-way timeshare in Majorca is a foolproof idea. *Nobody knows you. They have no preconceptions. All people can see is how you behave. If you just behave how everyone else behaves, people will like you.* And, as any responsible counsellor will tell you: *It doesn't matter who you really are inside; it's what's on the outside that counts.*

In the weeks leading up to my first day I spent every waking hour wrapped in glittering fantasies about how wonderful my university life would be. Before I arrived, I had already lived that first day in my head a thousand times over, each time with increasingly fantastical and implausible events, which had started to become indistinguishable from real life. By the time the big day actually arrived anything short of being told it was actually a magic university and I was being given the key to powers that had been within me all along would have been a letdown.

With my dad in tow I lugged box after box of pink fluffy tack I'd bought to decorate my room. I was so concerned with fitting in that I had made sure all my new belongings were strictly on brand. One box was filled exclusively with posters of shirtless men I'd never heard of and a similarly distasteful *Hollyoaks* calendar. I didn't even watch *Hollyoaks*. My halls were off campus. They weren't the poshest halls, where catered meals were served to the richest students by their less well-to-do peers, but I did have the luxury of my own en suite bathroom with a shower so scalding hot that the tiny cubicle doubled up as a makeshift sauna. We unlocked the door to find ourselves in a small dilapidated room overlooking a busy roundabout. My dad's face fell as he took in the shabby surroundings – the noise from the constant stream of traffic outside, the well-trodden carpet, the squeaky plastic mattress. All I saw was a room with a door that locked. 'A place of my own!' I beamed. 'I have a place of my own!'

My brave outlook lasted as long as it took for my dad to leave. I made an abrupt U-turn from 'I can't wait to get away from my old life' to 'Hold on, are you not going to go to university with me?' I put on as brave a face as I could manage, indistinguishable from my not-at-all-brave face. I watched from the window as my dad's car circled the roundabout and was out of sight, before sinking to the floor and sobbing.

Once I had stopped snotting and hiccoughing, I decided to go and meet my new hallmates. A group of pretty, impossibly posh girls with messy backcombed hair, pashminas and Ugg boots sat in the common area, chatting. *Right*, I said to myself, *just play it cool and* . . . 'HI, I'M SARA. OH MY GOD, ISN'T UNIVERSITY SO COOL? I FEEL SO GROWN-UP. MY DOOR LOCKS AND EVERYTHING! HEY, ARE YOU GUYS GOING CLUBBING TONIGHT? CAN I COME? WHERE ARE WE GOING?'

SHIT.

It became immediately obvious that the girls already knew each other through mysterious posh-people channels. If I thought I was missing the handbook before, now I was missing the handbook *and* the secret handshake. 'What school did you go to?' was shorthand for 'Are you worth talking to?' That night I followed the girls to a club by the Quay. It was nothing like the clubs back home, where I knew everybody and which played the same corny retro hits every week, like the DJ was a ghost who'd died in the mid-eighties but kept diligently showing up to work to play that week's top chart hits. This club was packed with strangers. The floor was sticky and shook with the bass of music I'd never heard. I drank alcopops and showed everyone who indulged me how they had turned my tongue blue. When the girls suggested moving on to another club, I followed them outside, relieved. They piled into a taxi together. 'Sorry,' they said. 'There's no room for you.' Then they sped off, their handbags piled on to the extra seat, leaving me drunk and alone in a strange part of town with no secret magical powers at all.

I had no idea how to unpack, so I spent my first week digging through my boxes, leaving debris everywhere. I couldn't figure out how to make my bed. Securing one corner of the bedsheet successfully meant another corner would come pinging off. Instead I lay my sheet in an uncomfortable, creased mess on top of the slippery plastic mattress, gave up on my duvet cover entirely and lay awake all night every night listening to the cars whoosh past and the whooping of passing drunk students who I hated for having the audacity to be having a much better time than I was. Most teenagers leaving home for the first time are pretty clueless, but I majored in having no idea how to do anything. The oven might as well have been a spaceship. The huge industrial washing machines were a mystery to someone who, until their late twenties, still thought the numbers stood for miles per hour and the little circle next to them represented the clothes going round and round. I lived off microwaved meals and takeaways. On one shameful day I was so exhausted by the pace of my new life, I fell asleep with my elbow in half a Domino's pizza. *Excellent*, I thought, wiping marinara sauce from my elbow. *Breakfast*.

After a bewildering day at the bustling freshers' fair, I found myself handing over a fiver to the Jewish Society because I figured that, whether they wanted to be or not, they were my people. I hadn't been involved in Jewish life since my bat mitzvah. While at home we celebrated the important holidays, we were very much the only Jews in the village. But these were desperate times, and, as I was one of them, if they rejected me, they would risk going to Jew hell. If there was a Jew hell. I'd have to remember to ask.

'Here,' said Jonathan, the society president, handing me a flyer. 'We're having an event. You should come.'

'*Jews on a Booze Cruise*,' I read aloud. 'Sure, I'll be there.'

'What's a booze cruise?' I asked my mum in a panicked phone call later.

'It's when you go to France to pick up cheap alcohol,' she explained.

France? It was my first week of university; I didn't have time to go to France! Would we have to stay overnight? How much was this expedition going to cost me? I frantically looked for a number on the flyer, but I couldn't find any way of contacting the society president with my ever-growing list of questions. I had no way to cancel, and I couldn't just not show up; they might have booked a seat on the Eurostar for me, or accommodation. After much flapping and hyperventilating, I packed a small bag with a few nights' clothes, my toothbrush and my passport, just to be safe. I withdrew notes from the ATM in case I needed to exchange currency. I texted my parents to let them know I might be uncontactable for a couple of days as I had to go to France.

The meeting point for the booze cruise was a small pub near my halls. A group of locals sat hunched over the bar narrowing their eyes at me as I lugged my over-stuffed handbag. I quickly spotted the Jewish Society, which comprised Jonathan and a very jumpy Israeli guy fresh from his military service, who looked suspiciously at my bag, as if he was dying to search it. We had a drink at the pub for locals, where the angry glares made it very obvious we were breaking the sacred student–local covenant of 'you stay in your bars and we'll stay in ours', before moving on to the next location. As the evening wore on, so did my anxiety. When were we going to get a move on? And who would be driving? We had long since passed the point of 'above the legal limit' and were now reaching levels of 'best not to light a match near us'. Would we be taking a coach? Finally, I blurted out, 'When are we going to France?' The others looked at me as if I was utterly mad and bellowed with drunken laughter. That's when it dawned on me that there was no trip to France. 'Booze cruise' just happened to rhyme with 'Jews'. They hadn't meant it literally.

That night, as the pubs began to empty, and we were the last stragglers, Jonathan told me that he was about to retire his three-year role.

'There's nobody left to take it over,' he said, sadly. 'I think it will be the end of the Jewish Society.'

'Oh no,' I said, genuinely saddened at the loss of this grand institution I had been a part of for about three hours.

'There's not much uptake here,' he confessed. 'It's not a very Jewish university. I think Jewish people who come here do it to escape their upbringing.' Then his eyes lit up, as if he'd had the brightest idea in the world. 'You could always take it on,' he suggested, hopefully.

I didn't want to be the president of a society, let alone one with about five active members, but, put on the spot, I've never been any good at saying no. And that's how, in my first week of university, I adopted the Jewish Society.

After a few days that seemed like a lifetime, I made a friend. Or, rather, he made me. A few days into my university disaster, there was a knock at my door and there stood a handsome young Italian man. He introduced himself as Filippo and asked if I wanted to hang out. Yes. Yes, I did. Filippo and I went to the cinema, where I introduced him to sweet popcorn and he, not knowing how to tell me he hated it, 'accidentally' spilled it all over the floor. After a brief, confusing two weeks where I did my obligatory routine of crushing hard, getting rejected and moving on to my next unsuspecting victim, he became my best friend. Filippo was kind, goofy and open-hearted. If it hadn't been for my friendship with him, I probably would have gone home in the first week.

My first term passed without much incident. A brief crush on the university's welfare officer, which was snuffed out after I showed up to what I thought was a date and what he thought was a welfare appointment, led me to run for a position on the student council. This would have been a potential source of friends, if I hadn't blown it by treating it like a courtroom drama where my job was to aggressively hold everyone to account. The Jewish Society rumbled along with about three members. We had gained a new member, a non-Jewish girl – I'll call her Anna – who was thinking of converting, who was just . . . well, very mean. I enjoyed her company for her acerbic sense of humour and vast intellect, but she was so unnecessarily cruel to everyone she encountered she kept scaring new joiners away. I would go on to waste years of my time and energy in a toxic on-again-off-again friendship with her, which ended for good in my late twenties after she blocked me from all social media channels following what I thought had been a lovely day out together. When I asked her what had happened, she sent back a cryptic response that basically boiled down to 'If you don't already know, I'm not going to tell you.' I'd like to say this is on her, but that has happened to me a lot.

It wasn't long before Filippo introduced someone else into my social circles, Katerina. Katerina was simply the most strikingly beautiful person I have ever met in real life. She was Greek, with long dark hair, soft brown eyes and dimples when she smiled. She was also kind, funny, compassionate and non-judgmental. I instantly hated her.

'You were just jealous,' I hear you cry to which I say, 'No shit, Sherlock.' Of course I was jealous. I had just made my first university friend and he had met this perfect human being, next to whom I looked like a thumb in a wig. Despite my initial hostility, I was unable to stop myself from liking her. It's very hard to dislike someone who's objectively wonderful, and it wasn't long before two became three.

Katerina and Filippo were delightful company. They were quirky, hilarious and adored me for who I was. I never had to pretend or apologise for myself in front of them and they went along with my zany schemes. During my obsessive *America's Next Top Model* phase, Katerina would let me do her make-up (despite the fact that I was very, very bad at it) and pose for my digital camera while I yelled nonsense at her like 'smize' and 'you look fierce'.

It quickly became obvious that there was a budding flirtation between Katerina and Filippo. Maybe, like me, they had seen too many romantic comedies, because they started flinging unnecessary obstacles in their own way: boyfriends and girlfriends from back home, denial of their attraction, an insistence that they were just good friends. For whatever reason the two of them seemed determined to deny what was clear as day to everyone around them: that these two gorgeous souls were meant to be.

True to form, I dated a lot at university and contin-ued to crush hard on anyone male and breathing, but it wasn't until my second term at university that I met Sven, not his real name and not his real nationality, at a student union meeting. He was the kind of guy Taylor Swift would have sniffed out immediately as trouble, before having a passionate love affair culminating in a Grammy-winning album. Sven was Danish, tall and good-looking in an unconventional, off-beat kind of way. Like all the bad-news big loves of my life, he had an intellectual superiority complex that made me feel small enough to want to earn his approval. Politically, he was much further to the left than I was, and he had this very sexy way of making me feel like an utter failure of a human being for my complicity in the capitalist machine. After the meeting, a group of us went to a cocktail bar, where I spent the night arguing with Sven about the many, many topics on which we disagreed. It should have been a red flag, perhaps, that vehement disagreement was basically foreplay, but at the end of the evening we found ourselves the last ones standing and a fierce make-out session began.

Now that I think about it, Sven was one big walking red flag and not just in his politics. For example, I asked for Sven's number and he said he didn't have a phone. I partly blame myself for wanting to believe the lie. Sven said he would meet me the next day outside the student union and it's a testament to just how low my self-esteem actually was that I thought he was the most amazing guy in the world ever just because he actually showed up. From that moment on we spent all our free time together in a heady bubble of new romance. It was the most intense love I had felt yet and, unusually for me, it really felt reciprocated. I started to tumble into a world of fantasies about what our future together would look like. I started reading far-left philosophers and political thinkers. Slowly, I started to morph my personality into whatever I thought he would like.

A few weeks into the relationship, his pocket started buzzing. The mobile phone he didn't have was ringing. It was then that he acquiesced and gave me his phone number in a way that made me feel proud of earning the privilege of being able to contact my own boyfriend. We dated for several turbulent months in a destructive cycle of arguing, passionately making up and total co-dependence on my part. My moods became increasingly volatile. Sven would flirt openly with other girls in front of me and I became paranoid and jealous.

The honeymoon period was soon over and, while I was still madly in love with Sven, I started to disgust him. We had several dramatic break-ups and make-ups, each more traumatic than the last. After one blazing argument, his voice dripping with disdain, he said 'My GOD, you're annoying.' This word, this triggering awful truth, set off the meltdown of a lifetime. Sven threw me out of his student house, and I sat in the street howling with misery. I knocked and knocked at the door, begging him to come out and speak to me. As if he just hadn't heard me and was going to pop his head out and be like, 'So sorry, I didn't realise you were out here'. It was my least dignified moment in a lifetime of extremely undignified moments. Eventually, an alarmed neighbour, another student and a mutual friend, ushered me into her house to calm me down and stop me from embarrassing myself. I genuinely do not recall how but maybe I do have magic powers after all because I managed to get Sven to talk to me. Even more miraculously, I managed to convince him not to break up with me and spent weeks trying to make it up to him and be the perfect girlfriend.

Things fell spectacularly apart during the Easter holidays. I went back home to spend Passover with my family and Sven went back to Denmark and stopped answering my messages and calls. I finally got hold of him in the middle of a Passover Seder with our entire extended family. In hushed whispers in my cousin Shelley's bedroom I received the dumping to end all dumpings. I staggered back downstairs, my eyes bulging and red, completely unable to find the plug I needed to stop me from crying. Nobody knew where to look as I sat at the Seder table in spasms of grief and rejection, as my family so kindly put it at the time, ruining Passover.

I got through the holidays by convincing myself that if I could just see Sven face to face again, he would remember all the good times (!) and fall back in love with me. Over the holidays, however, Sven had reconnected with his ex-girlfriend of many years – a woman he had described to me as 'crazy' and 'fat'. Years later, I still regret screaming at Sven that *he* was fat, because I knew he found it hurtful. Growing up, the message was everywhere that the worst thing a person could possibly be was fat. It was the thing everyone seemed the most terrified of and the most hostile towards. It was a thing I unnecessarily starved my young body trying to avoid. Knowing what I know now about how fat people are treated in society, the ugly prevalence of fatphobia and how utterly wrongheaded it is, I wish I could go back in time, take those thoughts out of my head and those words out of my mouth. I can't do that. All any of us can do when we've behaved abysmally, through ignorance or cruelty, is apologise unreservedly and do better next time. This is me doing that here and now. I truly am sorry.

Sven's attitude towards his ex is another red flag a savvier young woman might have spotted, but to my sheltered little brain it was just a positive sign that he wasn't still in love with her. You'd think the fact that he was back with his ex would be enough of a reason for me to leave him alone. You'd think. But I kept seeing him and sleeping with him. I did all the chasing. He would flick over an occasional 'I love you' or 'You know I can't resist you' and I would pour all my hope into those breadcrumbs. When he finally rejected me to be with her, I became suicidal. I careered wildly between begging him to love me again and, to my great shame, yelling at him when he didn't. I started to dissociate. I had no idea who I was any more without this relationship defining me. Sven, feeling responsible for me, took me to his house and put me on suicide watch. I must say it was incredibly healing playing the role of the unstable ex-girlfriend tucked up in his bed while he went into another room to Skype his actual girlfriend.

Sven graduated that summer and moved back to Denmark and I spiralled out of all control. I manufactured a reconnection with an old classmate from school, one of those 'left before he could figure out I was bad currency' exchange students I had loosely stayed in touch with who just happened to be Danish. As luck would have it, he had blossomed from a gangly teenager into a gorgeous man. He visited me at university and we had a lovely rebound fling. Had I left it at that, it would have just been the postscript to a messy break-up, but I didn't. I visited him in Denmark and we had a casual relationship for a few weeks while I texted Sven things like *Hey, I just happen to be in the area*. After Sven put some very understandable distance between us, I decided I'd rather have him in my life as a friend than not at all. And so, once I was back home, in the halls of residence I had opted to stay in alone over the summer because I desperately wanted to feel like I had actually moved out of home, I hopped on Facebook and befriended his girlfriend.

This may sound manipulative, but I actually, in my heart of hearts, had convinced myself that I could put any romantic feelings for Sven aside in the name of 'preserving our connection' and I genuinely began to like his new girlfriend. We chatted amiably for a couple of weeks and, for a while, it seemed like my plan might actually work. They were a lovely couple, I told myself. I started to honestly wish them well and, as hard as it might be to believe, to consider her to be a real friend. I have no idea what the breaking point was in my parade of stalker-level behaviour but one evening she sent me a series of abusive messages in Danish, which after running through Google Translate I discovered were very hurtful. Then she blocked me, cutting me off entirely and taking Sven with her.

Alone in my dorm room with my parents busy with their new relationships, my close friends away for the summer holidays and nothing but the echoing silence and my own self-loathing for company, I decided to die. This was different to previous loose thoughts of suicide. This was rock bottom. With no friends to gently help me tidy and make my bed, my room had descended into squalor. My recent behaviour came rushing back to me in shameful waves. The crying. The begging. The insulting. The TRANSPARENTLY FOLLOWING A MAN WHO DIDN'T LOVE ME ANY MORE TO DENMARK. *I should be in jail*, I thought. *I'm a monster. He's probably laughing at his crazy ex right now and he's right.* How could I carry on living after making such a colossal mess of my life? My shiny new fresh start lay in tatters on the floor. Probably. I couldn't see the floor. I was disgusting. Pathetic. I didn't deserve to live. It would never get better because *I* would never get better. I texted two friends – Anna, and the poor bastard I had used as my ticket to Denmark. I told them both I planned to kill myself. The only problem was, I didn't have a plan. It was a spontaneous act of desperation and I hadn't thought it through at all. I gathered all the pills I could find – antidepressants my doctor had just put me on and a bumper pack of paracetamol, and decided to take them all at once.

There was just one issue – I've never been very good at taking pills. I have an enormously sensitive gag reflex and it takes a long time to gear myself up to swallow a pill. It took twenty minutes of spluttering, coughing and nearly vomiting, before an ambulance arrived. My on-again-off-again friend had called them. By the time they arrived I had taken two pills – the recommended dose for a headache.

'How much have you taken?' asked the paramedic.

'I think I threw them up,' I mumbled, mortified. 'I'm fine. I'm so sorry for wasting your time.'

They left.

God, I thought, *I'm so useless, I can't even kill myself properly.*

It was decided that I would spend the rest of the summer living with a nearby relative, where I moved on in a super-healthy way by hooking up with Sven's former housemate, a complete and utter dullard whose only appeal was that he reminded me of Sven, and who I was due to move in with in my second year. I hacked off all my long hair, before running to the hairdresser, mortified, where they charged me the last dregs of my bank account to snip it into a fresh Agyness Deyn pixie cut that didn't suit my round face. When the dullard housemate dumped me, it was not only humiliating but completely awkward. We would go on to spend the rest of the year avoiding each other.

(In brighter news Filippo and Katerina returned from the summer holidays as a couple. They had arranged to go on holiday with a group of friends who had all dropped out at the last minute, leaving the two of them alone together on a romantic beach holiday. The rest was history. Ten years later, Filippo and Katerina are happily married after a beautiful ceremony in Tuscany that I was honoured to attend. They have a beautiful little boy together. Their romantic-comedy beginnings actually resulted in a happily ever after.)

This would not be my last depressive episode. Though it would, thankfully, be the last time I actively tried to end my life. I have had moments since where my physical or emotional pain was so extreme that I wanted to disappear, but I have been lucky enough to always find small pinpricks of hope in the darkness. Somehow, some part of myself has been able to hold on to facts like little flotation devices. I remind myself that death is forever, not just a temporary fix to end the pain. I think of my loved ones being told what has happened to me and the agony it would cause them. I think of all the times in my life I've felt this way and all the wonderful subsequent things I would never have experienced had my life ended then. I think of small inconsequential things to look forward to: what might happen on a TV show I love or something as simple as ordering a pizza. This may sound trivial, but when life is so overwhelming that I want it to be over, thinking of the big things in my future isn't always helpful. Thinking of the small joys I would never experience again tends to draw me back. When I feel at the bottom of my hope, I take advice given to me by a friend and I make my world smaller. I focus on what's immediately in front of me. I cling tight to the mast and wait for the storm to pass. Sometimes none of this works and I'm also fortunate that my particular brand of depression makes me so tired that acting on my despair seems too overwhelming and exhausting. By the time I have the energy to harm myself the urge has usually passed.

I appreciate that I am lucky that any of this helps. Depression is an illness and if these things don't work for you, you are not a failure. You are not responsible. You are not broken. You are also not alone.

10

FEMINIST

It's 1999. I'm eleven years old and canvassing for my first-ever political campaign. It's an issue extremely close to my heart. The previous year, cereal manufacturer, Kellogg's, had changed the name of my beloved Coco Pops to Choco Krispies. At the time I had been incensed. The packaging was different. The advertising jingle no longer scanned. 'I'd rather have a bowl of Coco Pops', a classic, had been mangled by the addition of an extra syllable that didn't belong there. I could have sworn the cereal even tasted different.

But now something incredible is happening. Kellogg's have announced a public vote on whether or not to change the name back. The number is free to call and you can also vote via the website – and as many times as you like. I am doing my bit, sitting by the phone day and night, hitting redial over and over and voting for 'Coco Pops'. Sure, clogging up the line may be costing my parents a few important work calls, but this isn't about the money. This is about something money can't buy: justice. It occurs to me, however, that somewhere out there, there might exist an equally tenacious eleven-year-old hitting redial for 'Choco Krispies' – so just to be on the safe side, I am in full campaigning mode. I hand out the number to my, frankly, apathetic classmates, explaining to them why this issue affects us all. I go door to door, making my case to the neighbours, and standing over them menacingly while they dial the number.

After what feels like an agonising wait, the votes are counted and it's a landslide for Coco Pops. 92%. A million votes have been cast. I'm pretty sure most of them were by me. I am elated. It's my first taste of electoral success and the adrenaline rush of justice being served. I will go on to spend the rest of my life trying to recreate it.

In my second year of university my dad started visiting often. Once every few weeks he would drive the four hours to Exeter, picking me up and taking me for long walks on Dartmoor where we would talk for hours on end about our lives. Our relationship had been steadily improving since the day he rescued me in Brighton and he was starting to feel like a real friend. Gone was the dad who shouted at me and couldn't bear my company. Instead I had a dad who had mellowed with age – someone who rushed to see me if something was wrong, who took me out for meals and loaned me food money when I completely mishandled my finances. Someone who would hang out with me and my university buddies and regale us with interesting tales about how his phone could tell you what time it is in any country. Shira, missing the sunshine, had moved back to Israel, and he was tentatively thinking of going to join her. 'I think you should go,' I told him. 'I'll miss you, but you'll be happy with her there.'

After the events of the summer, I started seeing a Gestalt psychotherapist, who made me have awkward out-loud conversations with 'different parts of myself'. To this day, I still don't quite understand what Gestalt therapy is. I basically chose her because she was on the first page of Google. In any case, I dreaded my sessions with her, which was a good motivation to get as mentally healthy as possible, so I never had to put on a weird squeaky voice again and have a chat to my inner child (who, incidentally, still doesn't know how to shut the fuck up).

It was at a Rosh Hashanah, Jewish new year, service at the local synagogue in Exeter, on my twenty-first birthday, that I met Poem Boy.

I noticed Poem Boy straight away because he was one of the only people at the synagogue under the age of fifty. He was dressed in turquoise New Agey clothing, had long-ish mid-brown hair and was cute in a 'second hottest member of a boy band' kind of way. Poem Boy was called to the bema to read a self-written poem about Rosh Hashanah. 'Oh good,' said a woman sarcastically, behind me, saving me the trouble of coming up with a pseudonym years later. 'It's Poem Boy.'

Naturally, I was curious about Poem Boy. Who was this probably university-aged Jewish man and, more importantly, why hadn't he joined my Jewish Society? I made it my business to corner him after the service. Poem Boy was soft-spoken with kind blue eyes and an earnestness that made me unsure if I wanted to hug him or beat him up and take his lunch money.

Poem Boy told me that he was a carer and trainee psychotherapist. When he asked what I did, 'student' suddenly sounded unforgivably lame.

'I'm a writer,' I blurted out. 'It's what I do.'

I felt a familiar tingle of humiliation creep across my cheeks as I heard the words come out of my mouth. In retrospect 'student' would have been fine. In ten days there would be a Yom Kippur sleepover at the synagogue. Yom Kippur is the Jewish Day of Atonement – a day of fasting, self-reflection and asking for your name to be written in the book of life for another year. I seized upon the opportunity and asked if he would be attending, while doing the mental calculations to figure out how many hours of repentance shamelessly using the Yom Kippur sleepover as a dating opportunity might cost me. He said yes! We exchanged numbers and I skipped off to my twenty-first birthday party on a cloud.

We spent the next ten days texting back and forth. I was twenty-one now, high time, I arbitrarily decided, for me to settle down. Poem Boy was definitely Husband Material. He seemed exactly the kind of man my parents would approve of. Jewish – tick. Vegetarian – tick. Spiritual – tick.

'Stop this,' I told my crush monster.

'Have we learned nothing from the Sven fiasco?'

'Fuck you,' said my crush monster. 'You can't control me; I own you.'

Disappointingly, Poem Boy ducked out of the Yom Kippur sleepover at the last minute. 'Ah yeah, I wasn't going to go either,' I lied unconvincingly. At least it spared me a one-way ticket to Jew Hell. If it exists. I really should ask about that.

Finally, Poem Boy and I went on a date, where he told me that he was actually thirty-three. I was stunned. Until then, I had been wondering if he might be too young for me. 'Can I see some ID?' I asked. I wasn't going to fall prey to some stupid teenager's prank again. He was telling the truth. He really was just a baby-faced thirty-three-year-old. Despite me carding him, we had our first kiss in the Wetherspoons beer garden and met up again a few days later for a second date in his home town nearby.

If I had thought my bohemian, cult-centric hometown was weird, it didn't hold a candle to Poem Boy's neighbourhood, which boasted a high street full of independent shops, New Age businesses and a lavish buffet of complete and utter weirdos. And that's coming from me, the Weirdo in Chief. One of the first things I saw on my arrival was a man wearing wizard robes walking his pet wolf. Poem Boy waved at him and shrugged it off in a way that said 'Oh, him? That's just Gary.' A few months later, my dad, who believed in psychic readings and tarot, would visit me there and whisper loudly to me, 'Sara, is anyone here *normal*?'

Despite my crush monster running away with itself as it always did, I was a little more cautious with Poem Boy. This relationship felt different. Poem Boy was an adult with his own place and a job. It was one of the first relationships where I didn't constantly feel like he was checking out other girls or figuring out a way to dump me. But, despite my best intentions, I found myself morphing into someone I thought he would like. I started wearing New Age clothes and talking in insufferable soundbites, which made me sound like I'd swallowed an entire plate of fortune cookie messages then thrown them back up. I dived headfirst with him into Five Rhythms dance classes, darshan singing sessions, long, uncomfortable talks about our feelings. 'You're being weird,' said Anna with her characteristic honesty. 'You're changing yourself for him. This is Sven all over again.'

She was sort of right. It was Sven all over again in that I wasn't being myself. But Poem Boy, for his eccentricities, really did care about me. He genuinely wanted me to be myself – and I think he truly believed that the elusive 'myself' was this deeply spiritual, introspective seeker and not someone who just wanted to watch *Neighbours* reruns on repeat. Poem Boy was extremely trusting. So trusting he once lost £500 to a pyramid scheme, because it was sold to him as an 'abundance flower'. He was always looking for the next big thing, the next way to explore himself and the universe and I was constantly torn between wanting to please him and, honestly, just wanting to eat crushed Wotsits with a teaspoon in my sweatpants. I was often sceptical about people selling spiritual wares, physical or otherwise, and he put any disagreements about this down to my immaturity and lack of connection with myself, to which I say, 'SO'S YOUR FACE.'

I started making friends with Poem Boy's friends, an assortment of sweet-natured kooks who would have their issues out with each other in passive-aggressive 'I' statements through half-closed eyes. All of them were heavily invested in their own personal growth in a way that made me wonder, as I sometimes do with very religious people, if they were so invested in thinking about the meaning of life that they might be missing out on living it. One particular highlight of entering Poem Boy's social circles was being invited to a fortieth birthday party where the birthday girl's dearest wish was for the women in attendance to slather mud on her naked body and bathe her in a river as a coming-of-age ritual. I had no objection, in theory, to this request. Each to their own. It was, however, perhaps the biggest ever test of my socially awkward limits. I, someone who finds the singing of 'Happy Birthday' so mortifying it is only made bearable with the immediate reward of cake, found myself ankle deep in a river, politely averting my eyes as I tentatively rubbed a bit of mud on to her back, muttering, 'There, there.'

Poem Boy and I experimented with drugs together. We took magic mushrooms. He took me to an underground ayahuasca ceremony, where the participants wore white robes (no matter where I land in life, I can't seem to outrun the hippies in white robes) and drank a disgusting tar-like substance that made everyone weep hysterically, projectile-vomit and come out the other side wanting to do it again. I took one tentative sip before deciding this definitely was not pizza and so it wasn't going down no matter how hard I tried. I softened the blow of my chickening out by smiling a lot with my eyes closed and saying things like 'I'm a hummingbird'.

That summer Poem Boy and I went to a New Age festival called Buddhafield (no link, as far as I'm aware, to the American group of the same name). Even I, who had grown up surrounded by hippies, was so ludicrously far out of my comfort zone I had to get off the train and buy a whole new ticket to Awkwardville. People at Buddhafield seemed to *love* being naked. In principle I applaud this body-positive attitude and think there's absolutely nothing wrong with it. In reality a stark-naked boomer man jiggled joyfully towards me at a Five Rhythms session, creating a one-off set of circumstances that made it appropriate to skip away in terror.

On the second day of the festival Poem Boy and I had a massive row after attending a session on non-violent communication, which I non-violently communicated that I thought was a pile of wank. Poem Boy thought my attitude was closed-minded. He broke up with me and stormed out of our shared tent, leaving me sobbing and alone in a field full of hippies. After some kindly tent neighbours calmed me down, Poem Boy and I decided to see out the rest of the festival and I texted my dad, who decided to join us for the final day before taking me home.

Unlike me, my dad was *delighted* by all the nudity. I had invited him to a field full of naked women. It was an odd situation. I was miserable because I'd just been dumped. My dad was having the time of his life, surrounded by all the woo, mysticism and muddy boobs. Poem Boy and I decided (well, he decided; I was just there) to end our relationship 'on loving terms' by attending a couples' intimacy workshop taster session, where the main event was a huge blow-up afterwards because one girl had been late to meet her boyfriend for the session and so he had had 'no choice' but to go ahead and do the workshop with his ex.

'See?' I gave Poem Boy a watery smile. 'It could be worse.'

My dad drove me home that evening. I wrote angsty poetry in the car as he told me about his relationship woes with Shira, who he had stormed out on after a mysterious argument in Israel. We spent the rest of the summer together writing songs and recording them. My dad's newest interest was recording equipment, and he became obsessed with 'immortalising' my terrible music. I started singing again in earnest. We went to open-mic sessions together, where audience members shouted encouraging things like 'You sound a lot better than you look, love!'

Poem Boy and I stayed in touch all summer and when I returned to university we started hanging out again. Hanging out very quickly turned romantic, but he was reticent to get back together, despite my constant pushing. Then, for my twenty-second birthday, Poem Boy's gift to me was us getting back together. I thought it was the most romantic present in the world. In a rare right of reply Poem Boy would like me to make it clear that it was just a lovely moment of reconnection that felt right to him and that his intention was not to give me the gift of himself as a birthday present. And, in his defence, that he also recreated a birthday-table concept my parents had introduced as a child and got me multiple other gifts. I will concede that here, despite that being significantly less funny, mainly because it is likely we will be friends into our nineties and he will never, ever let it go.

The rest of the year passed quickly. With Poem Boy and me on shaky, precarious ground, I signed up to a clinical trial of CBT group sessions. CBT was a breath of fresh air compared to Gestalt therapy. It gave me practical ways to cope with my anxiety and I didn't have to use my hands as little puppets. Moreover, the group sessions gave it a competitive classroom element, which I thrived in. OK, I'm pretty sure it was intended to be supportive and not competitive, but I wanted to please my CBT teachers and be top of my class in coping with life. Every week I diligently filled out my CBT forms and vowed to be even emotionally healthier the next week as I was applauded for my good work.

Poem Boy and I continued to try to make it work, despite our growing differences. I was becoming exhausted with all the pretending and, inconveniently, a sense of my own identity was starting to kick in. Before we broke up we went to a two-day couples' tantra workshop about the sensuality of food. Now, before you say anything, I had no idea what I was signing up for. Honestly, I thought it would be a couple of days of meditating with our eyes closed and maybe some painful eye contact and cringey talks about our connection. Perhaps it would be a masterclass in *really* appreciating our food. It was a bit like the time I signed up for a life-drawing class and, as the model dropped his robe, I asked the teacher when they would be bringing out the bowl of fruit for us to draw. The tantra workshop was a glorified orgy. As other couples slathered food all over each other, showing me how that elusive 'it' was *really* done, I looked at Poem Boy in panic. We both stifled an embarrassed laugh and sat in a corner of the room eating strawberries and trying not to look at the sea of writhing bodies all around us.

We finally broke up after Poem Boy became involved with a new self-help-type group that he found life-changingly wonderful. I went along to an initial session with him but despite my almost complete literature degree I could not discern any meaning from the jumble of words I was hearing. When we were asked to write a gratitude letter for the next session, my logical brain couldn't cope with the oxymoronic request of being *told* to be grateful. I revived my excellent non-violent communication skills to tell him that I had weird vibes from the meeting and wouldn't be going back.

Poem Boy did not appreciate my attitude. We argued. I screwed up my mandatory gratitude letter and threw it at him. I missed. I am as good at throwing as I am at catching. He broke up with me.

I coped surprisingly well with what was the end of my first serious long-term relationship. I wallowed for a few days, eating a lot of ice cream and watching *The First Wives Club* on repeat but, largely thanks to women like Caitlin, who introduced me to *The First Wives Club*, and Annie, a gorgeous and glamorous Québécois PhD candidate who showed up like a fierce mama bear with basketfuls of fruit and flowers, I didn't fall apart. After the requisite grieving period, when my friends gathered around my bed like I was a dying Victorian, and a brief blip jumping right back into my pattern of finding a rebound boyfriend, I was surprised to find that I was mostly OK. Poem Boy and I found a way to genuinely stay friends. Not 'I have to keep him in my life and try to win him back' friends, actual lifelong friends. Over the last decade we've had our ups and downs, our screaming rows and fallings-out. But we've also been there for each other through life crises, illnesses and bereavements. It wasn't the happy ending I'd fantasised about when I first saw Poem Boy that day at the synagogue, but what I gained in the end was much better.

In the background of my turbulent love life, my campus career had rumbled on. My degree was a side note to my political activism. I had been the Jewish Society president, a student councillor and NUS delegate. My final year of university had also introduced me to previously scoffed-at concepts, like feminism. I had grown up in such a sheltered environment that my perspective on feminism was 'why do we need it? The girls in my class are much smarter than the boys.' Apparently, I was the notable exception. I was so clueless; I honestly thought that the battle for women's rights was long over and that believing in feminism was its own sort of man-hating reverse sexism. That was until I met Caitlin. Caitlin had founded the student Feminist Society and was an absolute force of nature. She was fierce, articulate and so persuasive she managed to score a meeting with a visiting Emma Thompson and single-handedly convinced her to remove her name from a petition of support for Roman Polanski.

Caitlin was incredibly patient with me. If I had been her, I probably would have written me off after our first conversation, but she saw that my views came from a place of ignorance and, in places, self-loathing and shame. She challenged me kindly enough that I didn't become defensive, but firmly enough that I understood there was something I needed to re-examine. She high-lighted the ongoing injustices against women around the world. She explained that 'feminism' was the word to use instead of 'equality' because that was the imbalance that needed redressing. And, most crucially, she helped me to understand that I was *always* allowed to say no. It may sound unbelievable that I was twenty-two when I learned this, but nobody had ever explained it to me. The messages I had received all my life were 'Don't get boys too excited or they can't stop' and 'Don't dress that way if you don't want people to think you're asking for it'. The idea that I could be sexual, flirtatious, dress in ways I enjoyed and take joy in my own body without having to then acquiesce to whoever happened to want something from me was revolutionary. It was Caitlin, who gently explained to me for the first time that I had been raped.

I won't go into detail here. It is not even something I feel comfortable discussing in therapy. Even now, in my thirties, I feel uncomfortable using 'the R word', so deeply ingrained is the sense of shame and self-doubt surrounding the situation. It was so long ago that I don't even truly trust my memory of what happened. Did it really happen the way I think it did or was I not clear enough about saying 'no'? I remembered telling people at the time that this had happened to me, feeling really instinctively upset by it and having the experience brushed off. I thought I was just being dramatic, so I buried it and tried to never think about it again. I reframed the whole thing in my mind, despite intuitively having known that something awful had happened.

'But,' I explained to Caitlin, starting to feel dizzy and sick, 'I was already in bed with him. I'd got him all worked up.'

'That doesn't matter,' she said. 'If you say no, he has to stop.'

'But,' I argued again, in tears now, 'boys can't stop once you've got them started.'

'Of course they can,' she explained.

Oh my God. I started thinking through other encounters – times where I had gone through with it but not really consented and definitely not enthusiastically.

It may be a punch in the gut to some readers, particularly parents, that it's even possible for an academically bright young woman to reach their early twenties without a proper understanding of consent but, looking back, it's painfully clear to me how this gap in my education came about. For a start it was a different time. That may sound implausible given how far we've come since in terms of public consciousness around feminism, but even in 2009 to say you were a feminist was brave. The community I grew up in was hardly at the cutting edge of social discourse. Remember, I came from the tradition of dainty movements for girls, scimitars for boys. Our sex education was delivered in lifeless diagrams and wishy-washy stories about spirits choosing their parents. Everything I learned about consent, I learned from TV, where rape meant being dragged off the street by an armed stranger, not coerced by someone you're already in bed with when you've withdrawn your consent.

Everything my parents told me about boys was probably designed to warn me about predators, but the way I translated it was that boys have no self-control. If they were unable to restrain themselves when they were aroused, then it stood to reason that if I got them too excited, anything that happened from then on was my fault. If I'd led them on, I just had to deal with it. I get it – conversations with teenagers about sex are awkward and it's understandable that parents get squeamish and offer vague, euphemistic advice, but I speak from bitter experience when I say these messages are too important to risk getting lost in translation. Not all kids are able to read between the lines, but *all* kids can understand hard and fast rules.

I wish somebody had explained consent to me in this way: it is never OK to pressure or force someone into doing anything they don't want to do. If you're not 100% sure someone is happy with what's happening, you must stop. You are always allowed to say no, no matter how far you've already gone, no matter who or what you've already said yes to. It is perfectly fine to change your mind. If your partner doesn't stop when you ask them to, they are in the wrong, not you. What you see on television is not necessarily an example of how to behave and doesn't always represent healthy or consensual sexual relationships. If someone breaks up with you, it's not a big romantic gesture to follow them to Denmark; it's just creepy. I wish someone had told me this firmly, clearly and often. It is too late to go back and change that formative part of my education now – but for parents reading this it's not too late to make sure your girls and, more importantly, your boys, fully understand the importance of enthusiastic consent.

11
INAPPROPRIATE

I have had many, many jobs in my life, most of which have ended badly. There was my first job at Iceland, where I was told to stack everything by its sell-by date, which is how I wasted my entire first shift looking for the expiry date on a pack of toilet roll. There was my waitressing job at a local café, which quickly turned into a dishwashing job after I 'accidentally' spilled a drink on a ten-year-old boy in a bow tie who had clicked his fingers at me and called me 'waitress!'.

There was my one week of work experience at a law firm. My mum had been away on holiday and the night before work I had taken advantage of the free house and had my then boyfriend to stay over. My mum was due to come back that afternoon, and so, in a panic, I hid a condom we had used in my handbag in case she found it. My plan was to sneak off from work first thing in the morning and chuck it in a public bin. Except my lift to the office was late, and the moment I arrived I was asked to go with a colleague to take some documents over to court. I couldn't dispose of the offending item in front of her and, having never been to court before, had no idea what to expect. My heart stopped as I saw the security guards checking bags at the entrance. After several tense seconds where I refused to hand mine over, it was wrenched from my death grip. Because of my suspicious behaviour what would have just been a cursory glance turned into a full-scale excavation. For a moment I thought I had got away with it. And then he found it, lifting it in its tissue, in full view of my colleague and going bright red before whispering to his colleague, who doubled over laughing. *Maybe my colleague won't tell anyone*, I lied to myself. I endured a day of the staff at the law firm giggling and pointing. I never went back.

Then there was my university job at a boutique clothing store, where the manager told me I needed to interact with the customers and then was horrified when I relentlessly followed people around the store, suggesting random items they might buy by yelling things like 'SO, JEANS, HUH?', until they understandably fled, never to return. After witnessing that disaster, my boss called and asked for a chat, explaining that my social skills were lacking and also that my personal sense of style was very odd. I never went back.

There was my work experience at a regional newspaper, where I got my first-ever byline, which came to an abrupt end when I was gently taken aside and told my incessant chattering was distracting people from their work. The familiar feeling of shame and self-loathing prickled through me. I sat in tearful silence for the rest of the afternoon and, can you guess yet? I never went back.

With my relationship with Poem Boy in the past and graduation round the corner, my attention turned to the future. What did I want to do with my life? All I knew was that I wanted to write, but I had no idea how to make that happen. A few days after I sat my final exams, I took a tentative look at the *Guardian*'s job section, where I saw a copywriter position advertised at a small recruitment company. The company, on paper, looked ideal, with selling points like a 'relaxation dome' and many attractive benefits. It was a 'we're not your average workplace' type of workplace, which appealed to me. The job was basically writing job ads for other, better jobs, but it was a start. I sent in my application and the very next day was invited for an interview.

I rushed to London for the first-round interview with a nice HR lady who was visibly excited about me and ran off to get my would-be boss to meet me. I was given a spelling and grammar test, which I sailed through without issues and, a few hours later, was asked if I could stay in London for a second interview. The interview, I was told, was a bit different. I would meet with senior management and give them a creative presentation on my life. 'The more imaginative, the better,' insisted the HR lady. I decided on an illustrated storybook and, I honestly cannot remember what possessed me to do this, perhaps stress squeezes out unrelated trauma like too much toothpaste, mid-interview, I spontaneously burst into a round of 'Tomorrow' from *Annie*. They gave me the job on the spot, sending away the poor second-round applicants in the waiting room without seeing them. That discourtesy towards the other applicants, who had probably spent days preparing their own presentations, should have rung alarm bells, but it's hard to be too upset when you're the one benefitting from the rudeness. Plus, I like to think that Susie Perfection, who scored the role of Annie in our teens, was among the unsuccessful applicants, restoring balance to the universe.

I started my new job full of the same hopeless optimism with which I had approached college and university. My fresh, fresh, *fresh* start! OK, at this point I'd had more fresh starts than a retro IKEA ad, but this time *would* be different. All I had to do was be quiet and mysterious and act like everybody else. How hard could it be?

Refreshingly, there were a lot of women in roles throughout the company. I, however, was placed in a male-dominated team, made up of a group of 'lads' whose days consisted of back-and-forth banter. On my first day it seemed to me that no topic was off limits. Their jokes were rude, lewd and often sexist. I was way out of my depth.

The first thing to conquer was my IT training. I was introduced to John the IT manager, a scruffy, nerdy-looking guy with round wire-rimmed glasses and a goatie. I smiled nervously at him.

'Do you know how to use a Mac?' he asked, grumpily.

'Yes,' I replied.

'Good,' he said, before walking off.

Jerk, I thought.

My first day was bewildering and exhausting. I was so flustered I kept walking into stationery cupboards I had mistaken for office doors and forgetting people to whom I had been introduced moments earlier. The promised 'relaxation dome' turned out to just be a spare office with a couple of beanbags in it. The shine was starting to come off my fresh start. Still, it was a job. Most of my graduate friends would go on to spend months, in some cases years, looking for an entry-level opportunity. I was lucky.

John the IT guy continued to antagonise me. I did not like him one bit. In my first week we got into a debate about the Israel–Palestine conflict in which he proposed a one-state solution was the answer. 'Then you're either an extremist or an idiot,' I snapped at him. He looked momentarily stunned, then smiled at some private joke in his head and walked away. *Dickhead*, I thought.

And then, a few days in, I got a call on my work line from my brother. My Israeli grandmother had died. Less than a week into my new role, I was sobbing my eyes out in front of the entire floor. I had made one promise to myself: that I wouldn't cry at work. I hadn't lasted a week.

A few days later, I moved into a small flat in Brixton with my friend Alex, who I'd met through events run by the Union of Jewish Students, a national umbrella organisation that, among other things, supports university Jewish societies, and one of my brother's old university friends. In theory, I loved the hustle and bustle of Brixton, with its busy market and the thriving traders at the unofficial market as you left the tube station, selling their wares, even if those wares happened to be Jesus and pot. In practice, I hated having to shove my way through the crowded streets, to have to line up to get into the tiny supermarket, to have to queue for fifteen minutes each morning just to get on a rush-hour bus and that I was a part of the gentrification problem in the area. The flat was beautifully decorated and a nice calm space, all hardwood floors and Habitat furniture, but it didn't quite feel like home. I had been bad at sharing a space with people under fairly relaxed circumstances, but juggling a job *and* housemates was more than I could manage. I couldn't get my head around the etiquette of how much interaction was expected of me and I didn't have the energy to pretend to be normal. I would come home, lock my door, slump on to my bed, feeling like the smallest noise or flash of light would tip me over the edge. I felt guilty every time I ignored my housemates and panicky every time I talked to them, in case I'd talked too much and annoyed them.

Back at work, I was excelling at the actual job side of my job. What nobody tells you about having a job is that the actual job bit is only a tiny part of the job. I had never had much energy, but now I was starting to become chronically unwell. By the time I arrived in the morning I was already so exhausted from the rush-hour commute I could barely function. The fluorescent office lighting gave me a headache after about five minutes. If only there had been an actual relaxation dome in which to rest and recharge. My posture had always been slouchy, but now a combination of stress and sitting in front of a screen all day teamed up to cause excruciating neck and shoulder pain. Knots started appearing in my back and neck that are still there to this day. I developed an RSI in my wrist from typing. I found myself entirely unable to think straight and concentrate on the constant challenge of not making an arse of myself.

By the end of each day I was so frazzled that I would often get lost on my commute home, accidentally taking the wrong train and limping home hours later, replaying conversations from the day in my head and flushing with shame over all the embarrassing things I had said while too tired to stop myself. Back at home, I would have just enough energy to smoke a joint and eat a take-away before having to start all over again the next day. I became insular and withdrawn, avoiding all contact with my housemates, locking myself in my room and leaving the house as early as possible in the morning to avoid having to tell anyone how it was going.

In the office I tried joining in the boys' banter. See? I'm one of the lads, not a whimpering wreck who's ruining everyone's fun! But no matter what I said it went down like a shit sandwich. I couldn't work out what I was doing wrong. As far as I was concerned, they had set a standard of 'anything goes', but that didn't seem to apply to me. Maybe it was my delivery, or the fact that I wasn't really 'in' yet, but where there seemed to be no red line for them, my attempts to give as good as I got were met with tuts or awkward silences.

Office life was full of unspoken rules. One colleague, an older woman who had worked at the company for a hundred years, despite it only having been trading for twenty, complained that I wasn't answering the phones enough.

'But . . .' I protested, 'that's not part of my job.'

It was true. I had studied that job description like a sacred document. I never would have taken a role that required me to answer phones. I react to a ringing phone like it's a poisonous snake.

'It's called being a team player,' snapped the woman. 'You can figure it out.'

Things went from bad to worse when my laptop broke. My faithful pink Sony VAIO laptop, which had seen me all the way through university, died midway through an episode of *The Simpsons* and my feeble attempts to resuscitate it did absolutely nothing. I was alone in a new city with no friends, a crappy job and now no way to connect to the outside world. The next day, I came into work, cradling my laptop in a way that said 'please, my Sony VAIO, she is very sick', and, swallowing a huge serving of humble pie, asked John the IT guy if he'd take a look at it.

'I'll pay you,' I promised.

'Nah,' he said. 'Just buy me a drink next time we're out.'

John spent his lunch break with his head buried in my laptop, before returning it to me with a triumphant smile on his face. 'Fixed,' he said, proudly. 'Also, it was filthy. I cleaned it for you.'

My cheeks flushed at the shade thrown at my poor laptop hygiene. I looked in disbelief at the technological miracle in my hands. 'My hero,' I joked, giving him a hug, before I realised what I was doing. He blushed.

Somewhere deep inside, my crush monster yawned and stretched. 'Who dares wake me from my slumber?' he roared.

'Nobody. Go back to sleep,' I snapped.

'Well, I'm up now,' he said. 'Might as well see what all the fuss is about.'

Curious, I took John for a drink to say thank you. Outside the office, he was a completely different person. His brusqueness, which I had read as rudeness, was actually extreme shyness. John was seven years older than me, sweet, funny and a bit weird. He had grown up in Saudi Arabia and lived all over the world because of his dad's job. He had originally trained as a pilot, before moving back to the UK for a relationship, which had ended a year previously. We started hanging out more as friends, spending our lunchtimes together, walking through the park and talking. Slowly, slowly, my crush monster started to feed on him. I tried, a few times, to tell John I was starting to *like* him, but kept losing my nerve. At the office summer garden party, to which I brought my brother as my date because I didn't have any actual friends, I made a feeble move.

'Hey, John,' I tried, 'I heard there are some horses in the next field. Do you want to go and have a look?'

'No thanks,' he smiled, turning back to the conversation I had interrupted.

I scuttled off, mortified.

A month into my new employment, I was asked into a meeting with one of the managers. Let's call him Tony. Tony was as different from me as it was possible to be. If I could describe him in three words they would be 'estate-agent energy'.

'So, Sara . . .' he began, awkwardly. 'How do *you* think it's going?'

'Uh . . .' I stuttered, blind-sided, 'good I think. I've been getting good feedback on my work and—'

'Yes, yes,' he interrupted. 'Your work is very good. How do you think you're fitting in with your team?'

'OK,' I said. 'We're very different people, but—'

'It's not really OK, though,' he said.

My stomach lurched like I'd just realised the plane I was on was hurtling towards the ground. Tony, deciding he wasn't being obnoxious enough, pulled out an apple and started chomping loudly with his mouth open as he explained that I was annoying, my jokes were inappropriate, I was overfamiliar, I talked too much and I gave opinions when I hadn't yet earned my place. Tears spilled mutinously out of my eyes.

'Also,' he said, 'I've noticed you leave bang on six every day.'

'Yes,' I said, defending myself, 'that's when work ends.'

'If I were in your position,' he said, bits of apple flying from his mouth, 'I would stay late and kiss arse.'

'But I arrive early every day,' I protested, sobbing now, 'and I usually finish all my work for the day long before—'

'It's not about how much work you do,' he snapped. 'It's about being seen to care.'

This made zero sense to me. I was being paid to do a job. I was doing that job well. Did he want me to be so inefficient that I had to stay after-hours to finish it?

'OK,' I mumbled.

'Just some stuff to work on,' he said cheerfully with another crunch.

I rushed out of the meeting, blinded by tears, trying to navigate my way to the nearest bathroom where I could have a long, uninterrupted sobbing session. With my hands covering my swollen face, I bumped straight into John.

'Hey,' he laughed, 'watch where you're—' And then he noticed. 'What's wrong?'

I broke down completely. John put his arms round me as I sobbed into his shirt.

'Come out for a drink after work with everyone else later,' John suggested. 'Sit with me. Don't let them know they've got to you.'

It was the hottest day of the year. John and I sat by the river with our drinks, a little distance away from the rest of our colleagues. He tried to console me as I relived the toe-curling rebuke out loud. John put his arm round me again and I felt a sudden stirring of hope.

'You're a good kid,' he said, sending my moment of hope fizzing out of my grasp and shooting into the air like a deflating balloon.

After my meeting with Tony, I vowed to do better. I would do a better job of fitting in. I would do a better job of shutting up. I would do a better job of working out what was OK when other people said it but not when I said it. But being constantly on edge only made it worse. The more I tried to put a lid on it, the worse it got. *Maybe if I get to know them one on one*, I told myself, before following one of my poor unsuspecting teammates to the break room to watch the football with him and chattering anxiously at him like an irritating commentator who'd never seen the game before.

'Ooh, I think he was upside there,' I chirped. 'Oh my God, they've ended the first part on a cliffhanger. What a great episode of football! Just to make sure, the red team are the good guys, right?'

The only person at work who seemed to actually like me was John. By now we were spending most of our spare time together and people were starting to notice. There was the moment he taught me to hold a bat during the office rounders game, which elicited a round of wolf whistles, our 'platonic' trip to the cinema to see *Toy Story 3*, where John wept like a baby, my offer to 'help' him clean his house (ha!) before his parents visited from overseas, which culminated in a heavy, undeniable flirtation. John wasn't like the boys I'd been out with before, because he wasn't a boy. He was a proper adult with his own home, a steady job and had already had his first long-term relationship, which had ended after eight years a year previously. Someone else had already done the hard work of house-training him and he was ready for a serious commitment. John was measured and calm and genuinely seemed to adore me. He had seen me at my worst and, despite my constant vocal questioning as to what on earth he saw in me, it hadn't put him off. A few days before John's thirtieth birthday, John, who had taken a day off work to finish getting his house ready for his parents' visit, came all the way into town to spend my lunch break with me at the pub. Finally, we had our first kiss, and from then on it was on.

A couple of weeks into our relationship, at my flat in Brixton, someone, it doesn't matter who (all you need to know is it wasn't me) had a bad stomach and left our shared toilet looking like that scene in *Dogma* where the Shit Demon invades a strip bar, before apologising sheepishly and leaving the house.

John was the only one brave enough to confront the grisly scene. 'Don't come in,' he shouted, heroically swinging into action. John left the house and came back a few minutes later with a bottle of extra-strength Drain-o and a tin of extra-strength lager. I'm not sure which one he drank and which one he poured down the toilet, but after half an hour of retching noises and waving away my half-hearted offers of help ('I don't want you to see this'), John emerged looking victorious.

'Marry him,' said my crush monster, 'before he realises.'

John and I made some truly rubbish attempts to hide our relationship, like staggering our entrances to work in the morning and conspicuous, showy 'see you tomorrows', when we knew full well that we would be seeing each other in five minutes. People very quickly worked out that we were a couple and this hot gossip sparked the interest of a couple of the girls on my floor.

'Oh my God,' they said, as we gathered in a corner on a coffee break after one of our super-work-appropriate, clear-boundaried, company-sanctioned chill-out sessions where a colleague did dramatic readings of Mills & Boon novels. 'Tell us *everything*.'

'I don't know . . .' I said, blushing. 'We're a couple. It's nice.'

'Soooo . . .' said one of the girls, suggestively, 'have you . . . you know?'

'Yes,' I said. A direct question had been asked, so of course my only option was to give a bluntly honest answer.

The girls all squealed. *This is great*, I thought. *I'm in! Look at me, just one of the girls having a girlie gossip with her girlfriends.*

'How was it?' asked another.

'It was wonderful,' I said. 'I've got a rough history with that sort of thing, I've been taken advantage of in the past, but I felt really safe with him.'

There was a long awkward silence. The conspiratorial 'we're just girls having a chat' vibe vanished. I went back to my desk, my cheeks burning, wondering where the invisible line had been and how I'd managed to cross it.

John and I endured all the expected teasing and ribbing about our new relationship. We were mostly too happy to care, but once, caught off guard by a manager making a lewd comment about us, I replied reflexively, in what I thought was a joking tone, 'Fuck off.' Tony's eyes snapped up from his desk and, again, an awkward silence descended. A few days later, I was, admittedly, ranting to John about a headline I'd seen in the *Daily Mail*, which had been left on someone's desk, when the colleague who had once complained about my failure to answer the phones snapped and started sounding off at me in the middle of the office about how I was a know-it-all.

It seemed I was crossing that invisible line on a daily basis. I found myself constantly mortified and wondering what John, who told me he had fallen madly in love with me, saw in me at all. There seemed to be a gargantuan disconnect between how my colleagues perceived me and how John did. I would go home with John every evening to spend the night curled up with him and his three cats, Guinness and Boo (from a previous relationship) and Lily, a fussy, poorly behaved rescued Bengal cat with an unfortunate predilection for pissing on the curtains. It was so incongruous to have those evenings of comfortable bliss and then to go into the office the next day a gibbering, self-conscious wreck.

Then in September, a few days before John and I were due to go on our first holiday together to Turkey to celebrate my birthday, it was time for my first official appraisal. The appraisal was a peer-review system, where all my colleagues gave anonymous feedback about my work and my character. It was delivered by both Tony and another manager. Small mercies at least; this time there was no apple.

'I think I've improved a lot,' I said, shakily. 'I've been really trying to get to know people and connect with them on their level and . . .'

Tony shook his head sadly, before pulling out the epic document. My peer-review notes. Or, to be more accurate, a case against Sara. I sat in stunned silence, tears rolling freely down my cheeks, as he recited page after page of venomous comments. I knew that I'd been having trouble fitting in, but it was a shock to find out how universally loathed I was. The moment I thought

I'd connected with the girls in the office was in there; they had felt weird about how much I had shared. I was needy, annoying, too chatty, an oversharer, I didn't know how to dress smartly, I was a know-it-all, I just wasn't fitting in, I made people uncomfortable and, worst of all, I never answered the phones.

It was like my worst nightmares coming true at once: a dossier of my most potent fears and insecurities, things I had hoped I was managing to hide, things I'd told myself nobody had noticed, all there in black and white. CBT had taught me to see my anxieties as irrational, that most people don't even pick up on the things we ruminate about, but now a whole year of therapy was unravelling in that one hour. All my self-loathing was validated by the people I had to face every single day. Tony finished reading but he wasn't done.

'I've seen all this for myself,' he said. 'The way you talk to your line manager makes me cringe. It's also unfair on John. He's a respected manager in this business and you're embarrassing him and ruining his reputation.'

'I'm sorry,' I whispered, staring at my feet.

'We're extending your probation,' he said, formally. 'We'll see how the next few months go.'

Like hell we will, I thought.

For a second time I found myself running for the bathroom to hide my tears. I hid for the rest of the day, unable to face anyone. As I sat, blotting my eyes hopelessly, like a plaster over a gushing wound, I reread every single comment, trying to place which of my colleagues had made them. In that moment I never wanted to see John again.

'We have to break up,' I wept to him, when he eventually found me. 'I've ruined your reputation. I'm so sorry.'

'Don't be ridiculous,' he said. 'I love you. I'm not going anywhere.'

That weekend I took John home for the first time to celebrate Jewish New Year, my birthday and to be in situ to fly out to Turkey from Gatwick. Before we left the office together with our suitcases we found a parting gift from our colleagues, who had left condoms on top of my bag. Every day that invisible line became more baffling. It genuinely did not seem to apply to anybody else.

The trip home was a triumph. My family immediately adored John, who in turn fell head over heels in love with my family's welcoming, blunt, shouty Mediterranean vibes and the Jewish New Year customs. My dad, meanwhile, had entered a new relationship with a lovely woman from north London called Belinda. John joined us on our customary trip to Pizza Express to meet her for the first time, where I tested the waters by telling my dad that I wasn't really enjoying my job that much.

'The work just isn't that satisfying,' I lied, badly. 'I think I'll quit.'

'Sara,' he said sternly, 'you don't just quit a job with nowhere to go. You have rent to pay now. You have to stick it out.'

'I . . . I don't think so,' I said, trying not to cry. 'I'll work something else out.'

'What happened?' he demanded. 'You were so excited about your fresh start!'

I looked away, my cheeks burning with shame, as John tactfully changed the subject.

After a refreshing, head-clearing week away, I handed in my notice. The moment I'd done it, I felt an overwhelming sense of relief. I agreed to work for as long as it took for me to find a new job or for them to find a replacement. Over the couple of months this took, I started to notice more and more hypocrisy from the people who had called me inappropriate. One company meeting, one of the senior managers announced that a group of new graduates would be joining the following week. She gave a summary of each new yet-to-arrive hire, introducing one girl as 'Boobs' and doing an impression of the young woman none of us had met, bouncing her boobs around. The boys in the office, John informed me, had been circulating an email, having a secret 'Rear of the Year' competition, where they ranked all the women in the office according to who had the nicest arse. Fed up, I reported this to the nice HR lady who hired me, asking her why I had all but been fired for being inappropriate yet this was OK. She gave me a casual 'boys will be boys' sort of fob-off.

'You won, by the way,' I said, dully. She giggled, gratefully.

I spent a couple of months job hunting with no success, so I decided to go to Israel temporarily to work for my aunt's business. It was my only way to keep paying rent on my lease and, after what I'd just been through, the idea of being as far away from London as humanly possible for a month or two was extremely appealing.

I arrived in Israel bruised, exhausted and with the lowest self-esteem of my life. John and I were still together, but I had never felt like I deserved love less. I told myself I had gone to Israel because it was the only way to make money, but really I just couldn't face John. Still, he phoned every day, as I did my best to keep my head down at my aunt's company and just get through it without offending anyone.

Israel was easier. The culture is different. Israelis have a looser sense of interpersonal boundaries and are far harder to offend. If anything, rudeness is a prerequisite. Thanks to a culture where 'excuse me' will be met with confused stares and queuing is a sign of weakness, I found I didn't have the same high anxiety about putting a foot wrong.

A few weeks into my stay, John flew out to visit me. He was enchanted by the whole experience, telling everyone who'd listen how he, a Saudi-raised bearded frequent flyer with a pilot's licence, had been given the highest possible security risk number and the full bag-search treatment. I was taken aback at how relieved I was to see him. My whole life, whenever I had felt homesickness, it had been in the form of a longing for my childhood home, my parents. When John showed up at Ben Gurion Airport, grinning about how he'd been escorted on to the plane last by El Al security, my home-sickness evaporated. Somehow, in the few months I'd known him, John had become my home. My extended family were all charmed by John and by his obvious care for me. 'Marry him,' they instructed, 'before he realises.'

A month into my Israeli adventure, I got a call from home offering me a job at a small PR firm north of London. I took it. John and I decided the long commute would be marginally easier from his place – still an hour and a half each way on a good day – and so, just like that, we moved in together.

I had never lived with a boyfriend before and I struggled to adjust. John's ex had moved out a couple of years previously, and there was still some of her stuff lying around, which hadn't bothered me until I moved in. I felt like I was squatting in another woman's marital home. A coffee table she had mosaicked herself took pride of place in the living room and pictures of the two of them and pets they had owned together lined the walls. Even her make-up brushes sat in a jar in the bathroom, as if she was about to walk back in at any moment. This was compounded early on when John, trying to say how much the cats liked me, put his foot in his mouth and said, 'It's like you're their stepmum.'

A few days into our new living arrangement, while I was at home waiting for my new job to start, John came home from work to find me curled up in a ball on the couch, sobbing. It all came spilling out. I felt like I was living in the shadow of his big long-term relationship and I couldn't understand why he needed all these reminders of her everywhere. I didn't want to sleep in what was basically their marital bed. I didn't want to be the cats' stepmum.

John looked at me, blankly. 'Oh God, I'm just that much of an idiot,' he said. 'It's just stuff I was too lazy to get rid of.'

John went around the house, removing the happy couple framed photos and boxing up her things to give back to her via a mutual friend. He found a sage smudge stick in my old hippie belongings and waved it around the house. 'Cleansing the energy,' he laughed, trying to cheer me up, even though he absolutely didn't believe in that. He then dismantled the old bed, packed up the coffee table in the car and got rid of both of them. We went shopping for our own bed and our own coffee table. It was a symbolic new start together. An ACTUAL fresh start!

Best of all, we got our own baby – a fur baby. I hadn't raised a kitten since I was five years old, and so we decided we would bring a new addition into the home. I named her Tonks, after the Harry Potter character, because of her patchy, multicoloured fur and she quickly became the centre of my world.

'MARRY HIM,' said literally everyone I knew, 'BEFORE HE REALISES.'

'OK, OK,' I said.

I started leaving conspicuous hints around the house. Most men would have run a mile at this. John bought a ring.

At the end of January, just six months into our relationship, John took me on a weekend away in the Sussex countryside. We stayed at a little boutique hotel and John took me for dinner at my favourite pizza restaurant in Brighton. He knew that I had a childish fantasy of being proposed to on Brighton beach (he knew this because I told him many, many times) and so, after dinner, we went for a walk. It was fucking freezing. I knew a proposal was coming because I had so aggressively planted the idea. I had dreamed of this moment my whole life, but I had never imagined I would be thinking, *Hurry the fuck up*, as it happened, or worrying about losing a toe to frostbite. I can't remember the speech John made when he proposed to me. Why? Because he ended it with the words 'without further ado', and I found this so irrationally hysterical that I burst out laughing and that became my presiding memory. John sank down on one knee and pulled out a jewellery box. Behind us, a group of drunk clubbers wolf-whistled. I didn't care. We were engaged!

Planning the wedding instantly became my new obsession. I made John pull over at a petrol station on the way back to the hotel, where I bought every wedding magazine they had, making sure to put them on the counter ring first, like a little girl playing dress-up. None of my friends had the remotest interest in my wedding and so, in search of like-minded souls to jabber at about place settings, I started a blog about my wedding-planning journey. I know. But to my great surprise the blog started picking up a following and pretty soon I was updating it on a daily basis.

While all of this was going on, I started my new job. Because my commute was so epic, it was agreed that I would work from the office three days a week and the other two at home. The job was nice enough. It was a PR account executive job at a tiny firm in St Albans, staffed by about six people. It was naturally lit and much quieter than my previous job with fewer personalities to navigate and not enough people for cliques to have formed, but by the time I staggered into work after an hour and a half on three different trains I was already run ragged. I was good at my job and I got on fine with my colleagues, but the trauma of what I had just been through soon reared its ugly head. I was scared to say two words to anyone. If I opened up or became animated, which I couldn't help but do, I would panic for hours afterwards that I had said something annoying or inappropriate. I felt I couldn't relax for a second or people would see the real me and it would all go wrong. I cherished my two days a week at home, where I would get my entire week's writing work done in about an hour and then eke it out slowly throughout the rest of the week in between managing clients and planning events.

Meanwhile, my back and neck pain became almost unmanageable and my energy was nearly non-existent.

When I wasn't working, I was lying flat on my back in a darkened room, unable to open my eyes as the slightest pinprick of light would send me into some sort of uncontrollable fit. Every time I had one of my weird episodes, I would squirm with shame for days afterwards, wondering why on earth John wanted to stay with someone who cried and screamed and hit themselves for no reason. Where previous partners had reacted with disgust, John showed me nothing but love and patience.

'You just get overwhelmed,' he explained. 'Don't worry about it.'

The harder I worked at my day job, the less able I found myself to cope with anything else. Two minutes under the bright lights and scanning the overwhelming colourful shelves at the supermarket would set off one of my meltdowns. I would forget how to do basic things, like cook for myself or how to put on my clothes. Laundry started to pile up in great mounds. Bills would go unopened, the terror building every time I looked at them. I could either work, or I could look after myself. I simply could not do both. Quietly, without complaint or judgement, John took on the daily tasks I found impossible. I responded with denial. *It's just how he shows love*, I told myself. *He does NOT look after you. You can look after yourself.* But I couldn't look after myself. John knew it and deep down I knew it. It became a source of terrible shame for me and I started to do everything I could to hide it. I hid behind bravado, pretending I just enjoyed bossing John around. I hid behind excuses: I wasn't well today, but I would get better. I hid behind denial: I had cooked dinner once that month; I was definitely pulling my weight.

Three months into the new job, my appraisal came around. I spent the night before pacing our bedroom, feeling nauseated with anxiety. After a sleepless night and breakfastless morning, I trudged through my commute like I was walking to the gallows. The appraisal was delivered off site by the big boss, a kindly but stern older man, who preferred the 'compliment sandwich' model to the 'devastating character assassination' approach. The good news was I was excellent at my job. The bad news? I could be inconsistent; completely engaged and energetic one day and barely able to string a sentence together the next. The good news? I was confident and outgoing and the clients liked me. The bad news? I talked too much.

Shit. Shit shit shit shit shit. But I had been so careful! How had my awful personality still emerged when I had been trying so hard to suppress it?

'God gave you two of these,' said the big boss, pointing at his ears, 'and one of these,' he added, pointing at his mouth.

I swallowed, hard, trembling like a leaf and trying not to let the tears that were beginning to march their way towards my eyeballs spill out of my face.

'It feels like you're not really listening to other people. For example, what's my daughter's name?'

I knew the answer. The big boss talked about his daughter all the time. It wasn't that I wasn't listening;

it was just that I had no idea what I was supposed to say back. 'I have received this information' seemed like a weird thing to say, but it was all I had. I immediately gave him the answer.

'Oh,' he said, surprised. 'Maybe you take in more than it seems.'

I did take in more than it seemed. I took in everything. I just wasn't sure what was expected in response. I silently vowed to learn how to better 'perform' listening in the future. Not in this job, though. In my head I had quit the moment he revealed I had ruined it all with my talking.

'We love you and the work you do,' he continued, 'and to show how much we appreciate you we're giving you a thousand-pound raise.'

For most people this would have been a victorious appraisal. Sure, some stuff to work on, but valued so much they were willing to put it in monetary terms. But despite this show of confidence all I could think was: *They've found you out. You have to leave before they fire you.* I held it together for the rest of the day and wept into my lap the entire commute home.

I didn't quit right away; I couldn't face the mortification of leaving another job after just three months. Instead I worked on my blog in every spare second that I had. The blog quickly gained traction and soon was attracting thousands of hits a day. People started asking about sponsorship and it occurred to me that, with a small supplement to my income, I might actually be able to quit my job and make a modest living from my blog. Then, miracle of miracles, I found the perfect solution. A local one-woman-band wedding PR company was recruiting a new part-time account executive. The commute was much shorter, just half an hour in comparison to my marathon hour-and-a-half thrice-weekly slog. The subject matter was one of my most obsessive interests. Best of all, it would supplement my income as I monetised my blog. I went for an interview and was immediately offered the job.

A few days before I was due to start, my new boss, an intimidatingly posh and polished woman, invited me to a wedding industry party, where a few of the agency's clients would be in attendance. The evening was going well until I was mid-conversation with my would-be boss and one of her clients when two rival wedding bloggers walked in at the same time. There had been some very public beef between them for years and, without thinking, I blurted out, 'This should be interesting; they hate each other.' The client looked uncomfortable and my new boss looked scandalised. I knew instantly that I'd fucked up. I'd been indiscreet; I had named what was going on in front of me in a way that looked like idle gossip. That's a big no-no in PR. The next day, I received a short, curt email explaining that on second thoughts me monetising my blog presented a conflict of interest with one of her clients and sadly she would have to retract the offer of employment.

'Thanks for letting me know,' I replied simply, before rushing to the bathroom to be sick.

I had already quit my job. I had bills to pay.

Rummaging through my bag, I found the business card of another wedding PR firm. Its CEO had been at the same party the night before and had mentioned they were recruiting. Within a few hours I had secured new part-time work. OK, it paid a measly £10 per hour, but it was a job I could do from home. I wouldn't have to interact with anybody long enough for them to find me out. That would do.

Over the next few years I would take on the occasional temp job to supplement my freelance income, but my first job left deep emotional scars. Just one year into my fledgling career, I decided to do everything in my power to never have to work another office job as long as I lived.

12

CARER

It was the May before ~~my white dress party~~ our August wedding and the preparations were in full maniacal swing. Our lives became an eternal checklist. I had everything planned down to the final details, and a plan B for every plan A, including a list of backup grooms. We were young, skint and on a tight budget, so we decided to take advantage of the old scholar's discount and get married in the beautiful grounds of my old school, just outside the Seriously Haunted Mansion, making use of the outdoor theatre. I'm not sure why I chose a place associated with so many unhappy memories to host the Happiest Day of My Life™. Perhaps it was my way of cancelling out the bad memories by creating a whole new association with the place. Or, maybe, it was my way of compensating for the fact that in our Class Ten staging of *A Midsummer Night's Dream*, I had been cast as a random background fairy and even in my twenties I still wanted to be the star of that outdoor stage.

My mum heroically offered to cater the wedding herself, sacrificing six months of her life to preparing and freezing enough food to feed an army. Having insisted on clumsily crafting every last decor detail myself for the purposes of blogging and having total control over what I infuriatingly started referring to as 'the aesthetic', our house became a Dickensian-style workhouse. Nobody was safe from being made to cut, glue, print, sew and anything else I could dream up, all under my terrifying supervision. Hundreds of man hours were spent gluing little fabric hearts to recycled pasta and jam jars. My dad joined in with surprising gusto. He was not a flowery man, but he was deeply practical. It was he who measured out the dimensions of my 'exact replica of the actual tables, complete with mini tablecloths' table plan. It was he who got on the phone and politely scared the living daylights out of suppliers who were messing me around. And it was he who made templates for my crafts.

'Here,' he said, handing me a cardboard heart from which to trace outlines on to fabric. 'Now they'll look like they were made by the same idiot.'

It was around that time that my dad started dropping hints about his health. He texted me that his stomach wasn't feeling too hot. He was trying some new vitamins his cousin in Israel had sent to him. They were testing him at the doctor for Helicobacter pylori – or maybe an ulcer. He didn't go into details about his symptoms, but something felt very wrong.

Eventually, under great duress and far too late, my dad agreed to go for an endoscopy. By this point it was late July, just weeks before the big day and his weight had dropped dramatically. He looked ill. Really ill. A few days before the endoscopy, we had our final venue visit. As we walked around the Seriously Haunted Mansion, a place that had once struck terror into my heart for utterly fictional reasons, my dad was emaciated and could barely cope with a few steps without sitting down. He sank down on the stairs, the ones that I had once believed led to the bedroom of the ghostly lady of the manor, looking grey and tired. My mum, who just a few months ago could barely stand to be in the same room as my dad, sat down next to him, full of compassion and worry. All that animosity that had festered over so many years suddenly didn't matter. That's how I knew with certainty that this couldn't be good. For my mum to feel sorry for my dad he would literally have to be at death's door. 'He's really not well,' she said, tearfully, as soon as he was out of sight.

'It's something not good,' were my dad's exact words, when he phoned me after his endoscopy.

'What do you mean "not good"? But it's not definitely serious, right? It could be an ulcer, like you said? Or maybe they got it wrong? They have to do a biopsy still; they might have got it wrong.'

'It's not good, Sara,' he repeated. 'I'm in deep, deep shit.'

The next day, my dad came to visit. I ushered him in, sitting him down on the sofa with the cheeriest smile I could plaster across my useless-at-hiding-anything face, for the first time in my life all small talk. How was the traffic and had it been raining in East Grinstead when he left and would he like some tea? I'll make some tea.

'Sara,' he said. He gave me a look that said a million things that had been left unsaid over my lifetime, a look that said, 'I'm so sorry. There's no pretending. I am fucked'.

I burst into tears, the kind of remember-them-for-the-rest-of-your-life tears that feel like they're being wrung directly out of your heart. I sat by his side on the sofa. He put his arms round me and rocked me like a baby while I howled into his shirt. I breathed in the smell of him, trying to make it last forever. Once upon a time, that kind of carry-on would have made him apoplectic with rage, but in that moment he was the dad I'd always desperately needed him to be. The one that hugs you and makes everything better. Except he couldn't make everything better. Nobody could. He was that dad for that one heartbroken, healing, crushing hug. It would never happen again. After that day, our roles switched irrevocably, and I became the parent to him that I always wished he'd been to me.

The next few weeks were a blur of wedding preparations and hospital visits. My dad insisted that all the festivities should go ahead exactly as planned and we respected his wishes. Family and friends began to descend on us from all over the world and our house was packed to the rafters with guests while I tried to process the wrecking ball that had smashed its way into our lives. Just as I was getting my head round the diagnosis, my dad dropped another bombshell: he didn't want to seek treatment for his now diagnosed oesophageal cancer. We begged him to reconsider but he was adamant that he would rather die than go through invasive treatment and live the rest of his life with severe health problems.

My dad was a stubborn man and once he'd decided something he had his own ways of ensuring it happened as he intended. I was optimistic that he might still be convinced, particularly given his prognosis of five years survival without treatment, until one particularly harrowing phone call where he shut down the issue forever. 'Sara, if you guilt-trip me into getting treatment and I live the rest of my life in suffering, I will hate you.' All was lost. There was no competing with his romanticised imagination of how he would die of cancer. His plan was to treat his cancer with alternative 'medicine', which he was sure would buy him time and keep him in good health until he was ready to gently fade away on a beach somewhere. This is genuinely how he believed he would go – peacefully, surrounded by nature, on his own terms.

The big day finally arrived on the hottest day of the year. The perfect day to wear a giant meringue with about a thousand layers of fabric. The morning was surreal. I had been so excited and anxious about every detail of it for so long and suddenly the pomp and ceremony of it barely seemed to matter any more. I got ready in a daze, everything a chaotic tumble of tulle and make-up brushes and 'Has anyone seen my . . . ?' and 'Who's next for the bathroom?' and 'Oh, dear GOD, have you seen the size of my zit?' I sat uncharacteristically calmly in the eye of the hurricane, sipping on chamomile tea, mildly dissociated from reality. 'I think she's broken,' I heard someone whisper.

My brother had taken my phone away and was dealing with any last-minute dropouts. Every few minutes he would show up to the lionesses' den, nervously break the news that so and so had the flu or this and that had a family emergency, expecting me to start hyperventilating.

'OK,' I responded calmly. 'Bring me the seating plan. I'll rearrange it.'

Just as I was out of hair and make-up, my brother asked to speak to me and took me outside. '*Abba* hasn't been feeling very well this morning,' he explained gently. 'He's going to do his best to be there, but I just wanted you to be prepared in case he can't.'

For once in my life I didn't cry.

One of the advantages of getting married at my old school was that I knew all the hidden routes and shortcuts to get around unseen, which is no mean feat when you're dressed like a giant toilet roll. We traipsed through the muddy school garden, a comedic flotilla with me at the front in a dress that said 'I'm getting married young and therefore have no idea what suits me yet', my bridesmaids in mismatched floral dresses and petticoats like they'd travelled to the wedding from the eighteenth century. It took two of them to keep my ridiculous train from getting ruined before the wedding had even started. Then we hid behind the stage door to the outdoor theatre, the same spot where years before I had so resented my role as Background Fairy Number Five, nervously waiting for our cue to enter. In Jewish tradition both parents walk the bride down the aisle, so I had my mum by my side, but the moment of truth had arrived. I had been so laser-focused on everything else that I hadn't let myself think about whether or not my dad would be there. At the last second I asked my cousin Ella to check if my dad had made it. She surreptitiously darted out and came back two minutes later with him, and he took his place by my side to walk with us down the aisle and, finally, I could breathe.

The day was everything I had hoped it would be. We had a civil ceremony before our Jewish blessing under a chuppah I'd made out of table legs and a tablecloth. Basically, we got married under a table. Adrenaline must have kicked in because my dad lasted magnificently into the evening, even joining in the Jewish dancing and finding it in him to neurotically force food down strangers he felt weren't eating enough. And then there was his speech for which he rallied with astounding courage to be his most charming and good-humoured self. What was probably intended to be a light-hearted toast, however, was suddenly loaded and imbued with meaning in the light of his diagnosis.

After the wedding, my dad announced his plan to go to a holistic clinic in Germany for 'alternative' medicine. Despite the protestations of more scientifically minded members of the family, who understood that when medicine works it's just called medicine, my dad's mind was set. With my brother busy with his PhD, my parents long divorced and Belinda having her own three kids to look after, it was decided that I would accompany my dad to Germany for three weeks while he underwent a strict programme of alternative bullshit. The 'treatment' my dad had chosen was an adaptation of the controversial Gerson method – a mixture of homeopathy, fruit juice and coffee enemas, with a sprinkling of mysticism and victim-blaming. The doctor, who claimed to also be a qualified medical doctor, was said to be a miracle worker. Tales had reached my father of the multiple patients he had supposedly cured of their terminal cancers without a day of chemotherapy. My dad explained that he wasn't expecting miracles, but he was hoping to prolong his life through natural means. Even though the treatment sounded like nonsense, on a very deep level I still believed my dad knew everything and therefore must have known something I didn't.

I didn't want to go to Germany. I didn't feel old, brave or qualified enough to manage the situation by myself. But there was nobody else to do it and I couldn't bear to let my dad go alone. I said a tearful goodbye to

John at the airport. I felt much the same as I had on my first day of university saying goodbye to my dad. I was in over my head. I was someone who could barely look after myself and suddenly I was solely responsible for the wellbeing of a terminally ill man who was having a nervous breakdown. My dad was so anxious that he wanted to leave nothing to chance. Everything had to be locked in before we left. We planned the trip to the clinic in careful detail, a key component of which was a German SIM card, which we would need to make arrangements at the other end, and which John had pre-loaded and put into a folder for me.

On the journey my dad's anxiety was palpable. Every two seconds he asked me if everything was OK, if I had things under control. He asked the same questions over and over. Which platform did the train leave from? What time exactly did it leave? Was there a backup train in case that one was cancelled? How would we get food? Was I ready to phone a taxi to take me to the supermarket as soon as we arrived? Had I let our new landlords know we were on the way?

'It's all under control,' I said for the thousandth time. 'You need to relax and trust me.'

As we came towards the end of the flight, I decided to get ahead of myself and swap out the SIM card in my phone for the German one. I opened the folder containing my passport and travel documents and, to my horror, discovered that the SIM card was missing. I had definitely packed it. I had checked at home and at the airport. Somewhere along the way, it must have fallen out.

'What's wrong?' my dad demanded.

'Nothing,' I lied badly.

I waited until my dad went to the bathroom before frantically looking in every crevice and crack of my bag and seat.

'What are you looking for?' asked the woman in the seat next to me.

I burst into tears and explained what had happened.

'Poor dear,' she said, rubbing on my back. 'This is too much for someone so young. It's not the end of the world,' she comforted me as I became hysterical.

'You don't understand,' I sobbed. 'It's my job to keep him calm.'

I broke the news to my dad as gently as I could and promised I would get a SIM card the second we landed. He did not take it well. I could feel the woman in the seat next to me staring at us as he wrung his hands and told me what a catastrophe it was, while I stared tearfully at my shoes, apologising over and over.

At the airport I overheard two older men speaking English and asked them where there was a mobile phone shop. They directed me and, miraculously, I managed to fix the problem without any drama. But now we were late for our train. All my dad's fears were being validated, as were my own worries about being an incompetent caregiver. As soon as we arrived at the flat, I went straight to the local supermarket, where, away from my dad for the first time that day, I sat on the wall outside for half an hour and cried my heart out. I navigated the supermarket through thick tears. Supermarkets, with their fluorescent lighting, overwhelming selection of products and constant noise and crowds were not easy for me at the best of times and now there was the added obstacle of a second language. I started to hyperventilate again. I texted my friend Tom, who is fluent in German, and despite it making a large dent in his phone bill he translated each product on my shopping list. By the time I was done I had been gone two hours and my dad was absolutely frantic.

'I THOUGHT YOU'D DIED,' he screamed at me, as I lugged the first of the bags through the door.

The next morning, we walked across the picturesque town square to the clinic for my dad's first appointment. In the waiting room I was stunned to see one of the two English-speaking men who had helped me find the mobile phone shop at the airport. The man was tall, probably in his fifties and incredibly full-on. He had the energy of someone who had been a lifelong player. A classic bastard. Why he had been hurled into my path in this way, given the unlikely odds that someone I'd spoken to at the airport two hours away would be going to the same incredibly niche place as us, I had no idea, but I didn't like it. He was delighted to see me, giving me a big hug and shouting about synchronicities and the universe. My dad's expression stiffened. As we waited for my dad's appointment time, the man talked incessantly at him about how healing was a matter of self-belief, all the while putting an arm round me or a hand on my knee in a way that made my skin crawl. I looked at my dad helplessly, doing that thing that so many women do in a situation like that – be polite, don't make a scene, wait for him to get bored and go away.

'You seem defeated,' the man lectured my father. 'How many strokes do you think I've had? You'd be amazed. I healed myself just with this method and my mind.'

'Listen,' my dad snapped. 'You need to back right off from us from now on.'

There was a silence. The man looked like he had been slapped.

'I have to focus on my treatment,' said my dad. 'So you need to stay away from me, stay away from my daughter and leave us alone. Do you understand me?'

All the colour and life drained from the room and took up residency in my face. My dad was absolutely right, but, Christ almighty, was there not a gentler way of getting rid of the guy?

'Sorry,' the man said, looking like he was about to cry. 'I've been told that before.'

That was the moment the doctor chose to call my dad in to his appointment, leaving me to mop up the awkwardness alone. I almost felt sorry for the man until he tried to put his arm round me the second my dad had closed the door behind him.

From the waiting room I could hear every word of my dad's consultation. The doctor asked my dad a series of incredibly personal questions. He asked about his up-bringing, his relationships and many other things I tried my best not to hear. The point, he said, was to pinpoint the exact moment my dad had 'given himself' the cancer. I drew in a sharp breath. That's . . . absolutely not how cancer works. I didn't know much but I knew that.

After a long, mortifying interrogation, the doctor settled on a more recent moment, the argument with Shira that had split them up. 'That's when it happened,' he pronounced with confidence.

Panic surged through me. What had I been thinking bringing my dad to this stupid, dangerous place? But before I could assemble any coherent thoughts, the doctor was at the door, calling me in.

The doctor was exactly as you'd expect a snake oil salesman to look. He was tall, thin and stern, with the air of a professor who's had tenure for so long he no longer gives a fuck about performing his job competently but still expects total respect from everyone he meets. His treatment, he explained, worked on a diet of zero processed foods. This meant no added sugar (cancer, he claimed, feeds off sugar), nothing that came in a packet, only certain fruits and vegetables, liquids only, a special blend of fruit juices mixed with freshly picked nettles, coffee enemas, expensive bottles of vitamins and minerals, homeopathy, ghee butter, Ayurvedic massage and some sort of dodgy berry substance that would make my dad violently ill. I still have no idea what was in it. He barked instructions as I scribbled them down as fast as I could.

My dad seemed to be having the same doubts that I was. 'This is very extreme, doctor,' he said.

The doctor seemed stung. He leaned forward, looking my dad in the eye, and reeled off a list of extraordinary claims. All the people he had cured without any conventional treatment whatsoever. 'Call one of them if you don't believe me,' he said, casually, but his eyes were dark. 'One of them is on a cruise now. She's not even supposed to be alive, according to conventional medicine.' He then made my dad a promise. If my dad followed his treatment to the letter, the doctor could guarantee, 100%, that he would 'lick the cancer'.

'That's a very big claim,' my dad said, unsure.

'As long as you follow the treatment exactly,' the doctor said, reiterating that only people who had gone against his advice had died. He couldn't make such claims publicly, he added, as 'the establishment' would be after him, trying to shut down his great work.

As we stood up to leave, the doctor congratulated my dad again on his 'brave and correct' decision to forgo conventional treatment.

Despite the treatment having been sold to us as a bespoke, one-on-one intensive two-week programme, we barely saw the doctor after that. He was nearly impossible to get hold of if there was an issue, like my dad not being able to tolerate some of the advised 'treatments'. One of the only times I actually managed to speak to the doctor, he took the opportunity to express disgust at my dad for being a 'crybaby'. 'I thought he was a tough military man,' he snorted. For my dad's sake I suppressed the wave of hot rage that rose up in me.

The doctor would show up a couple of times a day, whenever the whim took him, sometimes late into the evening, to drop off disgusting liquefied meals for my dad, the only things he was allowed to eat. My dad would wait hours for these meagre rations, his anxiety filling up the small apartment and my desperate attempts to soothe him having absolutely no effect. The rest of the treatment was administered by me, or at a local Ayurvedic health spa, where my dad emerged close to tears from degrading coffee enemas. I would make up solutions for my dad that would cause him, already painfully underweight, to vomit for hours on end. I worked day and night, dutifully administering the doctor's plan, coaxing horrible liquids down my dad's throat, encouraging him to keep going. My life was non-stop. If I wasn't chopping vegetables, preparing pills, cleaning or shopping, I was walking him to treatments.

'Sara is incredible,' I overheard my dad telling Belinda on the phone.

I didn't feel incredible. I felt like I'd been shoved onstage to perform a one-woman show without having had time to memorise any of my lines.

I also felt suffocated – and guilty for feeling suffocated. The only time I had to myself was while my dad was at the spa. I would sit on a bench, overlooking the frosty hills, listening to the church bells chime and quietly releasing my tears, like a pressure valve. My dad woke every night with screaming nightmares. Suddenly I was the one trying to administer a calming bedtime routine. Night after night, I sat by his bed and we recited the bedtime verse he had written for me as a child:

Fairies, angels, wind and waves
Flowers, yellow, red and white
Gently close my sleepy eyes
Cover me with love and light.
Fear, I've none, I'm strong and brave.
Sun and moon, stars shining bright
Take me to a paradise
Of golden days and silver nights.

There were a few other patients staying in the same apartment block as us. My dad befriended a sweet-natured German woman, who was accompanied by her young teenage son. She explained how her cancer was now in remission.

'Wow,' said my dad. 'Without any conventional treatment?'

'No,' she responded sheepishly. 'I had an operation and chemotherapy. But I didn't have the optional extra radiotherapy and I'm still here.'

My dad and I dutifully followed the doctor's orders, which, despite him having stressed how they needed to be complied with to the letter, seemed to change whenever we actually managed to speak to him. Towards the end of the trip my dad went for a session with the doctor's business partner, a 'healer' who worked on him for an hour before announcing that my dad's immune system was 'kaput' and that he would be dead within a few months. 'Unless,' he said, slyly, 'you stay in Germany for another few months and come to see me every single day.'

My dad emerged from the session shaken. 'We've been had, haven't we?' he said, sadly.

I agreed, but to say so out loud felt too horrific, too damning and too final. I looked across the health spa lobby, where the 'healer' was tucking into his lunch. I watched him chew in a self-satisfied way that made blood rush to my ears. It took every ounce of self-restraint I had to respect my dad's begging and not shout at him then and there that he was a dangerous, lying fraud. Hot, angry tears spilled out of my eyes as it sunk in how much time we had wasted – and how my dad's precious reserves, the last of his body fat, his faith in the system, had been stolen by these crooks.

A few days before we were due to travel home, John arrived to help us with the journey, bringing with him an unseasonable blizzard that lasted several days. I had never been so relieved to see anybody in my life. The moment he arrived, John took over my practical duties and I collapsed into bed, finally able to give into the exhaustion that had been consuming me for weeks.

'Sara,' my dad chided, as John prepared dinner, 'aren't you going to help him?'

This comment was enough to tip me over the edge. I flew into a rage. John and I had our long-established dynamic. He could see that I needed a break. How dare my dad tell me off like I was a spoiled child, and not the person who had been nursing him round the clock for weeks on end? I stormed out of the apartment, where I sat in the town square, flakes of snow landing in my tears, leaving cold, salty streaks down my face. My dad's voice carried across the white square, begging me to come back, echoing in the way voices only do in the silence of a snow storm. I returned to the apartment, taking off my sodden coat and boots. My dad put his arms out to hug me and I collapsed into them, both of us crying and apologising.

At our final meeting with the doctor he took one last chance to upsell us expensive bottles of minerals and to remind my dad that under no circumstances should he have chemotherapy or even go to the hospital. 'Once you go in, you won't come out,' the doctor said to my dad, reiterating his congratulations for resisting the medical establishment.

As we landed back in the UK and stood up to exit the plane, my dad caught my arm. 'Sara,' he said, 'my life is in your hands.'

Despite what had happened in Germany, my dad moved in with us and I carried on my round-the-clock nursing, nettle-picking, catering service. The routine the

German doctor had left us to follow was punishing and relentless. I wondered if my dad might benefit from talking to people locally who had followed the diet. When I looked up if such an organisation existed, I was stunned to find that not only was it a thing, but that the address listed for it was on the same street we lived in, about a thirty-second walk down the road. Amazed by yet another synchronicity, I walked down the road and knocked on the door.

An elderly couple answered the door and told me that they were the facilitators of that organisation, inviting me in for a cup of tea. We chatted for a while and, when I mentioned my dad had rejected conventional treatment, the elderly man seemed troubled. He had been treated for the same type of cancer and had undergone the recommended operation and chemotherapy.

'I would highly recommend that he only uses alternative medicine as a supplement,' he said, diplomatically. 'I don't think you can survive a cancer like that without treatment.'

I went home feeling hopeful for the first time in months. These people landing on my literal doorstep *had* to be more than a coincidence. If people who were so enthusiastic about alternative remedies that they owned an organisation dedicated to them still thought he should have conventional treatment, that would have to make my dad sit up and listen. I arranged with the couple to come back the following day and bring my dad around for a chat. The next day, I got a text from the elderly man's wife. He had suddenly, and completely unexpectedly, died.

All of us were saddened and in shock, but my dad was beside himself and I felt wholly responsible. I had done such an efficient job of raising his hopes that this man could help guide him; I had been so convincing about the idea that this synchronicity was a sign from the universe, that there was now no way I could backpedal.

'It's a bad omen,' he repeated over and over, wringing his hands.

The death was enough to shock my dad into reconsidering his approach to his treatment. Under heavy duress he agreed to go and see a world-leading specialist in oesophageal cancer at UCL hospital. All of us hoped that with the promise of being in such safe hands my dad might finally change his mind. My dad was a ball of nerves on the way to the hospital, unable to sit still and barely able to wait his turn once we arrived. The consultant was troubled to hear about my dad's alternative treatment plan, insisting that the best available treatment was still the operation and chemotherapy my dad had already been offered.

'But you're an expert,' my dad begged. 'I was hoping there would be a trial or a cutting-edge treatment, not the same thing I've already turned down.'

'It's the best available treatment,' the specialist reiterated gently.

My dad thanked him for his time and staggered back out into reception like a condemned man. 'I thought there would be something . . .' he said, before throwing himself on to a bank of empty seats and howling like a wounded animal, weeping into his hands.

I stood helplessly in the echoey vast reception area, watching my dad, my strong, dependable dad, break in front of my eyes.

People stared. Someone giggled. My ears rang. I wanted to pounce on them like a lioness defending a cub and tear their throats out. 'You're seeing him in the worst moment of his life,' I wanted to scream. 'This isn't who he is.' Instead I scooped my dad up, suddenly frail in my arms, and, miraculously, managed to get him back to the station and home, where he could be free to fall apart in private.

Back at home, life somehow went on. We stuck to the daily routine from the German doctor. We played music and sang together. We worked on processing my dad's feelings, writing down small blessings and positive things that had happened that day. That was until my dad started to turn yellow. It took the collective efforts of everyone in his life to convince him to go to the hospital. The German doctor, my dad pointed out, had said not to do it. The doctor, we pointed out, had not answered a single email from us since we had returned from Germany. Finally, on my dad's request, I phoned the doctor in Germany, who was most reluctant to take my call. He sounded aggravated and told me that under no circumstances was I to take my dad to a hospital, and that once he went in he would not come out. I thanked him tersely and hung up. That was the last time I ever spoke to him. After a few visits to A & E, days before his fifty-ninth birthday, my dad was admitted to a hospital.

To say my dad was not an easy patient would be the understatement of the century. It became clear that my dad, who I thought had always been taken with the idea of alternative therapies simply because he enjoyed magical thinking, was seriously phobic of medicine and hospitals. The doctors were already under enormous strain and did not have a great deal of patience for someone who had to be coaxed into even the most routine tests. Despite having never been able to do so for myself, I found myself having to learn to advocate for my dad, while also taking on the role of gently persuading him to allow the doctors to do their jobs. I was cast in the stressful role of mediator between my dad and the hospital, trying to soften his brusque manner and deliver his distress diplomatically, while doing the same in reverse to keep him calm.

I took it upon myself to keep everyone's spirits up, working overtime to make everything OK for everybody else. By my dad's birthday he had been moved to a ward for gastroenterology patients and, through sheer luck, ended up in a private room with just one other patient. While my dad showered and dressed, I decorated his bed with birthday banners and balloons. He was absolutely livid, wanting no part in the celebration, but begrudgingly opened his cards and gifts and even let me pin a 'birthday boy' badge on to his jumper, which he wore with a stubborn, jarringly comical frown, as if someone had forced Grumpy Cat to wear a party hat.

After a few days of tests, a team of doctors came in to see us and explained that my dad's cancer had spread beyond the point where treatment would be effective. They didn't know how long it would be. It could be anything from days to months. None of us had been expecting that. My dad's prognosis had been five years and it hadn't even been four months. Nobody was more stunned than my dad. He looked completely dazed, like he had been slapped awake, while simultaneously being in a living nightmare.

'If you want to do something with your life,' he told the attending nurses, 'you have to do it right now. Don't wait.'

The visiting Macmillan nurses helped arrange for my dad to be placed on a waiting list to be transferred to the local hospice, which meant my time as his full-time carer would be over. I was both relieved and utterly devastated. I felt like I had failed in my promise to take care of my dad, like he didn't trust me to look after him in the final weeks of his life. Worst of all, he had told me that his life was in my hands. That life was now ending. Putting two and two together and making five, I decided that if my dad didn't want me to look after him any more and he'd been relying on me to keep him alive, that meant it was my fault he was dying and he blamed me. I realise now, of course, that this can't be true. My dad could not possibly have believed that I had magical healing powers but at the time it felt like a damning rejection.

The night before my dad was due to be transferred to the hospice, he was moved from his private twin room to a packed ward. My dad was absolutely furious, unable to rest with the constant noise and bustle of the busy environment. To add insult to injury the elderly lady, for whom my dad had been asked to give up his private suite, was there for five minutes before multiple alarms shrieked, and teams of doctors rushed to her room to attend to the emergency, before leaving, their heads bowed.

My dad turned to me, his eyes shining with hope and asked, 'Does this mean I can ask for my room back?'

The next day, my dad was transferred to the local hospice. I had read somewhere that it was important to make a patient feel as at home as possible in their new environment and so, as soon as we arrived, I began unpacking framed photos of our life together. Pictures of us at my wedding. Pictures of my brother and me on the beach as children. Holidays. Birthdays. Family outings. All our most precious moments. It was the worst thing I could have done. My dad was devastated at the reminders of the life he was losing.

'Take them away,' he screamed at me in a way he hadn't shouted since I was a child.

I burst into noisy, stressed tears and my uncle, visiting from Israel, hugged me. 'She's trying to help,' he explained, softly.

My dad curled up on the bed, looking away from us.

The hospice was the gentlest and kindest place to die. My dad had a private room and bathroom. He was allowed visitors at all times. The staff were universally compassionate and highly competent, taking time to get to know my dad and his quirks and understanding quickly that the best way to convince him to do something was via me. I, in turn, continued to advocate for him, a role he both needed and resented, referring to me bitterly as his 'spokesperson'. The hospice cooks provided bespoke meals for my dad, making sure to get them right each time. The long-haired elderly dame hospice cat, Mitzi, strolled lazily from room to room, like she owned the place, offering companionship and comfort to everyone who needed it.

For someone who has always been so phobic of seeing death, and who is so terrified of their own mortality, making myself at home in a hospice was a surreal challenge. While my dad had company at all times, I was struck by how many of the patients were completely alone. It was eerie how quickly I got used to it. I would walk past the same rooms every day. One day, the patient would be sitting up brightly, eating a meal. The next, they would be resting, peacefully. The next, they would be unconscious, skeletal, their mouths open in a haunting 'O', the look everyone adopted when they were at the end. Then, quite without warning, a nurse would come round and close all the doors. We would hear the sound of wheels trundling past the room. The nurses would come back and open up the doors again and the next time I walked past that room, it would be empty.

'One day soon,' my dad said, 'those wheels will be for me.'

I didn't know what to say. He was right, but I didn't want to think about it.

As time passed, my dad plunged further into depression and despair, sitting listlessly for hours on end, barely able to interact with us and unable to even leave the hospice grounds because he found it too upsetting to see all the healthy people going about their lives. Autumn turned to winter and we found ourselves celebrating a lonely Hanukkah and then Christmas together. The previous year, my dad and I had celebrated Hanukkah at Belinda's warm, welcoming house. I had bought him a jumper. We had eaten doughnuts, sung songs, played games. The difference could not have been starker. At Hanukkah Belinda phoned to let me know she was on her way to the hospice. I suddenly realised that my dad had not been able to buy her a gift.

'I'll fix it,' I said, my impulse to make everything better for everyone taking over. With my dad's permission

I took a couple of notes out of his wallet and rushed to a nearby antiques shop. Belinda loved the Art Deco aesthetic, and so I bought her a crystal twenties-style perfume bottle I knew she would like.

'Sara got it,' my dad said, miserably. 'It had nothing to do with me.'

'But you told her what I would like,' said Belinda. 'This is how you live on – through your children.'

As my dad's health deteriorated, his appetite decreased. He stopped eating his daily meals and was only able to stomach soft fruits, like packets of sliced watermelon. His mental health continued to decline as the illness progressed, probably a combination of severe malnutrition and possibly the cancer having spread to his brain. He wanted the same watermelon every day, but he very angrily insisted that I must not go to any trouble and wasn't allowed to buy any more when it ran out. To get around these incompatible wishes, I got into a routine of sneaking out to the supermarket whenever I went to get my own lunch, buying more watermelon and bringing him the same packet every time, as if it just magically refilled itself. The hospice staff were all in on this odd and necessary deception. One day, my dad cornered a member of staff who had just returned from maternity leave and therefore hadn't been briefed, asking if he had any watermelon left.

'Of course,' she responded. 'There are about twenty packets in the fridge.'

When I arrived a few hours later, my dad confronted me about it. 'Well,' I said, panicking, 'you wanted watermelon and it was the only way you'd have it.'

'You're very clever,' said my dad, sleepily, cracking a hint of a smile for the first time in forever. 'It's like what I did with your bakbuk.'

I corrected him. 'My bakbuk went to a starving baby.'

He looked at me, perplexed. 'Sara, we made that up. We threw your bakbuk away. It was disgusting.'

I started to see the hospital counsellor, Susie, on a weekly basis. Susie was a lovely woman who just seemed to 'get' me without much effort on my part to have to make myself understood. It was also completely different to conventional therapy because this counsellor was physically there to witness what I was going through. She had met my dad and my whole family. She was around all the time to see the ins and outs of what happened. She didn't just hear about it; she lived it with us. Susie's support was like an antidote to a lifetime of slow poisoning. My whole life I had been told, explicitly or otherwise, that I was doing everything all wrong. Susie's approach to counteracting this was relentless encouragement. She taught me how to listen to my gut and trust my own perception of events. She told me, as often as it took to sink in, that I was a good person with good intentions. She rubbished the idea that I was bad or broken. She made me feel heard, valued and fiercely protected. She was, and still is, my biggest cheerleader, making sure I stop and absorb my achievements, big or small – reminding me that my feelings matter just as much as everyone else's. Slowly, session by session, Susie helped me to build a solid foundation of self-esteem. Never underestimate the significance in life of having someone on your side. That therapeutic relationship became so important to me that, eight years on, I still see her as a private client.

One day, when I was particularly exhausted, I took longer over going out for lunch than usual. Lunchtimes were the only time I had to myself – my one hour to breathe, refresh and find the strength to carry on for another day of sitting by my dad's bed. As I signed back into the hospice, I heard a commotion down the hall and one of the healthcare assistants came running out and asked me to come to my dad's room immediately. Fearing the worst, I ran in a blind panic, to find my dad shouting and wrestling off two nurses who were trying to subdue him.

'They're trying to take me away and lock me up,' my dad told me, wild-eyed. 'They want to put me in a mental institution.'

The nurses hovered warily by the door as I put my arms round my dad. 'Why do you think that?' I asked. 'It's not true, I promise.'

It turned out that after my dad had refused his lunch, one of the nurses had made a face at the other and he had interpreted this as a secret code between them. He had become paranoid that they were going to put him in a home. I wondered where he thought he was.

My dad grasped the back of my neck and removed my glasses from my face. 'Swear on your unborn children that you're not going to put me in a home,' he said, staring me in the eye.

'I swear,' I soothed, trying to sound calm, while feeling like I'd just stepped off a hamster wheel.

This mollified him and he sank on to the bed and cried. I put my arms round him again as tears poured silently down my face. I texted everyone I could think of to come and help me, but everybody else was busy with their jobs, their lives – all of which had gone on while mine had been obliterated. I felt like my dad and I were alone in a tiny boat, stranded at open sea with no hope of rescue.

As my dad's illness progressed, he started to sleep most of the time and, having spent almost three months watching others cycle through the phases of death, I realised we must be nearing the end. It was amazing how, even when expected, each new stage of horror was a colossal shock to the system and even more amazing how quickly that stage became the new normal. We would get used to the next level of the nightmare, adapting quickly before everything changed, leaving us to acclimatise all over again. You would think this situation would take its toll on a brand-new marriage, but John was amazing. He took as much time off work as he could, spending every spare second he could at the hospice with us. He dropped me off every morning and collected me every evening. He looked after me at home, spoiling me, massaging my tired shoulders, making sure I ate something, holding me as I sobbed out my grief night after night. He carried my dying father to the bathroom. When John had said 'for better or for worse', he had really meant it.

One day, I popped to the supermarket to pick up my dad's watermelon to find the shelf empty.

I approached the teenager stacking the shelves. 'Excuse me. Is there any more watermelon?'

'Um . . .' he said.

I burst into tears. 'I'm so sorry,' I said, mortified. 'It's just . . . I really needed it.' I looked up, expecting this poor kid to be looking back at me as if I was mad.

'Give me a minute, I'll just check out back,' he said.

I didn't think he was coming back. Not without security, anyway. But I was desperate so I stood and waited. Minutes later, the young man came back, carrying a huge box of watermelon slices in his arms, grinning like a hero returning with the spoils of war. 'How many do you need?' he asked, looking so pleased with himself my heart cracked open.

'Thank you . . .' I croaked. 'You have no idea . . .'

'Just doing my job,' he responded pleasantly. 'I'll keep some aside for you every day, so this doesn't happen again.'

Every now and then I think of that young man and hope that, wherever he is now, he is living the best life imaginable.

My mum visited often at my dad's request. It speaks volumes about how compassionate she is that she was able to put the past behind her and spend hours sitting by my dad's bed while he cried and apologised to her over and over for how he had treated her – how he had treated all of us – during their marriage. 'I was shameful,' he said to us again and again. My mum, my beautiful, heroic, empathetic mum, held his hand and forgave him.

I had not given much thought to my parents' break-up since it happened, but now I sat in the corner, feeling like I was five years old again, my heart suddenly sore for everything that had gone wrong for them, for my dad's pain at being the architect of his own demise.

'When you were little,' he said to me, 'I shouted at you and you were so scared you clutched on to your mother's skirt.'

'That doesn't matter now,' I insisted.

'It does,' he replied. 'I was a horrible father. I damaged you. You're so broken.'

'I'm not that broken.' I frowned, offended.

'Yes, you are,' he wailed. 'You're so broken!'

A few days before my dad died, I asked my uncle to come over from Israel again to spend my dad's final days with him. My dad had said he didn't want any visitors, but I was so sure this was another watermelon situation and that once my uncle was actually here my dad would be thrilled to see him. When I broke the news that my uncle would be arriving later that day, my dad was devastated. In one final burst of energy he stood up, shaking, and screamed at me that I had betrayed him and he would never trust me again. Usually when he was in this state I would be the only one who could calm him, but this time I was the problem. I shook with tears in my mum's arms while other people consoled him. However, when my uncle arrived, my dad was exhausted but, ultimately, happy to see him.

That evening I asked my dad if he was angry with me.

'Please, Sara,' he mumbled, barely able to speak any more, 'I can't take that with me.'

'I love you,' I told him.

'I love you too,' he replied.

When I arrived the next morning, my dad didn't wake up. He lay on his back, his mouth in that telltale horror-movie 'O' that was so familiar by now I could sketch the expression with my eyes closed. The hospice staff took us to a private room, where they discussed what would happen to 'the body' when he passed away. Talking about my dad as 'the body' was too much for me. I had to leave the room while my brother arranged the difficult details.

It took three days for my dad to slip away. According to my grief counsellor, there tend to be two types of death – peaceful and agitated. My dad had an agitated death. He twitched and moaned and cried out in his sleep, like he used to when he would wake with nightmares. I sat by his bed day and night, holding his hand

and singing his favourite Beatles songs, while reading up on how to know when the end is imminent. I didn't want him to be alone for that.

'He's not in pain,' the staff reassured me. 'It looks worse than it is. It's just the body shutting down.'

I really wanted to believe that, but looking at him it was impossible for me to believe he wasn't in distress. Even in his final hours, as he lay unconscious and skeletal, struggling for breath, my phone was constantly abuzz with 'helpful' suggestions from friends and family members, recommending alternative remedies that they insisted would save his life. My brother and I replied tersely, thanking them for their input and reminding them that they were not oncologists. If they could have only seen how their chirpy suggestions were juxtaposed with the reality of my dad's last hours. It was all I could do not to hurl my phone out of the window.

On the third night I noticed his breathing change. It's called Cheyne–Stokes respiration. I had read about it the day before. A pattern of breathing characterised by deeper or faster breathing with long periods of apnoea in between the breaths. I called my brother, uncle and husband in from the day room. 'It's time,' I told them.

We sat round his bed, holding his hand, telling him we loved him, that we would be OK and that we would look after each other and that it was OK for him to let go now. We watched as the spaces between his breathing grew longer and longer, wondering if there would be a next breath at all. And then, just six months after his diagnosis, at around 10 p.m. on 6 February 2013, my dad took his last breath, leaving me stunned to find that he was gone and, despite having walked to the edge of the cliff with him, I was still here.

13

BURNED OUT

After my dad died, I was bewildered to find myself still alive. I had spent the past six months of my life accompanying him down the dark tunnel of death, only to lose my grip on his hand at the last second and find myself stumbling alone back into the light, dazed and confused, like when you leave the cinema in the afternoon and find yourself back in bright daylight.

In six months I had barely thought of myself. My every sense had been tuned permanently into his needs, his pain and his journey. My blog had been neglected. My fledgling marriage put on the backburner. The pause button had been pressed on my friendships. Suddenly, my dad was gone and, most unexpectedly, I was still here. I had gone through the whole process of dying, hadn't I? I had shed my own life, bit by bit, as his life had ebbed away from him. Except, I hadn't, really. I had just been a close witness to his tragedy. I hadn't had to suffer the physical pain and the visceral fear of dying. I hadn't had to watch my own body waste away in front of my eyes. I hadn't had to think of those I loved continuing on without me and all that I would miss. I hadn't really had to face the reaper, because no matter how involved I had felt, it wasn't my time to meet him.

But still, I felt a strange sense of abandonment. After all we'd been through together, he had really just died and left me behind. That period of my life passed in a blur of grief. I, like many others, I'm sure, didn't experience grief in a neat, linear process. Nor did it hit me in one overwhelming sucker punch. My grief was like a tumble dryer, knocking me about from emotion to emotion with absolutely no rhyme or reason. One moment, I would be convinced that a flock of Canada geese overhead represented my dad coming for a visit, the next I would be ranting about how there's no afterlife and when we're gone, we're just gone. Some days, I would be so numb to it; I would feel guilty, wondering if I had ever cared at all – and then the missing him would surge up like a tidal wave, and I would forget that I had ever felt anything but this overwhelming, tortuous pain.

The world, which to me had always felt fraught with peril, now felt like a death trap. The worst had happened to my dad, so why not my mum? My brother? My husband? My dad's death hadn't just crushed the very last crumbs of my sense of safety into a fine powder, it had also shone a harsh and unflattering light on the belief system my dad, and I, by proxy, had held all my life. Until now, I had believed in magical thinking. Even after his death, for the first few weeks my coping mechanism was to visit a psychic, his psychic, as it so happened, desperately grasping at straws to interpret everything she said as a sign from him.

After a session with the psychic where she was so far off the mark, she wasn't even in the same shooting range as me, I started to wonder exactly how much of my life to date had been a massive con. I began googling everything I'd taken for granted without ever thinking to question it. Vaccines, it turned out, were lifesaving and necessary. Gluten is no threat at all if you're not a coeliac. Homeopathy has been conclusively proven, time and again, to be horse shit. Not only that, but it was the most transparent nonsense that fell apart at the slightest investigation. Homeopathy relies on the belief that water has a memory, which is why it is supposedly effective even if there is no trace of active ingredient in it, but that water only remembers the stuff homeopaths want it to. Homeopaths claim that 'like cures like'; for example an onion, which gives you a runny nose, cures a cold – a belief that has its basis in precisely nothing. According to homeopathy, the more something is diluted, the more potent it is. In place of scientific scrutiny is the mantra 'there are just some things that can't be understood.' How anyone could know all this and still have even a fleeting amount of faith in homeopathy as anything other than a mildly tasty placebo is beyond me.

I started to stew. I was angry, really angry, with the community in which I had been raised. I made it my personal mission to go around viciously debunking anyone who believed in any kind of woo. I took on anti-vaxxers on Facebook, flaring up with rage every time I saw one of their posts. I smugly informed people of how homeopathy is supposed to work. I started obsessively watching videos by Dr Ben Goldacre. I called a lot of people idiots. I ranted incoherently at people who already agreed with me about junk science. I withdrew from old friends, who seemed relieved that I'd been the one to cool things off.

Then there was the matter of how to fill my time. I rebranded my blog, but my heart just wasn't in it. Writing about twee dinner parties, wallpaper samples and other people's happy occasions had lost all its appeal. There was more to me now than window-dressing. I was full of rage, grief and disillusionment. Instead of finding a new direction, I floundered around, freelancing for PR companies and magazines; I became obsessed with photography because suddenly preserving people I loved seemed like a desperately urgent task; I wrote sad, embarrassingly earnest songs; and I tried to have a baby.

I say I tried, because I didn't really give my husband much choice in the matter. I just decided that the hole my dad's death had left in my life could only be filled by creating another human life that depended on me. The only lingering part of my identity that hadn't been squished like a bug was the idea of myself as a carer. John and I had started trying before my dad had passed, but now my life was a vast chasm of nothing having a baby became a preoccupation. I signed up to forums where would-be parents shared their 'trying to conceive' stories. I was so desperate I saw second lines in negative pregnancy tests like religious fundamentalists see the face of Jesus in slices of toast. Maybe, if you squint really hard and also lie to yourself.

My monthly disappointment intermingled with my grief until it was nearly impossible to separate the two. I couldn't understand why this shining, coveted goal of 'baby' wasn't happening. We were young and healthy, weren't we? Thinking I was probably being paranoid, I booked us in for fertility tests. After a lot of prodding and poking, the doctor explained, with a brusque and impatient bedside manner, that the issue was with both of us. I had severe polycystic ovary syndrome (PCOS) and it was unlikely that we would conceive naturally. As I began to quietly sob, the doctor irritably asked me what I was so upset about. At the time I was upset at the doctor's bedside manner, but I've since had time to calm down and see how irritating it must have been for him to have to deal with yet another hormonal woman getting all hysterical about nothing. What was there to cry about? It was just a little lifelong excess body hair, insulin resistance, painful, heavy periods, constant exhaustion and infertility. I realise now I should have taken the news about my extra androgens like a man.

Our inability to conceive a child coincided with everyone in my life suddenly becoming fertility experts. 'You're trying at the wrong ovulation window,' explained one relative. 'You're only tracking your body's ovulation. You want to be trying during your lunar ovulation.' Another expert opinion included 'babies come to those who are ready for them,' delivered with casual certainty as we walked past a girl who looked no older than sixteen, pushing a stroller containing two infants. 'Why do you really want a baby?' another friend asked, pointedly, pregnant with her second child. 'Do you want one because you want to bring a child into the world, or because you want one?' This struck me as a particularly hypocritical question. Of course my desire to procreate biologically was selfishly motivated. Of course the answer was 'because I want a family'. And, of course, if she was being honest, she would have come to the same conclusion about herself. The world is drastically overpopulated, hurtling towards a cataclysmic climate disaster and fraught with peril, pain and the inevitability of death. I defy anyone to list an altruistic reason to bring new life on to our shitshow of a planet.

'You just need to relax,' said another self-appointed obstetrician. 'You're never going to conceive if you're this stressed about it. Have a holiday.' So we took a small amount of my inheritance and booked a three-week US road trip, starting in San Francisco and driving down the Pacific Coast Highway to LA, where I would spend my twenty-sixth birthday, continuing on to the famous, kitschy Route 66 before ending our trip by flying to Florida to enjoy two days of the theme parks. We stayed everywhere, from themed fifties hotels to cockroach-infested dive motels, wigwam-shaped lodgings to a yurt in the middle of the Mojave Desert. We met sea lions on the beach, fell asleep in the desert to the ominous howls of coyotes. Most of our time was spent in the car, watching the magical, ever-changing landscape – mountains to oceans to desert to forests of giant sequoia trees – listening to music and enjoying long, comfortable silences. It was simultaneously the happiest and saddest three weeks of my life. Being surrounded day after day by awe-inspiring beauty, soaking in the new experiences and having a moment to breathe made my insides feel wobbly and raw. It was how I imagine it might feel learning to walk again on a broken leg, the cast of grief coming off and exposing the fragile limb below, taking its first shaky steps to rehabilitation. I cried a lot. I ate even more. I slowly started to learn to laugh again. The trip, however, did not result in a baby.

As my life became a 24-7 obsession about our inability to conceive, friends and family started to have their own babies and I began to hate them. My rational brain knew that someone else having a baby took nothing away from me, but I couldn't help it. I started to see happy new mothers as smug and cruel. I saw other people's baby photos as a personal attack. Woe betide anyone who complained to me about how hard it was to have a small child – that was salt in an already festering wound. I became bitter. I unfollowed friends who spammed their feeds with baby content. I started to look into adoption, but even that wasn't straightforward. We would also both have to be on board for an adoption and John wasn't convinced. He had always been ambivalent about babies, figuring he would work it out once it happened, but the whole adoption process spooked him. I had to physically restrain myself from hitting a poor, unsuspecting friend who said, 'You can always just adopt.'

A few months of drifting aimlessly around PR assignments, underpaid features writing and half-heartedly updating my blog later, I was on the last train back from London to Surrey. It was December and the train was packed with pub-goers and revellers on their way back from office Christmas parties. I was on my way home from a nineties-themed reunion gig at the O2 Arena, which had featured such big names as 911, 5ive (although there were only four of them) and Atomic Kitten. It had been a hoot. The bands had been decidedly D-list and just a little out of practice. At one point I worried we might have to ring the emergency services for one of the members of 911, but that we would all collectively forget the right number to call. At another point 911 had performed one of their lesser-known tracks, which is saying something as all their numbers are lesser known, and pointed the microphone at the audience expectantly, indicating that we were supposed to sing along. It immediately became clear that not one person in the entire O2 Arena had ever heard the song before. Several thousand people all looked at each other in awkward confusion, before mumbling something non-descript.

The music had evoked a strong sense of nostalgia of childhood Christmases that had left me in an upbeat mood and, despite being exhausted from the echoey, packed arena, I was still riding enough adrenaline from the final number, during which glittery paper poured from the ceiling to 'ooohs' and 'aaahs', to get me home. That's when I encountered the drunkest drunk girl I've ever seen in my life. She was, as she loudly informed the carriage, on her way back from London's legendary Christmas fair, Winter Wonderland, and seemed single-minded in her goal to befriend us all. She lurched unsteadily around the carriage, dancing from passenger to passenger, loudly broadcasting her mortifying, deeply personal secrets (why do that when you can just write a book?).

I opened Twitter, as was the only appropriate reaction, and typed: *There is the drunkest girl in the world on my train home yelling comedic obscenities at everyone. It's way too entertaining.* Then my stop arrived and, more than a little relieved, I got off the train. As I walked to the car, a notification popped up from a beauty blogger I'd never spoken to before called Klaire de Lys. *You too? Seems to be some kind of competition going on.* It took a couple more tweets back and forth for us to establish that we had been on the same train, in the same carriage, actually sitting opposite one another.

As disillusioned as I still was with the philosophy of my upbringing, this felt uncannily to me like something one of my teachers would have called 'synchronicity'.

A month later, while in charge of the guest list for a PR event at a hair salon, I made sure to drop Klaire an invitation. As it turned out, Klaire was not just another beauty blogger. She was an extremely skilled, self-taught special-effects make-up artist who had amassed a following of hundreds of thousands of fans and, quite incredibly, hundreds of millions of views on YouTube. Through the magic of make-up Klaire could transform herself into anything, from Disney princess to gory zombie. She could replicate horrific injuries in one video and bring out her best features in another. As luck would have it, I was responsible for organising a magazine photoshoot the following month and had yet to book a make-up artist. I contacted Klaire immediately and was delighted when she agreed to join us for our trip to Dartmoor, where we would be sleeping in yurts and creating ethereal shots on the windswept moors.

Once Klaire and I got chatting, it became clear that we had quite an uncanny amount in common. We were both creative misfits, often misunderstood by the people around us but deeply invested in art, music and making. We both loved fantasy, fairy tales and whimsy – and it was that shared love that brought Klaire to my house one evening for a binge-watching session of an obscure US fantasy show called *Once Upon a Time*.

Klaire noticed my keyboard set up in the living room and asked me if I played. As any amateur musician knows, asking such a question is obviously tantamount to a request for a performance. I didn't need asking twice.

Or once. I sat at my keyboard and played her a song I'd written. Her eyes grew wide.

'I sing too,' she explained. 'I've been looking for someone to play and write with.'

We started rifling through our brains for songs we both knew, settling on 'A Thousand Years' by Christina Perri. As Klaire sang and I harmonised we shared one of those once-in-a-lifetime knowing looks. I don't know what it sounded like, but to us it felt like magic. My inner fantasist kicked into gear again, except this time there were two of us with big dreams, wild imaginations and eternal supplies of optimism. Klaire and I would spend hours on the phone, discussing our plans for world domination, feeding each other's rich inner worlds and delighting in the shared experience of a creative relationship.

We set to work straight away, scheduling in songwriting sessions, a strategy for gaining an audience and, most importantly, choosing a name. With Klaire immediately vetoing Just Add Vodka, we went through the awkward process of two people who don't really know each other that well and don't want to offend each other making a vital creative decision. That's how we ended up with the name Malumi – pronounced mah-loo-my – a combination of the words 'magpie' and 'lumi', which in different languages means 'snow' or 'glow'. Of course nearly everybody pronounced it so it rhymed with halloumi, making us sound less like a mystical fantasy band and more like a mezze starter.

We both developed an obsessive focus on the band and it wasn't long before we had a library of songs ready to record. Most bands start out by playing live gigs and, if they're lucky enough, go on to record their music and make music videos. Being two stage-shy introverts, and given Klaire's unique following on YouTube, we did everything backwards. Before we'd contemplated so much as an open-mic night, Klaire and I had contacted a producer, a cheerful, funny and talented man named Graeme who worked out of a studio with a model dinosaur in the garden and a set of giant teeth overhanging the door. Graeme quickly became like a third band member, coaxing the best out of both of us, pranking us frequently and tolerating my irritating attention to detail. My nickname in the studio became 'bat ears', because I would hear issues, slight tuning problems and faults that nobody else would pick up on unless that track happened to be isolated and would not shut up until they were fixed.

The next couple of years were a whirlwind adventure. Klaire and I recorded an EP and an album. Our terrible homemade music videos, which usually featured me looking like a total dickhead, covered head to toe in glitter or wearing ludicrous elf ears, and Klaire looking positively radiant, received hundreds of thousands of views. We were featured on *BBC Music Introducing*. Our first single even made it to number one on the Amazon folk chart, knocking Joni Mitchell off the top spot. Sorry, Joni, I'm sure you'll make it big one day.

After we released our album, things came to a natural end. As much as I loved writing songs, I was no performer, which is kind of a vital skill in a career as a performer. Klaire got engaged and I . . . well, I stopped. Not just music, I just stopped. I stopped being able to person. In all the excitement of our rock-and-roll adventure I had shut down my blog and my PR work was negligible. When I had started, I had felt like a young person on a gap year, exploring the possibilities of life. Suddenly it was over. I was in my late twenties with no job, no direction, no baby and no idea what to do next. I sank into a deep depression.

Every day, John would head off to work, leaving me in bed, and come back in the evening to find me exactly where he had left me, curled up in a ball. On a good day, I would be curled up in a ball with various junk food wrappers littered around me. On a bad day, I would be so weak from hunger that I couldn't lift my head. My tolerance for noise, smells and light was now so low, I worried I had a brain tumour. I could barely open my eyes. My chronic pain was a constant feature, chipping away at my mood and ability to function. My odd little tantrums were flaring up on a regular basis. *Just stop*, a small, distant voice in my head would say as I screamed and cried and pounded my head. *Just stop doing this. I'm sure you can just stop if you want to.* But my body seemed totally disconnected from the commands my brain was barking. I needed to believe I had control over my moods, but I had no more control over them than the weather, which, despite the rumours, Jews are not actually in charge of.

When I tried to fantasise about the future, all I saw was a blank, endless expanse. 'I've ruined my life,' I kept saying, over and over. 'I can't be in an office, I don't have any skills, we can't conceive . . . What am I going to do?' I had never given much thought to my long-term future. That always seemed like a problem for Tomorrow Sara. But somehow years had passed and Tomorrow Sara had become Today Sara, and Today Sara had no idea what she was doing with her life.

'You don't need to figure it out just yet,' John reassured me. 'Take your time. Don't rush into the next thing until you know what it is.'

As my energy deteriorated, we acknowledged just how much John was having to look after me. He explained, as gently as he could, that he loved me and didn't mind taking care of me, but he didn't have it in him to look after me and a baby. I was furious. I could take care of myself. I'd taken care of my dying father, hadn't I? Surely when the baby came along, I'd find some energy in reserves, like I'd done for my dad. Or I'd find a treatment – some sort of magic bullet for my pain and energy and it would all be better. We agreed to put the idea of parenting on pause until we could work out exactly what that magic bullet was. Exhausted from the constant disappointment month after month, I agreed.

As for what came next? John had a plan. I was going to rest – take all the pressure off myself to have all the answers and just take a month out to relax, watch TV, read books, stop the clocks for a little while. At the end of that month we would go away on a little mini-break to Paris, and when I came home, I could refocus on figuring out my next move.

So, that's exactly what I did. I started small, lying in bed with my eyes closed listening to an audiobook – Tina Fey's *Bossypants*. And it was there, lying in the dark, listening to Tina talking about how she got into comedy, that the first sparks of what would become a burning fire were lit. Tina sounded like someone I could be friends with. And her job sounded fun – really fun.

'Don't be stupid,' snapped my depression. 'You're not funny.'

'Sorry, sorry,' I murmured back. 'I got carried away.'

Once I had finished *Bossypants*, I wasn't quite ready to leave Tina's world. I downloaded *Yes Please*, an auto-biography by Tina's best friend and frequent partner in crime, Amy Poehler. If Tina sounded like someone I could be friends with, Amy sounded like someone I could grow up to be. Amy was warm, empathetic and emotional, with a sharp wit and a fierce determination to succeed.

'OK, but her job sounds really fun,' I said. 'I wonder if . . .'

'DON'T BE AN IDIOT,' my depression barked back.

'Sorry, sorry, you're right,' I replied. But Amy's book seemed to have an answer to that. In her warm bath of a voice she explained how to ignore the muffled cries of that little voice of self-criticism by stuffing it in a drawer and conceding that you may be all the terrible things it's yelling, but you can deal with those when you're done writing. I'm paraphrasing – wildly. I heartily suggest that *Yes Please* be the next book you read.

I finished *Yes Please*, leaving a huge Amy-and-Tina-shaped void in my day. Slowly, like a bear waking up from hibernation, I crawled downstairs, wild-haired, with a duvet wrapped round my pasta-stained pyjamas, and devoured *30 Rock* in one sitting, before moving on to *Parks and Recreation*. And that was it. My depression was by no means over, but the little spark that had been lit in me had been stoked and nurtured and now was a roaring fire. The hope was enough to slap me awake. The comedy world seemed like a magical, shiny portal to a better future – and I wanted in.

14

TEACHER'S PET

I had found my calling – comedy. There was just one problem. I wasn't funny. Or was I? Friends often laughed at things I said and did but usually they were laughing *at* me, not with me. Or were they? It wasn't as if I blundered around accidentally playing the clown – I certainly played up to that persona. I thought back to my childhood, trying to impress my brother and his friends with my sense of humour, and the enormous sense of gratification I got when I managed to make one of them laugh. I had been raised on *The Simpsons* and *Friends*, hadn't I? Which meant that I knew what 'funny' was supposed to look and sound like.

As promised, John and I spent a week in Paris, staying in a beautiful, bijou (which is French for 'fucking tiny') flat above a boulangerie, where I was woken each morning by the wafting scent of fresh bread, wore an obnoxious floppy hat and imagined myself skipping through the Parisian streets like an ad for a perfume that would definitely give me a headache in reality. I ruminated day and night on thoughts of becoming a comedy writer, oscillating between the growing sense of excitement and purpose that tingled in my stomach and reminding myself that I had never written so much as a joke and I had no idea where to start.

On my return from Paris I googled 'comedy writing course' and landed on a site for the National Film and Television School. The course was a part-time comedy writing diploma, led by legendary producer of radio and TV Bill Dare. By the time I had finished reading through the course syllabus, the guest speakers and mentors, I wanted to get in more than I had ever wanted anything in my entire life. Applications were open for another couple of weeks for the course starting the following winter. There were just a few major snags: the application requested two sketches and an outline for a sitcom episode, none of which I had any idea how to write, and the website asked 'Do you think you're funny?' I didn't have an answer. Then there was the price tag. Over seven grand. My heart sank. My dad had left me some money, but that was supposed to be for our future. I imagined what my dad would say if I could tell him to his face that I had blown a massive chunk of his life savings, diligently scraped and saved over decades, on a spontaneous whim to go to clown college.

That afternoon I received a phone call out of the blue from my uncle. 'Your dad left you some extra money in his bank account in Israel,' he informed me. 'Just over seven thousand.'

I don't know if I believe in signs and synchronicity after everything that happened with my dad's illness, but if I did, this one was crystal clear. *Didn't you have dreams when you were younger, and everyone told you they were impossible?* My childhood words to my dad floated back to me.

'Right you are, baby,' I imagined my dad, replying. 'Go out there and get into clown college.'

I sent off my application containing the only two sketches I'd ever written and, miraculously, I was invited to interview for a place on the course. I decided to dye my hair, which was at the time bright pink, to a more muted auburn brown. I wasn't going to interview for clown college looking like some sort of . . . clown!

I am a subscriber to the philosophy of failing to pre-pare being preparing to fail. This approach has served me incredibly well in situations like exams, but inter-viewers tend to get spooked when you reel off the entire company history, unprompted, and address potential colleagues who you've never met by name. Still, I read everything I could find about the course. I listened to every available episode of *Dead Ringers*, Bill Dare's most famous show. I even found a Facebook group for current students, which I'm pretty sure they assumed was private as they openly spilled their thoughts, feelings and anx-ieties about the course. I read every single post, dating back a whole year. When I was up to date, I felt I had a pretty good beat on this Bill Dare character. The stu-dents spoke about him with a mixture of reverence and terror. Bill seemed like a tough-love type, like a stern dad that they were all desperate to please. The atmosphere was contagious. By the time I shut my laptop I'd never wanted to impress a stranger more.

The day of the interview did not exactly go to plan. In a last-minute panic I decided to watch *Mrs. Brown's Boys* for the first time. We happened to be hosting a friend of John's from overseas who I generally got along with very well – so, of course, the morning of an interview on which my entire future depended was the moment we chose to have a massive falling-out.

It started, as these altercations always do for me, with a comment I thought was uncontroversial. A character in *Mrs Brown's Boys* made a big song and dance about pulling out a chair for a woman during a date and tucking her in. I commented that I hate it when men do that, as I find it infantilising. I looked up, expecting a laugh, only to see our guest looking thunderous. He was furious that I would take a nice harmless gesture and turn it into such a drama. Had I been able to better read the room, I would have realised that this is probably something he's done on a date, hence the defensiveness, but instead I launched into a long infodump about benevolent sexism and how exalting women as dainty little helpless creatures is a form of misogyny. For some reason this only made him angrier.

Disaster struck for a second time when I realised the interview wasn't going to be held in central London, as I'd thought, but at the NFTS campus in Beaconsfield, a three-hour journey away on public transport. My interview was in two hours. I am someone who considers being on time to be lateness. I am always where I say I'm going to be. I always look things up several times, days in advance, to make sure I have a foolproof plan – and this was the moment I had chosen to drop the ball? One very tense hour later, I was in a taxi I couldn't afford, discovering the hard way that I wasn't a skilled enough make-up artist to do a lip so impressive it would distract from my swollen eyes. It is a testament to my dedication to timeliness that, despite the circumstances, I still arrived half an hour early.

Sitting in reception, breathing deeply, I was just beginning to approach a state resembling steadiness, when a sharply dressed older man approached me. 'Are you Kat?' he asked.

Of course. I was half an hour early. The candidate before me hadn't even arrived yet. I apologised for not being Kat.

'No, I'm Sara.'

'OK,' said the man. 'I'll just sit here and wait for Sara then.' He sat on the sofa adjacent to mine and began scrolling through his phone.

Multiple anxiety explosions began to go off in my brain at once. I knew exactly who the man was. He was none other than Bill Dare himself. But . . . the moment had sort of passed for a proper introduction. Was it weird that I recognised him? Or would he expect me to recognise him and to acknowledge it? Was this a test? Or was it inappropriate to speak to him outside of the context of the official interview? He had said he was waiting for Sara. Did he think Sara was late, and I was someone else? Would this count against me, the real Sara, when deciding who to let into the course? Maybe I should just pipe up and say 'Are you Bill Dare?' but he seemed buried in his phone and interrupting him felt awkward and impertinent. So I said nothing. I sat in excruciating silence, my inner monologue screaming so loudly I'm surprised he couldn't hear it.

The interview felt like a good-cop-bad-cop comedy sketch. The second interviewer was a kindly man named Dave Cohen, whose book on the comedy industry I had read cover to cover to ensure I didn't accidentally insult him, and who nodded encouragingly when I spoke. A minute into the interview, I began to feel out of my depth. What had I done in the industry? Well . . . I had been an avid viewer of comedy. Some comedy. Mostly sitcoms. Mostly American sitcoms actually. Did I think I was funny? Er . . . I mean . . . I guess some people say . . . uh . . . I could feel the energy in the room deflating like a giant balloon. This was an interview for a comedy course and I was giving off the energy of the widow at a funeral who had just found out her husband had left his worldly possessions to the local cat shelter.

'You realise you'd be the least experienced one on the course,' Bill put it to me, bluntly.

'I'll work harder than everyone,' I half shouted, sounding painfully like a mediocre *X Factor* contestant who can feel Simon's 'it's a no from me' coming.

'Hmmm . . .' said Bill, inscrutably. 'How will you pay for the course?'

'I HAVE THE MONEY,' I blurted out insanely in my excitement that I was finally able to answer a question positively.

The interview ended. I thanked Bill and Dave, shook both their hands, wandered outside and burst into tears.

A month went by in which devastation turned to mild disappointment and mild disappointment to acceptance. I decided not to waste time wallowing but to take Bill's feedback on board and start accumulating experience as soon as possible so that by the time next year's intake came round, I would be ready. I submitted satirical articles to a parody news site called *NewsThump* and was delighted when they were accepted and published. I submitted a sketch to a live comedy podcast for female writers and got lucky a second time – my silly little sketch was to be performed by actors in front of an audience. It was the most exciting evening of my life. My mum, my brother, his now wife and John all came along to the Clapham theatre to support me like I had won an Oscar. As they read out my sketch, I felt, for the first-ever time, that heady mixture of anxiety, elation and mortification. That addictive adrenaline that every writer and performer of comedy recognises – the feeling you then spend years chasing, only to need a bigger and bigger hit every time. Afterwards, my mum looked at me, her eyes shining. 'Did you see that woman in front of us? She was convulsing with laughter! Convulsing!'

Then, in late November, the email arrived. *Oh*, I thought dully. *Here's the rejection I've been expecting.* But there it was in black and white. I had been offered an unconditional place on the course, due to start in January. Happiness exploded inside me like fireworks. I read the email about a thousand times, just to make sure that I hadn't made a mistake. *Here we go*, said my inner optimist, boldly. *Another fresh start.*

The course took place in Soho once a week on a Tuesday evening in the large swanky boardroom of a production company. The kind of clinical, fancy boardroom that looks like it contains a secret button at the head of the table that opens a trapdoor under people's chair to send them to the incinerator. I made a typically 'Sara' first impression on my classmates, offering to take notes every single session for everybody and handing out 'please like me' home-baked goods. Despite my nerves, I immediately felt at home on the course. It was the only place I'd ever been where everyone was just as weird as I was, where oversharing was the norm (it's all material) and where everybody had the same burning, desperate ambition to prove themselves. Still, I felt behind. Everyone else had years of experience in the comedy industry and I was completely green. My sketches were unoriginal and unfunny, and the feedback from Bill and visiting mentors reflected this. I would travel into Soho once a week on a Tuesday evening, a bag of nerves, and would be back on the tube again a few hours later, crying in shame for the entire length of the Piccadilly line.

Sometimes, though, all it takes to really soar is to have someone believe in and champion you. For me that came in the form of Joel and Jason. Joel Morris and Jason Hazeley comprised a writing partnership that had written for pretty much every famous comedy show I could think of. They were best known as the writers behind Charlie Brooker's Philomena Cunk and the team responsible for the Ladybird Books for Grown-Ups. Our homework for our upcoming session with Joel and Jason was to write a Philomena Cunk monologue for them to appraise. I spent the whole week studying every Cunk segment I could get my hands on, before attempting my own. Joel and Jason were animated, engaged and gave detailed, thoughtful feedback. That week, there were building works taking place in the offices where we held our weekly sessions, which felt like someone taking literal drills to my very soul, but I focused with all my might to listen past the constant drilling and banging noises to hear what they had to say about my monologue. They loved it.

'Joke!' they declared, reading my opening line. 'Proper joke.'

I glowed with pride and embarrassment as they reeled off compliment after compliment and was delighted when they reiterated their praise in an email to Bill, specifically about me and another student, a kind and sharp-witted former TV critic named Alex. Alex and I were thrilled and asked Joel and Jason if they might like to come for a drink after class one evening. They very graciously said yes, beginning a wonderful friendship and mentoring relationship I cherish to this day.

Joel and Jason's belief in us gave me and Alex a priceless gift – confidence. And it was that confidence that led us to team up when we were given homework to come up with some *Dead Ringers* pitches, as a new series would soon be starting on Radio 4. Getting a credit on *Dead Ringers* was one of my biggest ambitions for the course and, while some people saw it as homework, Alex and I decided it was a job interview. Alex and I made an excellent team – I had never listened to Radio 4 before applying to the course, whereas she had an encyclopaedic knowledge of the industry and all the references we would need for a *Dead Ringers* sketch to make sense. And I had an almost deluded level of ambition that drove us both to believe we could breathe fire. She had a whimsical and delightful sense of humour; I had an eye for structure. Between us, we came up with around thirty sketch ideas, which we pitched to Bill during an evening class.

'That,' he said to the class, 'was an exemplary pitching session.' Coming from Bill there was no higher compliment.

Two weeks into the series, the episode after the Brexit vote, Alex and I sat in the front row of a *Dead Ringers* recording session as our first-ever broadcast sketches were recorded. While it didn't quell the absolute terror of the long political nightmare that lay ahead, I have to admit it temporarily took some of the sting out of it. There was no crying on the tube that night. I sat on the Piccadilly line, grinning like an idiot the whole way home, smiling at alarmed strangers, my whole body tingling with pride.

The year and a half I spent on the course was the happiest time of my life. I was smashing it in every area. My life was round-the-clock discipline. I was working out every day and I started to get strong and muscular. Alex and I started getting work and credits on other Radio 4 shows. I found I mostly worked well in writers' rooms. I would go through a process of panicking that I had nothing all day long and then started pulling jokes out of thin air, like a magic trick, at the last possible second. My loved ones were delighted with my career trajectory. 'You've proved us all wrong,' said my grandma, proudly. I still lie awake at night wondering what she meant by that.

Meanwhile, frustrated with the general lack of entry-level opportunities in the comedy industry, I teamed up with another writer I had met up on the course, Kat Sadler, the aforementioned Kat who had been late for her interview but early for mine, and together we started a satirical online women's magazine called *Succubus*. I use Kat Sadler's full name because she is already well on her way to being an incredibly famous writer and, when the time comes for her to collect her first BAFTA, while

I watch from home in my Gizmo from the Gremlins pyjamas, I'd very much like to have some bragging rights.

Kat and I clicked right away in that intense 'writers working on a shared goal' way, but also as friends. The first time I hung out with Kat one on one, we went to a Joe & The Juice bar. We tried to take a commemorative selfie, but no matter which angle we took the picture from, whether she had her hair up or down, no matter what we did, an optical illusion made Kat look bald. There is, of course, nothing wrong with being bald – but Kat wasn't bald and we couldn't work out why my camera was so determined to make her look so. It was probably one of those things where you had to be there, but after five minutes of doomed selfies we were both laughing so hard we could barely breathe.

Kat brought out the best, most fun version of me. Together we egged each other on to do over-the-top, spontaneous things, like the time we brought a fondant fairy princess birthday cake and used it in a ritual to cleanse ourselves of former romantic partners who had hurt us. We had lit a candle for everyone who had wronged us, before blowing them out and then, satisfyingly, hacking the cake to death. We haunted the streets of Soho, following our noses as they picked up irresistible scents of food and eating our way round town on random whims. We bought matching power lipsticks – Ruby Woo by MAC and felt like queens wearing them. We encouraged each other to explore our personal styles, telling each other we looked fierce when we did and giving honest 'not for you' grimaces when we didn't. During one shopping trip, we decided to ignore our guilt and go into a one-size-fits-all shop with tiny sizes, despite that being discriminatory and size-ist. 'I know it's bad,' I said to Kat, 'but they do such nice clothes.' Ten minutes later, we had both stomped out, ranting about how unethical the shop was and how we were too morally pure to shop there. Why? The trousers hadn't fitted us.

Kat and I worked day and night preparing *Succubus* for launch. Kat was the kind of friend for whom no topic was off limits. She was as keen to discuss bowel movements as she was business. She became a regular fixture in my home, one of the only people in the world who could stay longer than a few hours without me feeling suffocated or anxious. My friendship with Kat was as easy as breathing. We occasionally butted heads about the business. We had one notable showdown about the placement of commas, in which I acted like a total jackass and then spent the next few months second-guessing every comma and, panicking, unnecessarily putting them everywhere just to feel like I had been right. But most of the time it was like having a younger sister. In Kat I saw enormous talent and potential, the kind I wish I'd had the confidence to pursue years earlier. I had chutzpah and determination, which helped me to open doors and succeed, but Kat had the kind of raw talent you can't fake. Everyone who met her and read her writing agreed – Kat was the real deal. I wanted to do everything in my power to help her get to where she would inevitably end up, with or without me.

Meanwhile, in my personal life, a miracle happened. My baby nephew burst on to the scene, altering the landscape of my world forever. I took two trains to meet him at the south-east London hospital where he lay in his crib, a tiny beetroot of a thing, just twelve hours old and already the love of my life. I carefully lifted him like I'd been entrusted to guard a rare Fabergé egg, watching this alien creature who had stolen my heart squirming in my arms. I put him down and he grasped my finger. I burst into tears of joy.

Succubus launched to great acclaim throughout the industry. We threw a do-over prom, a party for all the rejected nerds of high school, and invited every writer, producer and comedian we knew. The site was an instant hit and secured us a spot on a satire panel at the industry-famous Craft of Comedy conference. Through that both of us got jobs writing for *The Daily Mash*, which led to credits on BBC2's *The Mash Report*. By the time I had graduated from the course I had already earned back the money I had paid for it and then some, just from comedy writing work. I felt good about myself. Really good. And then, out of nowhere, I started to crash.

Outside the safety of the course, I noticed myself falling into old patterns. *Succubus* was bringing out all my ancient insecurities. I had no idea how to be in a business partnership, how to navigate the give and take of that dynamic. My problem was that I cared too much – both about the business and the friendship. I felt constantly paranoid that I was upsetting Kat, and sometimes I did by saying something thoughtless or clumsy. That paranoia, as it had my whole life, made me behave oddly around her, which sent me into a spin cycle of anxiety. I would try to fix something that wasn't broken, thereby breaking something, causing further anxiety and more mortifying attempts to fix it.

It wasn't just Kat I was humiliating myself in front of. I began having the same anxieties about the industry in general. After every writers' room, every pub trip, every show recording, I would go home and panic for hours about whether I'd talked too much, said something inappropriate, whether I was good enough to be there, or if everybody hated me. The pressure of overcoming my self-loathing became a constant exhausting battle. No matter what I achieved, no matter how well I had done, I still walked away furious with myself, thinking about everything I could have done better.

The more time people spent around me, the more I was convinced that they couldn't possibly tolerate me much longer. Things came to a terrible head when Kat and I went to Edinburgh for the fringe with some comedy friends and I had the nervous breakdown to end all nervous breakdowns. Things started going wrong the second I arrived. It was a bright, sunny day – the kind of sunlight that always makes my eyes water and my head pound. Kat came to collect me from the train station and helped me navigate my way through the heaving crowds. It was like having my brain battered from all angles. As people lurched all around me with flyers, shouting about their shows and begging for an audience, I started to feel like I was suffocating. Kat took my bag, moving me swiftly through the crowds like a bodyguard, while I cowered and shook, unable to explain to myself why running this particular gauntlet was so hard. By the time I'd done my shopping and settled in at the Airbnb I'd rented, I couldn't contemplate going back out there. I called Kat and apologised; I just felt too sick to go and see her show that night.

'Oh . . .' she responded, disappointed. 'That's OK.'

But it didn't feel OK. Nor did it feel OK the next day when a group of us went to see several shows in one day and I sat in tearful silence at the bar while everyone else had a lovely time, wondering what on earth was wrong with me. Nor did it feel OK the day after that, when we went to the Scottish National Gallery, where the red walls and violent paintings made my head spin and my entire body seize up. I sat on a bench with my head between my legs, apologising profusely while my friends looked at me, probably just feeling helpless and unsure of what to do, but in a way that I read to mean 'what the hell is wrong with you?'.

By the end of day three I wanted to die. 'You guys go out without me,' I insisted, deciding to get an early night.

That night, when Kat and another friend returned, drunk and giggling, it was more than I could take. I felt like the biggest failure in the world for not being able to just jump out of bed and join in. I was a sobering, sad presence and I was ruining everyone's good time. I stormed out to the living room where they sat together and angrily slammed the door shut, before sobbing my heart out in my bed.

'What's happening to me?' I asked John in a whispered phone call. 'What's wrong with me?'

Too embarrassed to face my friends after my little outburst, I spent the rest of the trip alone at local beauty spots. I took a taxi to the beach, where I sat in relieved silence. I went to Arthur's Seat and hiked miles and miles by myself. And then I took an early train back to London without saying goodbye to anybody.

As soon as I got home, my health began to plummet. My back and neck pain revved up to full volume again. I stopped exercising. I started to feel sick most of the time. It felt like I was paying back the burst of energy I had enjoyed while I was doing the course with interest. Like someone had sold me a payday loan with excruciating repayment terms and I had failed to read the small print.

Back in my new role as Proud Aunt, I was loving every second I spent with my nephew, but I also felt dismally underqualified to care for him. Whenever we were left alone together, I would panic that he would hurt himself. No matter how closely I kept an eye on him, little things always seemed to go wrong on my watch. One time, I got my wires crossed about him having had lunch at his last caregiver and didn't realise he was hungry until he was howling with misery. Another time, I glanced at my phone for half a second to update his parents that he was fine and, by the time I'd looked up, he had flipped over his baby music table and got his head stuck in between the legs. My nephew was a dream baby. He was impeccably behaved, good-natured and easy-going. When I successfully kept him alive for a few hours, I would feel an overwhelming sense of pride. I texted my grandma. *I got the baby to sleep!* Her response arrived seconds later: *Did you tell him one of your jokes?*

When I looked after my nephew, my heart felt swollen with love and raw with the pain of leaving him behind. All the maternal instincts were there. I would have fought fully grown bears to protect that little boy. I would have lost, but still, I wouldn't have curled up in a ball yelling 'Take him, not me!' I think this signifies huge personal growth. And yet, after every babysitting session, I would be unable to function for days afterwards. I would be so exhausted after a day of nervously hovering over him that I could barely open my eyes, let alone manage the train journey home. Several times, John drove an hour and a half through central London to get me, because I would simply get stuck.

'I hope we find this magic bullet,' I told John, using the last of my reserves as he picked me up from my brother's one evening. 'Because otherwise I don't think I'd be up to having our own.'

A few months later, the dream of a lifetime came true when Kat and I were invited to watch a table read for *The Simpsons*. A writer for the show, Mike Scully, had found *Succubus* online and was an instant fan. A small group of us flew out to LA, where we lined up meetings with writers and producers, hoping to lay the groundwork to one day move there. The flight out was a nightmare. I have never been a good flyer and long-haul trips are indescribably difficult for me. The constant roaring of the engine, the dry air, the sickly smells, the confined space, the uncomfortable seating, the motion, the anxiety that any minute we will drop out of the sky like a stone and hurtle to earth in a ball of fire . . . Let's just say that thirteen straight hours of that is enough to drive me, and everyone around me, to distraction.

True to form, I had fantasised day and night about the upcoming LA trip. I was going to be the most fun version of myself. I was going to go out to bars, spend days at Disney, take Kat shopping. I was going to prove to myself and everyone else that I wasn't miserable, anxious and broken, that Kat hadn't made a terrible mistake by associating with me. The trip got off to a great start. As we stumbled out of the airport, I found the nearest bin and threw up. By the time we arrived at our Airbnb I could barely speak or move.

Usually, when I am too tired to function, I ask John for help. He has never minded, but I have always felt self-conscious about how much help I actually need. In the constant company of friends I had no way to communicate to John in my easy, normal way what I needed, and so I tried to do so in whispers and looks, which just came off as passive aggressive to everyone around us. I could feel everyone's eyes boring into me. *What's wrong with her?* I heard them think. 'I don't know,' I wanted to shout. 'I don't know, OK? I wish I knew!'

The rest of the holiday was as far from my promise to myself as was humanly possible. I had maybe one or two good hours in me before I had to find a dark space to lie down in. I could barely open my eyes in the hard LA sun, even with my sunglasses on. My pain and nausea were constant. I seemed to put my foot in my mouth every five seconds. I managed to pull it together for the table read and the meetings, watch myself long enough not to humiliate myself, and Kat, in front of anyone important, but I spent the rest of the time curled up in bed. My confidence fell to such catastrophic levels that I couldn't socialise without being high. As anyone who's ever been sober around a high person will be able to verify, this was a horrible idea. Stoned out of my mind, I convinced everyone to come to a grotty karaoke bar in a strip mall, where, upon seeing a stranger had booked a solo karaoke session and finding this inexplicably hilarious, I descended into fits of unstoppable giggles, while my friends looked on in stony silence.

On the last day, after we had left the Airbnb, I felt so unwell all I could do was lie in the car while everyone else got out for ice cream, frozen bananas, coffees and to enjoy their last day in paradise. The flight home was a gruelling nightmare. I upgraded my seat, partly to give myself a small chance at sleep, but mainly to spare Kat the ordeal of having to sit near me. By the time we got back to the UK I was so angry with myself and so embarrassed that I could barely look at Kat. I didn't deserve to be her friend. I didn't deserve to be her business partner. I wanted to be as far away from her as possible to protect her from having to know me. I was right back where I started – wallowing in a pit of self-loathing and wondering what had happened to yet another fresh start.

15

AUTISTIC

It's April 2018, a few weeks after our trip to LA. I'm chatting to a comedy pal, Graeme (not to be confused with Malumi's producer, Graeme), after a particularly stressful day battling my sensory issues and wondering aloud what could be causing them. 'I think you should watch this Chris Packham documentary,' he tells me. 'It's about his Asperger's and some of the stuff he said really reminded me of what you say about your experience of the world.'

'I don't have Asperger's,' I snap back, ending the discussion.

I spend the rest of the day bristling with annoyance. Why do people keep bringing up Asperger's?

'I just don't want there to be *another* thing wrong with me,' I found myself saying to John, without really understanding why I was saying it.

It was back in 2016 when somebody first casually suggested that I might have Asperger's. It feels antiquated now to even use that word, but this was back when Asperger's was still in most diagnostic manuals, just on the cusp of a change in language within the medical and autistic community. It was suggested by my cousin Dominique, someone I hadn't known very well growing up, after I attended her autistic son's birthday party. She had sent me a message asking if I'd ever looked into it as she'd noticed I had some autistic traits.

When I think of Dominique now, it's hard to describe the gratitude I feel towards her – for seeing me more clearly than I saw myself, for having the courage to tell me and for changing my life for the better. At the time, however, I threw what can only be described as a strop. I will hold my hands up to this right now: my reaction was ignorant and ableist. At the time I knew very little about autism and the little I thought I knew was way off the mark. All I had were small crumbs of what I assumed to be information, the way I often assume actual crumbs to be remnants of something delicious I have previously eaten, only to find out as soon as I put them on my tongue that they're just something the cat trod through the house. The less said about that, the better. The Frankenstein's monster impression of autism I had cobbled together from poorly assembled parts, was as follows: autistic people are rude, prickly people who are impossible to get along with. They completely lack empathy and the ability to relate to others. They are basically robots. They tend to be quiet, mathematical, technical and can never make eye contact under any circumstances. How could anybody who had met me, this noisy whirlwind of creative energy and big feelings, think that I am one of those people?

Looking back, I'm not sure how I let myself get away with that. It is not only out of character, but I knew a real-life autistic person who was nothing like that. My friend Amanda – an eloquent, artistic and kind-hearted woman who did not bear so much as a fleeting resemblance to the inaccurate caricature in my head. If anything, she reminded me of me. At least, the parts of myself I liked. But, instead of examining that, I decided that I must not know her very well and she must be a secret maths genius.

When it was suggested to me that I might be autistic, I was furious. I had worked very, very hard to blend in and have normal social skills and now someone I barely knew was calling them into question. How dare she? I was absolutely fine. Yes, I'd had a few issues growing up, and, yes, there had been all that business at work, but all that was years ago. I'd got past those. I felt judged. I replied tersely but politely that I didn't think that was me and pushed it to the back of my mind.

A few weeks after I had batted away Graeme's suggestion, I went to my great-uncle's ninetieth birthday party. Dominique happened to be there. She watched me closely as I shielded my eyes from the harsh sunlight coming through the window, as I tensed with annoyance while someone drummed their fingers on the table, as I spent the entire afternoon avoiding conversation, looking at my lap and pushing the too-posh food around my plate, before surreptitiously slipping it to John.

'You know you're autistic, right?' she said, conversationally, as if she was asking about the weather.

'Oh.' I flushed red. This again. And without the buffer of a keyboard and time to formulate a diplomatic response. 'No,' I said, 'I don't think so.' I explained all the reasons I thought I wasn't autistic.

She smiled knowingly. I scowled. 'That's movie autism,' she explained. 'If you knew how autism presents in girls and women, you'd probably find yourself identifying with it. Do you ever feel like you have too much empathy?'

'Yes . . .' I said, slowly.

'And that drumming on the table. Is it driving you nuts?'

I looked at my hands, which I hadn't realised were wringing together anxiously.

'How about this? I'll send you a quiz. It's not an official diagnostic tool, but it will give you an indication of whether or not you might be . . .'

Fine, I thought, bitterly. *If it will put an end to this, I'll take the stupid quiz. Then I'll never have to think about it again.*

With John back at work the following day, I decided to take a few minutes out of my busy morning to take the dreaded quiz. *What a waste of my time*, I thought, tetchily, thinking of my multiple looming deadlines.

Now, one thing I am uncannily good at is spotting patterns – in this case, understanding what something is getting at via the volume of questions asked about particular things. About five minutes into the quiz, I started to feel rattled. A lot of the answers were 'yes'. By the end of the quiz I was in tears. I clicked for the results and they came up on the screen, a graph in a satisfying, symmetrical seashell shape and the pronouncement: *You are most likely neurodiverse*. Not only that, my score was high. Off-the-scale high.

With shaking hands I opened some of the other links Dominique had sent me. I started with the link by a clinical psychologist and autism expert, Tania Marshall, about how what was then known as Asperger's presents in young girls. It was like somebody had written a profile specifically about my childhood self. *Intense emotions*, I read. Check. *Sensory sensitivities* – check. *Difficulty coping with change* – check. *Formal, overly articulate use of language* – check. *Regresses to baby talk when stressed* – *God help me*, I thought, my cheeks burning. *I still do that*. *May have begun talking very early* – *Hello, Jerica*, I could almost hear my baby self say, *would you like to come in? Good with words, bad at conversation?* Check. *Hyperlexia – may have taught herself to read early on? The pwinth wath incotholable*, I heard my childhood self read aloud, long before I should have been able to. *A bossy playing style* – hell yes. *Difficulty with boundaries and personal space? Too much touching? Run away from the kissy girl!* I heard the boys in the playground shout, as they did exactly that.

My eyes started to blur with tears as I read on. *Highly sensitive, especially about death?* Christ. *Big imaginary inner worlds she prefers to spend time in? Imaginary friends?* Can't answer that, Tiddlypong's trying to talk to me. Pegasus was specifically mentioned on the list and I cast my mind back to my imaginary flying horse, Destrier, and how vividly I had seen him when to everybody else I was just sitting sideways on a swing. *There may be some difficulty distinguishing between fantasy and reality*, the list read. Writing was given as something autistic girls may be particularly interested in, as well as nature and animals. I thought of the letters I had written to my cats.

As I carried on reading, I noticed the list mentioned musical and singing talent, often with perfect or relative pitch. I decided to test the skill. I pulled up my Spotify playlist and hummed the opening notes to the first song I saw. I pressed play. I had started on precisely the correct note. I tried again and succeeded. And again. I tried, perhaps, a hundred times. I was wrong twice by a semitone. Excited, I pulled out my phone and recorded my new party trick.

Determination, stubbornness, an argumentative streak, a need to be right all the time. Well, one need only glance at my school reports to verify these. *A discrepancy between facial expressions and feelings.* That sense I had my whole life that my face didn't match what I was trying to express? I hadn't been imagining it after all. *People assuming she's not listening or is in her own little world*, the list read. I had never grown out of that.

The list was seemingly endless, a catalogue of what I had thought were random, disparate personality traits that had nothing to do with each other but were all coming together in a flash under this umbrella of a potential diagnosis. I had always thought I was so unique that it would be impossible for anyone else to understand me, but there I was, a walking, talking checklist. I had been the exact hyperempathetic, highly intuitive, obsessively interested, intensely anxious and phobic, poorly coordinated, easily nauseated, sleep-disturbed little girl the list described. *May be extraverted to the point of annoying her peers or family members*, the list continued. This was when I started to weep. I could barely read the rest through my tears as it explained how young autistic girls are unaware of social hierarchies, may have trouble letting things go, might avoid demands, may seem simultaneously more or less mature than their age group, have strong moral compasses and are often interested in social justice. This was before I'd even clicked on a single link about how autism presents in adulthood.

I phoned my mum first and, barely able to articulate the enormity of what I was processing, read her the list. There was a long silence. Finally, she drew in a deep breath. 'Oh my God,' she said, the penny clunking to the floor loudly enough to be heard from space.

I phoned my husband next. 'That does sound a lot like you,' he admitted.

There was just one thing that didn't make sense to me. 'One of the articles I read talks about a thing called stimming,' I said. 'It's where people display self-soothing movements, like rocking or bouncing or flapping, but I don't think I do any of those things.'

'Sara,' he said calmly, 'you have a different bounce for every mood. When you're sad, you rock. You rub your hair. You jiggle your knee. You . . .'

'OK,' I said. 'Maybe I do that a bit.'

I wrote back to Dominique and to Graeme, admitting that maybe they were on to something. Dominique immediately wrote back with a list of Facebook support groups for autistic women. Initially, I was reluctant to join. First of all, I didn't have a diagnosis. What if I was wrong and I was just imagining it all? What if I was looking for answers where there weren't any? And then an even more daunting thought occurred to me – I *had* always thought I was too unique to be understood but . . . the checklist of autistic female traits had been *so* specific. If I related to it on such a profound level, that meant . . . Oh my God, were there other people out there like me?

As I scrolled through the Facebook page full of questions, discussions and articles, I could not believe my eyes. My whole life I felt like I had been abandoned on Earth by aliens and this felt like returning to a home planet I had no idea even existed. The posts were so uncannily familiar and about such *random* things. I devoured each post and article, reading for hours. Through a mixture of academic articles and anecdotal discussion, I discovered all sorts of things that only validated my conviction that

I *had* to be autistic. Autistic people tend to have food aversions, which means they simply *cannot* force themselves to eat foods with certain tastes and textures no matter how hard they try. Everyone had sensory issues with their own unique sets of triggers. Loads had seriously low pain thresholds, as well as chronic, unexplained pain. A lot of them had experienced a lifetime of obsessive crushes. Most had special interests – subject areas approached with a beautifully obsessive focus in which they were total experts. Many had serious executive dysfunction and could not live independently, needing practical help with things like cooking, cleaning, making appointments and paying bills. Exactly the kind of labour John had been silently taking on during the course of our relationship. Loads of the women had rainbow hair, hair in bright unnatural colours, to the point of it being a trope.

Through my reading I learned about meltdowns and shutdowns. Shutdowns can be silent, insular episodes where we lose our ability to communicate with the outside world. I thought of all the times I had 'lost my words', so to speak – or not. All the times my language had abandoned me when I felt overwhelmed, all the times I felt like I could not interact with anything or anyone for a moment longer. Meltdowns, on the other hand, look like temper tantrums but they're not. What had always been 'Sara's little tantrums' were actually medical events, an autistic body's response to stress. They are necessary for us to release tension, often triggered by emotional or sensory overload. Stimming can help release some of that energy, which is why it is important to let an autistic person move, but once a meltdown is happening it is beyond our control. According to the literature, the best thing people around us can do in that situation is remove all unnecessary sensory triggers and make sure we are safe from harming ourselves – and to be forgiving afterwards, making sure not to shame their autistic loved one. All the things John had already been doing intuitively. I thought of myself stuck in my sunken place, screaming at my body from somewhere far away to stop wrecking my life. I had no idea whether or not I was comforted by the fact that I couldn't help it.

The first few weeks after discovering I was autistic were surreal and jumbled. I careered wildly between big overwhelming feelings. I felt like Bruce Willis in *The Sixth Sense* finding out he'd been a ghost all along. I spent half my time reading about autistic traits and the other half, in light of the new information, turning over the deck of cards that had been my life to date to reveal pictures on the other side. On the one hand, I was elated. I had always sensed that I was different. I had always felt, as my friend Amanda poetically puts it, that I was on a treadmill set to a more difficult setting, wondering why I was chugging away like I was climbing Everest when everyone was strolling along beside me without breaking a sweat. But, on the other hand, I had always worked so hard to hide my differences that I had almost managed to completely fool myself. That in itself was a scary, unsettling notion. I had lied to myself so successfully that facing all these difficulties and demons head on now was the most confronting thing I had ever had to do.

I learned through my research that this is called masking, and it is the reason so many people, particularly women, reach adulthood without a diagnosis. We learn to hide, obscure and overcompensate. We often do it very well – until we don't. Until we hit a moment of exhaustion and say or do something weird or have a meltdown in front of the wrong person. We mask well until suddenly we are found out. I learned too that masking costs us – big time. Masking long-term and taking on more than we are naturally able to manage can lead to serious autistic burnout. A total collapse of our ability to function. This sounded an awful lot like what I was going through.

Despite ticking literally every box, despite finding a community of women with exactly the same experiences as me and despite all of this ringing true with both my mother and husband, I still doubted myself. I had endured a lifetime of labels. Could it really be that all these awful things I believed about myself, all the terrible ways in which other people had seen me, were because of this one much more understandable label? It felt like too much to hope for. Like a cop-out for my poor behaviour.

I was extremely lucky that autism rang true for my mum and husband. Both of them immediately started reading up on how to make my life easier and started making every effort to make my environment habitable when we were together. For so many women diagnosed in adulthood this is sadly not the case and many have become estranged from their families as a result. I started trying out the word with my friends with mixed results. For Kat autism immediately made sense. She had been closer to me in recent months than anybody and had seen my unusual behaviours up close, firsthand. Others were less convinced. It turns out that if people have a long-established view of you as a drama queen, a sudden self-diagnosis with a disability only validates their view of you. It's just another one of Sara's attention-seeking schemes. Another thing wrong with the girl who always has to have something wrong with her.

To hopefully save some future newly discovered autistic people the heartache that I went through here are a few things *not* to say:

1. I'm so sorry to hear that.
2. No you're not.
3. You must be very high-functioning.
4. That's offensive to my relative who's really autistic.
5. Aren't we all a bit autistic?
6. Autism is a bit of a fad at the moment.
7. Wow, you're so brave.
8. I don't like labels.
9. Don't go using that as an excuse for everything now.
10. I wondered what was wrong with you!

As irritating as it is to be told not to let my autism define me by someone with 'drinker of tea' in their

Twitter bio, I always find it tremendously unhelpful when I'm told what *not* to do with no direction on what I actually *should* be doing, so here are a few suggestions for alternative things you might say:

1. Congratulations!
2. That's a big thing to learn about yourself. How are you feeling about it?
3. You never have to cover up your difficulties in front of me. (You have to actually mean this one.)
4. What can I do to make things easier when we're hanging out? (You have to actually mean this one too.)
5. Is there anything you'd like me to read so that I can better understand you?
6. Please let me know if you'd like support or backup when telling other people.
7. Do you have any preferences for the language I use when I talk about autism?
8. You should be so proud of yourself for managing for this long without a diagnosis.
9. This is a huge psychological adjustment for you and you can talk about it as much as you need to with me. (Again, please try to mean this.)
10. How can I best advocate for you with people who are less understanding?

When I first discovered I was autistic, I found that all the friends who, just a few years previously, had been fertility experts, had suddenly changed fields and were now psychiatrists and clinical psychologists specialising in autism assessments. I finally had answers for why I had felt so different all my life. I was elated and they were raining on my parade of self-discovery. To shut them up once and for all I managed, and anyone who's tried to get a diagnosis will recognise this for the miracle that it is, to get a diagnostic appointment for May 2018 with an *actual* clinical psychologist specialising in autism in women. Even with my husband's private insurance from his job, the GP was reluctant to refer me on.

'You do know there's no cure,' he told me.

'I don't want a cure,' I replied. 'I want an answer.'

This is one of the major reasons I fully support self-diagnosis when it comes to autism. The barriers to official diagnosis are significant and regardless, diagnosis is based largely on self-assessment. If autistic people have to wait for a formal diagnosis in order to start making vital changes in their lives, they could be waiting forever.

Still, old habits die hard and I felt at the time like I needed external validation of my suspicions. I prepared for my appointment like it was a job interview and I was interviewing for the role of Legitimate Autistic Person. I compiled an epic dossier, around the length of this book, probably, of all my autistic traits, my sensory triggers and my childhood memories. My mum wrote a statement to take with to the appointment and John came with me to give his perspective.

As I was preparing, a sudden thought occurred to me. 'Didn't you wonder what was up?' I asked John.

He shifted a bit, looking uncomfortable. 'Well,' he said, carefully, 'I always knew you were different.'

'Didn't you wonder why, though? Like, didn't you think I was being dramatic or putting it on?'

'Sara, if you have been putting it on 24-7 for the past eight years, you deserve all the Oscars.'

'Right, but you helped me, even though we didn't have an explanation.'

John shrugged. 'I didn't need an explanation to help you.'

As we pulled up to the psychologist's home practice, I was a jittering mess. 'What if I'm not autistic?' I asked over and over.

'I'm not sure that's possible,' John responded.

Suddenly, horror of horrors, I looked on my lap and realised that all my written evidence, everything I had been relying on in case I forgot something, was sitting by the door at home. I burst into stressed tears. I sat in the car, crying and rocking, as John went to the door and explained to the psychologist what had happened. She smiled kindly at me and told him to tell me that it didn't matter at all; I could send her all the extra information later and to come in when I was ready. With hindsight I wouldn't be surprised if in her mind she diagnosed me in that moment.

The room was dimly lit, with large comfortable chairs. I took a tissue and dabbed my leaky eyes. They were the softest tissues I had ever felt in my life. My leg bounced uncontrollably as I answered her questions. Halfway through our chat, my blood sugar started to dip. I asked if she would mind if I had a quick snack and she told me to go ahead. She watched, a small smile on the corner of her mouth as I tried, and failed, to open a packet of oatcakes, which I then handed to John for help. The next question on the list was about whether or not I have issues with fine motor skills. I answered by gesturing at the oat cracker packet. 'Good point,' she replied, scribbling something down. About three quarters of the way through the appointment, she casually dropped into conversation that I was definitely autistic. As the word 'Asperger's' was being phased out, I was given the dual diagnosis of Asperger's and autistic-spectrum disorder or condition.

She told me that it was incredible that I had not only survived this long without a diagnosis, but managed to thrive professionally. She praised my grit and determination for carving a place for myself in the world, despite none of it being designed for me. It was a shock. I was so used to people telling me I wasn't trying hard enough that someone taking the opposite view felt like being shaken upside down in a snow globe.

We also discussed my dad. My dad with his heady, constant crushes. His stream of obsessive interests. His need for order and consistency. His plan B for every scenario. And, oh my God, his hatred of my noisy chattering at dinnertime . . . the blow-ups . . . the fear of medical intervention . . . 'It's impossible to tell without being able to speak to him but it's very likely,' said the psychologist, 'that your dad was also autistic.'

Suddenly everything clicked into place. The reason our relationship had been so difficult all those years. It hadn't been my fault that he couldn't cope with noise. It hadn't been my fault that he'd shouted. It hadn't been his fault either. And I would never be able to resolve it with him. I would never be able to sit down with him and talk about our shared autistic traits and how we set each other off. He had gone to his grave thinking he had just been a bad person and a failure as a father. As healing as the new information was for me, it was also incredibly painful to know that this closure went one way. He would never know.

John and I drove home in silence, processing everything. I looked out of the window, avoiding meeting his eyes. What was wrong with me? The past two months of uncovering all the facets of my autistic identity had felt like a blissful homecoming. Had I not been terrified of my instincts being invalidated? Why then, now that I had my official diagnosis in hand, did I feel so wobbly?

It hit me like a freight train at the most innocuous moment. One second, I was brushing my teeth before bed, the next I was letting out a wail of grief before collapsing to the floor and sobbing. I had spent my whole life trying to fit in and be like everybody else. I had just received official confirmation that this lifelong goal was impossible. I was never going to be my idealised idea of 'normal'. I had wasted thirty years of my life trying to achieve something that was far beyond my reach, instead of letting myself be comfortable with who I was. I wept for that lost time. I wept for how differently others might have treated me. I wept for the way important things, like consent, could have been explained to me if only we'd known. And then a second truth hit me: I might never feel completely better. My exhaustion, my unexplained pain, my sensory issues – they could all be for life. That magic bullet I was counting on might not exist at all.

In that moment I knew with a certainty that settled into my heart like cement that I was never going to be a parent. Even though, intellectually, I know that my comorbid health issues might improve, I don't personally feel I have the stamina, physical or emotional, that parenting requires.

This is where it's more important than ever to emphasise how much I do NOT speak for all, or even most, autistic people. I am in no way saying that being autistic is a barrier to parenthood. I know countless autistic parents who are absolutely incredible at what they do. Their empathy, sensitivity and imagination make them spectacular parents. While a lot of autistic traits are shared, not all autistic traits are as pronounced or even present in people with different profiles. My sensory issues, for example, are particularly severe, as is my executive dysfunction. But the truth is that for some people being autistic can present unique parenting challenges. For people who tend to struggle with noises, smells, unexpected changes in routine, medical appointments, socialising with other parents and so on, parenting can be even more of a struggle. For people who choose to have children these are important things to be aware of so that the right support can be provided and they can thrive as parents, just like anybody else. These struggles should *never* be used to deprive would-be autistic parents of that opportunity and I would be devastated if speaking about my own experiences were to be used as an excuse to discriminate in any way against autistic parents.

It is highly likely that others, even with difficulties as pronounced as mine, have the grit and determination to be fantastic parents regardless. For me, personally, I knew this would not be the case. If these issues were for life and were this severe, then my dream of having children would have to be left behind.

There is often an oversimplification when it comes to the conversation around people who are child-free. People assume you fall into one of two camps: never wanted children and delighted not to have them or desperately want kids but can't conceive. Nobody ever talks about the shades of grey in between, the instinctual yearning to be a mother juxtaposed with the reality of my lived experience: motherhood not being an impossible goal but also not quite being in my best interests and therefore not in the best interests of the human being I am considering creating. I softened the blow by telling myself that the world is overpopulated and doomed due to the climate emergency and that it would be selfish and cruel to bring new life into that situation. This is all true, but still, every now and then I see a mother holding a baby, a tiny little replica in her image, or my nephew grasps my hand and I have to take myself off somewhere for a moment of quiet honesty, to just let myself grieve. I compensate by being the best auntie to my nephew and my friends' babies that I can possibly be. I am the one who comes bearing presents and sugary snacks, knowing I don't have to be around for the comedown. I am the cool aunt who can tell long improvised stories, who is always available when my nephew wants a chat, and for whom he will always be number one, because he is the closest I will ever have to a child of my own.

After my diagnosis, I fell into a colossal depression, the likes of which I had never experienced, not even in the dark days post-Malumi where my bed had been replaced with a nest of crisp packets. It felt as though if I had managed to go my whole life with a neurological disability without even noticing, how could I ever trust my perception of reality? I started to doubt myself and my instincts. If someone upset me, how could I know if I was being unreasonable or not, given how differently my brain worked? Before my diagnosis, I had ready-made excuses for each life crash, but with this new knowledge could I really trust that I had read a social situation correctly? I started to gaslight myself, telling myself that I was always wrong in every scenario, that I couldn't be trusted to be around other people and I certainly could not be trusted with running a business. After an awkward meeting where I felt I'd embarrassed her yet again, I wrote to Kat and quit *Succubus*.

Once I had fulfilled the last of my obligations for *Succubus*, including a horrific incident at the Craft of Comedy festival where I was so overwhelmed that I had an epic meltdown in the conference centre and had to flee to the safety of the Airbnb, leaving poor Kat to conduct an entire networking event on her own and hiding until it was home time, I cleared my diary. I stopped taking work. I stopped going outside. And I stopped talking to my friends. I withdrew from everything and everyone I loved, not trusting myself to be out in society. The only person I felt safe around was John, who knew better than to push me out of my funk before I was ready.

For a while my inner world collapsed. The vast ornate fantasy world in which I had half lived my whole life, where I dreamed for hours on end of my bright, shiny future, had become completely inaccessible to me. It was like someone had boarded up my second home in my absence, a notice on the front door that read *warning – danger – do not enter*. My crush monster, who had lived on throughout my marriage, albeit attaching itself to safe, faraway targets who would never actually threaten my relationship, lay dead on the floor, an arrow through his heart. I had thought he was indestructible, but in one session with a psychologist I had finally killed him.

At the time I thought I'd killed him simply by becoming aware of him – but now, with the benefit of hindsight, I think the truth ran deeper than that. My crush monster was never really about men – it was about searching and yearning. It was a confused, directionless feeling that happened to latch on to romance as the key to my happiness. What I'd really been looking for was an answer. The minute I found out I was autistic, I had mine. The crush monster had nothing left to look for.

With my imagination proving impotent, I processed my feelings by writing about them. I started to write commissioned articles about what it was like to suddenly discover you're autistic. The articles had a distinctly more optimistic tone than the reality of how I was processing everything, but actually that seemed to help. It was the first time in my life that 'fake it until you make it' was surprisingly good advice. My only regret from that early time of learning my way around my own autistic mind was using functioning labels in my writing.

You have probably heard the terms 'high-functioning' or 'low-functioning' when it comes to autism. When I was first diagnosed, I thought that they were nothing more than medical labels, but actually many autistic people find them hugely offensive and unhelpful. Now, with the benefit of a couple of years of wisdom, I totally understand why. Autism is not as simple as a left-to-right, high-to-low gradient. It is not a spectrum where someone is affected a little bit to a lot. It is also not a rigid state of affairs, with you either very autistic or a little bit. My 'functioning', so to speak, changes on a daily basis. One day I can have a wholly productive and energetic day, the next I might not be able to verbalise a thing. Ultimately, you cannot tell, at a glance, how an autistic person 'functions' in the world, whatever that even means. I once had a tearful exchange with a famous journalist who, with no scientific evidence, rubbished the idea of the autistic spectrum, saying that people like me did not belong on it, telling me I had nothing in common, for example, with an autistic boy he knew who couldn't speak. I very quickly learned that 'high-functioning', in the minds of many neurotypical people, means 'able to articulate themselves'.

This is why I apologise now for ever having used functioning labels. I know now that they are used to write off people perceived as 'low-functioning', or to dismiss the struggles of those perceived as 'high-functioning'. I described myself as 'high-functioning', because shortly after my diagnosis, I was told by someone with an autistic relative that my diagnosis was an insult to their 'low-functioning' loved one. I was still processing my diagnosis and, after a lifetime of being told I was making a fuss over nothing, still felt like a fraud explaining exactly how autistic I was. When you spend your whole life working overtime to hide your struggles, it feels like an incredibly sharp U-turn to suddenly spill them to the world in order to be believed. I was terrified of appropriating someone else's struggle and making it about me.

I also discovered that a lot of autistic advocates, and I now count myself as one of them, do not see autism as a deficit. Neurodiversity activists see autism as simply having a different brain to the majority. We see the world differently and our struggles are different – some factors of it, such as severe sensory overload or executive dysfunction issues, definitely qualify it as a disability. But the idea that our no-nonsense delivery, our passionate belief in knowing right from wrong, our unique way of thinking, is something to be lamented, grieved or cured is offensive.

These days, when I re-read the original quiz I took to placate my cousin, or speak to an autism professional, I find myself cringing at the pathologising language used to describe autistic traits. I don't recognise myself in the descriptions that make me inherently in the wrong for directly getting to the heart of an issue, or refusing to compromise on a moral red line.

Having said that, I also find myself wincing when well-meaning neurotypicals describe autism as a superpower. The wider world seeing us as a magical, fascinating alien species, or assuming that we are all savants is equally incorrect and, even though people's hearts are in the right place, it can feel incredibly patronising.

It has taken me several years of exploration but I am at a place now where I see autism as neither an affliction nor a superpower. It's just the blueprint for who I am. There is no cure, but that's absolutely fine by me. To cure me of my autism would be to cure me of myself.

It was getting to know other autistic people that started the healing process. Through Facebook support groups and through Twitter I found myself ensconced in a community of like-minded women. Literally, with minds just like mine. And I loved what I saw. These women were just incredible. They were brilliant, nuanced thinkers, emotionally sensitive and caring, creative, inventive and just wonderful. If this was what autism looked like, what the hell was I moping about? Slowly, I started to poke my head out of hibernation and into the sunlight (while wearing sunglasses, of course). I started to accept work offers again and tentatively began to socialise. It was other people's small acts of kindness that were like hands in the dark. My healing could be catalogued in a series of moments: my friend Greg taking me to see fireworks and bringing my favourite hot chocolate in a mug decorated to my taste, telling me he loves watching my happy stims as I watch the display; my friend Bronwen travelling several stops out of her way on the tube to make sure I got home safely after we hung out together; my friend Simon picking up a ball containing a unicorn surrounded by glitter that I used to calm myself down, after it fell out of my bag, and instead of thinking I was weird, playing with the ball and trying to make the glitter land on the unicorn.

I wasn't just rebuilding my sense of identity, I was discovering it from scratch. For the first time I was living it authentically. I wasn't pushing myself into situations I couldn't cope with just to please other people. I wasn't squinting through bright light without my sunglasses, or interacting for longer than I felt comfortable. I started to buy colourful, expressive clothes, letting myself stand out instead of wearing myself out trying to fit in.

I found that the people who mattered were more than happy to hang out with me on my own terms, to travel the extra distance to spend time with me at my house, to be accepting and kind when I said no to something overwhelming or busy. And the people who didn't quickly fell by the wayside – I finally had the confidence to invest in friendships that were a good match, rather than taking what I could get. My friendships now are like buying clothes in the correct size, which fit me as I am, rather than buying a size down and starving myself to squeeze into them. My days of making myself smaller to suit other people are over.

I started to get more and more work opportunities. They weren't the same opportunities as before, but they were much more substantial. People wanted to hear about what it was like to be autistic and how my mind worked. They were actually interested in who I really was – and most of the time they seemed to genuinely like what they heard and saw. The more honest I was on Twitter, the more followers I amassed and connections I made. Knowing I was autistic gave me courage to speak out, not only about autism but about all the social justice issues that mattered to me. I had spent so many years pretending to be someone I wasn't when, all this time, I was absolutely fine as I was. Finally, I felt free.

My relationships with my neurotypical loved ones were utterly transformed. The excuses I made to myself to explain why John had to wait on me hand and foot have been replaced with a sense of overwhelming awe, gratitude and deep love. I always loved John, but now that I am able to accept how much help I need, I am also able to acknowledge that he is the one providing it and how exceptionally lucky I am to have somebody constantly supporting me through life. All my professional achievements would have been impossible without his practical and emotional support, his round-the-clock care and his unflinching acceptance of who I am.

My mum and I are closer than ever. She truly sees me for who I am and makes every effort to accommodate me, advocating for me when others make life difficult. It has been incredibly hard for her to process and she feels a lot of guilt about everything she would have done differently if she'd known – something I hope she can let go of in time. Our relationship is more affectionate now. She is gentler with me. With my vulnerability post-diagnosis came a desperate need for my mum and many hours spent curled up beside her on the sofa, just enjoying the simple comfort of having her there. I avoid those who don't believe I'm autistic. It's a shame, and in some cases it's been a real wrench, but I don't particularly want to spend time with people who think I'm a lying hypochondriac who's pretending to be disabled for attention. I don't see why if they think that, they would want to know me and, as it happens, I'm done seeing myself that way.

My imaginary world has slowly been rebuilt from the rubble and, much like my fledgling identity, looks very different to how it did before my diagnosis. I no longer fantasise about anything based on my real life or the people in it. It does me no good to idealise people and things, nor to set my expectations so high that exciting life events consistently disappoint me. Instead I have built an entirely fictional escape, full of characters I've created, a safe space that does not rely on my external circumstances to provide a happy refuge for me. It is a whole new way of relating to my inner world, one that provides stability and comfort, instead of confusion and chaos.

These days I am now almost completely comfortable being my autistic self. That's not to say I never mask – of course there are situations where it's still inappropriate to be, well, inappropriate. And it's not to say I never have bad days where I wish I was different, usually on days where my pain is particularly bad, or I've had a meltdown. But now I live my life at my own pace. I know what my boundaries are and how to convey them to other people. I do my best not to beat myself up for the things I'm not able to easily do. I remind myself that I would never expect someone with a physical disability to berate themselves for having differing needs, so why do it to myself just because mine is hidden? I am no longer in hiding. I exist in the world as an autistic person, without shame or compromise.

If I could wish anything for future generations of autistic people, it would be that we live in a world where saying 'I'm autistic' answers more questions than it raises. Imagine saying 'I'm autistic' and people actually knowing what that means in different situations! Where we see someone wearing sunglasses or headphones indoors and think nothing of it, rather than staring or commenting.

I dream of a society where autism is recognised as a complex set of traits, abilities and difficulties, rather than viewed in a limited, linear model that completely ignores the reality of most autistic people's lived experience, belittles some and makes a tragedy of others. I wish for autistic people to be believed – both before and after diagnosis – when they say something is harder for them than it is for other people. I never want to see another autistic person be accused of lying for attention, being weak or pathetic or lazy, diverting resources and awareness from other, more worthy autistics. The world would be so much easier for everyone if our first assumption was that people are acting in good faith and speaking honestly. Autistic people already face so many practical barriers to participating in society – it is incredibly frustrating when additional emotional barriers are created by other people for no good reason.

I wish for autism to be more readily recognised in people of colour, in women and in any marginalised group that doesn't fit the stereotypical understanding of what autism looks like. I wish for shorter waiting times for official diagnosis and for GPs who don't assume someone 'can't be autistic' if they can make eye contact or hold a conversation. I wish for more parents to love and accept their autistic child as they are, rather than mourning the child they wish they'd had instead. I wish for damaging and traumatic 'cures' to be banished to the dark ages, from emotionally scarring behavioural therapies designed to make a person appear less autistic to potentially life-threatening quackery like bleach enemas. I wish everybody knew that vaccines don't cause autism – and that even if they did (they don't), I wish people saw that having an autistic child is infinitely better than losing a child to a preventable illness. I wish for loved ones of autistic people to understand that reasonably small environmental adjustments can completely change an autistic person's life for the better. I wish that there will never be another autistic person who feels like a burden or an inconvenience for asking for things they *need* at the expense of things other people *want*. I wish for autistic communication to be seen as valid and valuable, for neurotypical people to recognise the enormous effort autistic people make to live in their world and to, at the very least, meet us halfway.

I hope that the more people share their experiences, the less stigma there will be around autism. I know many people will disagree with me on this, but I don't blame people for having a skewed perspective on autism. It is all around us – in the media we consume, in whispered 'I know I'm not supposed to think this but' conversations, in media representations of autism written and performed without the involvement of autistic people, in organisations that claim to want to help us but focus on trying to 'cure' us and mitigate our impact on other people. It is completely understandable that some people's reactions to discovering they're autistic might be negative. It is my deepest wish that finding out you're autistic is no more traumatic than finding out you're left-handed.

Most of all I wish autistic people lived in a world where none of us have to be the lucky ones who escaped with our lives and grew up to finally find love, support and acceptance. Luck shouldn't come into it.

Right . . . Well, it's getting late and I've got to get dinner on. Ah, crap, you're never going to believe that. You know I'm not the one who cooks dinner. OK, uh . . . I think my cat is asking for me. No? I have to go; my husband's on fire. God. Fine, you've got me. I have no idea how to end this book. I'm as good as getting out of conversations as I am at instigating them. I will leave you with these words – which I recently blurted out before hanging up on a confused GP's receptionist: 'K, love you, bye!

ACKNOWLEDGEMENTS

Thank you to everyone who made this book possible. To Sarah Emsley, the best editor I could have possibly wished for and the brilliant team at Headline.

Thank you to my agent, Rowan, for taking such wonderful care of me.

Special thanks to Neil and Rory.

Thanks to Dr Maria O'Neill for her thoughtful review.

To my friends of many years who helped me piece together the memories that make up this book: Tom, Greg, Meredith, Barbara, Sarah H, Carys, Rhiannon, Annie, Amanda, Caitlin, Filippo, Katerina, Marc and Bronwen.

To Rob, for loving me before I loved myself – and Michael, for loving him as much as I do!

To my writer friends for being the most excellent sounding boards: specifically Pete Wharmby, Simon Alcock, Graeme Watson, Lizzy Dent and Kat Sadler.

To Jane Morris-Brown, for igniting my love of writing. To Bill Dare, for taking the biggest chance on me and to Joel Morris and Jason Hazeley for convincing me he was right to do it.

To my family, especially Yotam, Heather, Jesse, Rosella, John Sr., Irene, Belinda and Dominique.

Thank you to my support network: my mum, Lorraine, who is there for me every single day and my amazing husband, John, for all you do for me to make my life magical and make it possible for me to write.